D1556943

THE FATHERS
OF THE CHURCH

A NEW TRANSLATION

VOLUME 109

THE FATHERS OF THE CHURCH

A NEW TRANSLATION

ST. PETER CHRYSOLOGUS
SELECTED SERMONS
VOLUME 2

Translated by

WILLIAM B. PALARDY
St. John's Seminary School of Theology
Brighton, Massachusetts

THE CATHOLIC UNIVERSITY OF AMERICA PRESS
Washington, D.C.

In memory of my mother and father

The paper used in this publication meets the minimum requirements of the
American National Standards for Information Science—Permanence of Paper
for Printed Library Materials, ANSI z39.48 - 1984.

LIBRARY OF CONGRESS CATALOGING-IN-PUBLICATION DATA
Peter, Chrysologus, Saint, Archbishop of Ravenna, ca. 400–450.
[Sermons. English. Selections]
St. Peter Chrysologus : selected sermons / translated by William B. Palardy.
p. cm. — (The Fathers of the church, a new translation, v. 109)
Vol. 1 published in 1953, by Fathers of the Church, New York, under title:
Saint Peter Chrysologus : selected sermons; and Saint Valerian : homilies.
Includes bibliographical references and index.
ISBN 0-8132-0109-8 (alk. paper)
1. Sermons, Latin—Translations into English. I. Title: Saint Peter Chrysolo-
gus. II. Title. III. Series: Fathers of the church ; v. 109.

BR60.F3P474 2004
252'.014—dc22
2004004195

CONTENTS

INDICES

PREFACE

In 1953 the Fathers of the Church series published their seventeenth volume, comprising the homilies of St. Valerian and selected sermons of St. Peter Chrysologus, thereby making thirty percent of the authentic sermons of Chrysologus available to an English-speaking audience. In the half-century since that publication Dom Alejandro Olivar, O.S.B., from Montserrat provided significant advances for studies in Chrysologus by publishing a critical study of the sermons in 1962 and by producing a critical edition of them in CCL, volumes 24, 24A, and 24B from 1975 to 1982. Thanks to Olivar's painstaking efforts, subsequent studies and translations in other languages have been made of these sermons.

With the publication of this and the subsequent volume all of Chrysologus's authentic sermons will be available in English in the Fathers of the Church series. This translation is based upon the text edited by Olivar in the three volumes of CCL. If a reading at variance with the CCL text is used, indication is given in a footnote. I have also used Olivar's extensive notes in the CCL edition for cross-referencing terms and similar ideas within Chrysologus's corpus, for pointing out parallels in classical and other patristic texts, and for signaling works of contemporary scholarship where appropriate. In addition but to a lesser extent I have benefitted from the recent Italian translation (which also includes the Latin of the CCL) by G. Banterle, who corrected the CCL text and added notes.

The citations from the Old Testament follow the Septuagint (and Vetus Latina) rendering and numeration. When the numeration differs from the New Revised Standard Version of the Bible, that of the NRSV is noted in parentheses. The translation of Scripture is based on Chrysologus's Latin text. Translations of other texts are mine unless otherwise indicated. In footnoting other patristic texts I cite the FOTC edition, if available; otherwise, in general, the best text available to me in the original Latin or Greek is referenced. In the introduction to this volume I note which sermons formerly attributed to Chrysologus are in fact spurious. The fifteen recently attributed sermons are given the designation "a" and "b" rather than the "bis" and "ter" of the CCL (e.g., *Sermon* 72bis is designated here as "72a" and 72ter as "72b"). Unless otherwise noted, "[ ]" are insertions I have made into the translation for the sake of clarity, and "< >" are additions that Olivar has made to some of the sermons' titles, which postdate Chrysologus anyway. Texts upon which Chrysologus preaches in sequence, such as the Creed or the Gospel reading of the day, are rendered in italics.

I began my studies of St. Peter Chrysologus while in a doctoral program at The Catholic University of America from 1988 to 1992. I am grateful to my dissertation director, the late Rev. Dr. Robert B. Eno, S.S., and my readers, Dr. Robin Darling Young and Mr. Gerald Bonner, for their invaluable expertise and insight. My appreciation also extends to the Rev. Dr. Thomas Halton, who encouraged me to pursue this translation project as early as 1992. More recently Dr. Carole Burnett, a fellow classmate at CUA and staff editor for FOTC, provided me additional encouragement and assistance as I began this project. I have also been greatly helped by the guidance and expertise of Joel Kalvesmaki, the current staff editor.

My thanks also extend to seminarians and other students at St. John's Seminary in Brighton, where I teach, especially those who have been exposed to Chrysologus's sermons in patristic or Latin classes, and whose interest in him helped further convince me that this translation project would be worthwhile. I am also very grateful for the support and insight of the former Rector, the Most Rev. Richard G. Lennon, and my other colleagues at St. John's throughout the course of this project. Finally, I am most appreciative of the resources available in our seminary's library and the O'Neill Library at Boston College, as well as the assistance provided by our seminary's Librarian, the Rev. Msgr. Laurence W. McGrath.

ABBREVIATIONS

ACCR	*Atti dei convegni di Cesena e Ravenna I (1966–1967)*. Cesena, 1969.
BSS	*Bibliotheca Sanctorum*. Ed. F. Caraffa. Rome, 1962–2000.
CCL	Corpus Christianorum, Series Latina. Turnhout, 1953– .
CSEL	Corpus scriptorum ecclesiasticorum Latinorum. Vienna, 1866– .
FOTC	The Fathers of the Church. New York: Cima, 1947–49; New York: FOTC, Inc., 1949–60; Washington, D.C.: The Catholic University of America Press, 1960– .
GCS	Die griechischen christlichen Schriftsteller der ersten drei Jahrhunderte. Leipzig and Berlin, 1897– .
LXX	The Septuagint.
MGH.AA	Monumenta Germaniae historica: Auctores antiquissimi. Hannover and Berlin, 1877–1919.
NRSV	New Revised Standard Version
NT	New Testament
NTApo	*New Testament Apocrypha*, revised ed. of collection of E. Hennecke, ed. W. Schneemelcher and R. McL. Wilson. Cambridge: J. Clarke, 1991; Louisville, KY: Westminster/ John Knox Press, 1991.
OECT	Oxford Early Christian Texts. Oxford, 1971– .
OT	Old Testament
PG	Patrologiae Cursus Completus: Series Graeca. Ed. J.-P. Migne. Paris, 1857–66.
PL	Patrologiae Cursus Completus: Series Latina. Ed. J.-P. Migne. Paris, 1841–94.
PLS	Patrologiae Latinae Supplementum. Ed. A. Hamman. Paris, 1958–74.

PRE	*Paulys Real-Enzyclopädie der classischen Altertumswissenschaft.* Ed. Pauly, Wissowa, and Kroll. Stuttgart, 1893–1978.
RSCI	*Rivista di storia della chiesa in Italia.* Rome, 1947– .
SC	Sources chrétiennes. Paris, 1941– .
ZKTh	*Zeitschrift für katholische Theologie.* Vienna, 1876– .

SELECT BIBLIOGRAPHY

Other than the references below to the text of Migne and the translations of Böhmer and Held, the items found in the Bibliography in FOTC 17.24 will not be repeated here.

Texts

Agnellus. *Agnelli qui et Andreas Liber Pontificalis Ecclesiae Ravennatis.* Ed. O. Holder-Egger. In *Scriptores Rerum Langobardicarum et Italicarum,* ed. G. Waitz. Hannover: Impensis bibliopolii Hahniani, 1878.

Peter Chrysologus. *Epistula ad Eutychen.* In *Acta Conciliorum Oecumenicorum II,* ed. E. Schwartz, II, vol. 3, part 1, 6–7. Berlin and Leipzig: Walter de Gruyter, 1935.

———. *Sermones.* CCL 24, 24A, and 24B. Ed. A. Olivar. 1975, 1981, and 1982.

———. *Sancti Petri Chrysologi Archiepiscopi Ravennatis. Opera Omnia.* PL 52:183–666. 1894. Supplemented in PLS 3:153–83, 4:659–65, 5:397–98. 1963, 1967, 1974.

Translations

Agnellus. *Il Libro di Agnello Istorico.* Trans. Mario Pierpaoli. Ravenna: Diamond Byte, 1988.

———. *The Book of Pontiffs of the Church of Ravenna.* Trans. Deborah Mauskopf Deliyannis. Washington, D.C.: The Catholic University of America Press, 2004.

Pedro Crisólogo. *Homilías Escogidas.* Intro. and notes by A. Olivar. Trans. J. Garitaonandia. Madrid: Editorial Ciudad Nueva, 1998.

San Pietro Crisologo. *Sermoni e Lettera a Eutiche.* 3 vols. Trans. G. Banterle et al. Intro. and notes by R. Benericetti, C. Truzzi, et al. Rome: Città Nuova Editrice, 1996–97.

Pier Crisologo. *Omelie per la vita quotidiana.* Trans. and intro. by Mario Spinelli. Rome: Città Nuova Editrice, 1978.

San Pier Crisologo. *I CLXXVII Sermoni.* 3 vols. Trans. A. Pasini. Siena: Cantagalli, 1953.

Saint Peter Chrysologus. *Selected Sermons and Letter to Eutyches.* Trans. G. Ganss. FOTC 17. 1953.

Petrus Chrysologus. *Des hl. Petrus Chrysologus, Erzbischofs von Ravenna, ausgewählte Predigten.* Trans. G. Böhmer. Bibliothek der Kirchenvater 43. Munich and Kempten: J. Kösel and F. Pustet, 1923.

————. *Ausgewählte Reden des hl. Petrus Chrysologus.* Trans. M. Held. Bibliothek der Kirchenväter 67. Kempten: J. Kösel, 1874.

Secondary Sources

Baldisserri, D. L. *San Pier Crisologo, Arcivescovo di Ravenna.* Imola: Stabilimento Tipografico Imolese, 1920.

Benelli, Augusto. "Note sulla vita e l'episcopato di Petro Crisologo." In *In Verbis Verum Amare,* ed. P. Serra Zanetti, 63–79. Florence: La Nuova Italia, 1980.

Benericetti, Ruggero. *Il Cristo nei Sermoni di S. Pier Crisologo.* Cesena: Centro studi e ricerche sulla antica provincia ecclesiastica Ravennate, 1995.

Bonner, Gerald. "Petrus Chrysologus." In *Theologische Realenzyclopädie* 26:290–91. Berlin: Walter de Gruyter, 1996.

Cortesi, Giuseppe. "Cinque note su San Pier Crisologo." *Felix Ravenna* 128 (1984): 117–32.

Del Ton, Josephus. "De Sancti Petri Chrysologi Eloquentia." *Latinitas* 6 (1958): 177–89.

De Margerie, Bertrand. "L'Exégèse de Saint Pierre Chrysologue, théologien biblique." Ch. 3 in *Introduction à l'histoire de l'exégèse: IV. L'Occident latin de Léon le Grand à Bernard de Clairvaux,* 75–108. Paris: Cerf, 1990.

Fitzgerald, Allan. *Conversion through Penance in the Italian Church of the Fourth and Fifth Centuries.* Lewiston, Queenston, and Lampeter: Edwin Mellen Press, 1988.

Jossua, J.-P. *Le Salut, Incarnation ou Mystère Pascal chez les Pères de l'Eglise de Saint Irénée à Saint Léon le Grand.* Paris: Cerf, 1968.

Koch, H. "Petrus Chrysologus." In *PRE* 38:1361–72 (1938).

Kochaniewicz, Bogusław. *La Vergine Maria nei sermoni di San Pietro Crisologo.* Rome: Pontifical Theological Faculty "Marianum," 1998.

Ladino, Rolando. *La iniciación cristiana en San Pedro Crisólogo de Ravenna.* Rome: Pontifical Gregorian University, 1969.

Lanzoni, F. *Le diocesi d'Italia dalle origini al principio del Secolo VII (An. 604).* Studi e Testi 35. Faenza: Stabilimento Grafico F. Lega, 1927.

La Rosa, Virgilio. *Il commento al Pater Noster nei sermoni di S. Pier Crisologo.* Rome: Pontifical Lateran University, 1965.

Lemarié, Joseph. "La liturgie de Ravenne au temps de Pierre Chrysologue et l'ancienne liturgie d'Aquilée." In *Antichità Altoadriatiche XIII: Aquileia e Ravenna,* 355–73. Udine: Arti Grafiche Friulane, 1978.

Lodi, E. "La preghiera in S. Pietro Crisologo." In *La preghiera nel tardo antico: Dalle origini ad Agostino: XXVII Incontro di studiosi dell'antichità cristiana,* 389–417. Rome: Institutum Patristicum Augustinianum, 1999.

————. "L'esegesi biblica nei testi rituali dei sermoni di s. Pier Crisologo." In *L'esegesi nei padri latini: Dalle origini a Gregorio magno: XXVIII Incontro di studiosi dell'antichità cristiana*, 2:617–53. Rome: Institutum Patristicum Augustinianum, 2000.

Lucchesi, G. "Stato attuale degli studi sui santi dell'antica provincia ravennate." In *ACCR*, 51–80.

McGlynn, Robert H. *The Incarnation in the Sermons of Saint Peter Chrysologus*. Mundelein, IL: Saint Mary of the Lake Seminary, 1956.

Old, Hughes Oliphant. "Peter Chrysologus." Ch. VI.II in *The Reading and Preaching of the Scriptures in the Worship of the Christian Church: Volume 2: The Patristic Age*, 416–24. Grand Rapids, MI: Eerdmans, 1998.

Olivar, A. "Els principis exegètics de sant Pere Crisòleg." In *Miscellanea biblica B. Ubach*, ed. Romualdo M. Díaz, 413–37. Montserrat: Abadía de Montserrat, 1953.

———. "Clavis S. Petri Chrysologi." *Sacris Erudiri* 6 (1954): 327–42.

———. *Los sermones de San Pedro Crisólogo: Estudio crítico*. Montserrat: Abadía de Montserrat, 1962.

———. "La duración de la predicación antigua." *Liturgica* 3 (1966): 143–84.

———. "La consagración del Obispo Marcelino de Voghenza." *RSCI* 22 (1968): 87–93.

———. "Pietro Crisologo, arcivescovo di Ravenna, Dottore della Chiesa, santo." In *BSS* 10:685–91. 1968.

———. "Preparación e improvisación en la predicación patrística." In *Kyriakon: Festschrift J. Quasten*, ed. P. Granfield and J. A. Jungmann, 2:736–67. Münster: Verlag Aschendorff, 1970.

———. "Reseña de las publicaciones recientes referentes a San Pedro Crisólogo." *Didaskalia* 7 (1977): 131–51.

———. "Die Textüberlieferung der Predigten des Petrus Chrysologus." In *Texte und Textkritik: eine Aufstatzsammlung*. Texte und Untersuchungen zur Geschichte der altchristlichen Literatur 133, ed. J. Dummer, 469–87. Berlin: Akademie-Verlag, 1987.

———. *La predicación cristiana antigua*. Barcelona: Herder, 1991.

———. "Les exordes des sermons de saint Pierre Chrysologue." *Revue bénédictine* 104 (1994): 88–105.

Olivar, A., and A. Argemi. "La Eucaristía en la predicación de San Pedro Crisólogo." *La Ciencia Tomista* 86 (1959): 605–28.

Paganotto, R. D. A. *L'apporto dei Sermoni di San Pier Crisologo alla storia della cura pastorale a Ravenna nel secolo V*. Rome: Pontifical Gregorian University, 1969.

Palardy, William. "The Church and the Synagogue in the Sermons of Saint Peter Chrysologus." Ph.D. dissertation, Catholic University of America, Washington, D.C., 1992.

———. "Peter Chrysologus' Interpretation of the Raising of Lazarus." In *Studia Patristica* 25, ed. E. A. Livingstone, 129–33. Louvain: Peeters, 1993.

Schlitz, E. "Un trésor oublié: Saint Pierre Chrysologue comme théologien." *Nouvelle revue théologique* 55 (1928): 265–76.

Scimè, Giuseppe. *Giudei e cristiani nei Sermoni di San Pietro Crisologo.* Rome: Institutum patristicum Augustinianum, 2003.

Sottocornola, Franco. *L'anno liturgico nei sermoni di Pietro Crisologo.* Cesena: Centro studi e ricerche sulla antica provincia ecclesiastica Ravennate, 1973.

Speigl, Jakob. "Petrus Chrysologus über die Auferstehung der Toten." *Jahrbuch für Antike und Christentum* 9 (1982): 140–53.

Spinelli, Mario. "L'eco delle invasioni barbariche nelle omelie di Pier Crisologo." *Vetera Christianorum* 16 (1979): 87–93.

———. "Il ruolo sociale del digiuno in Pier Crisologo." *Vetera Christianorum* 18 (1981): 143–56.

———. "Sangue, martirio e redenzione in Pier Crisologo." In *Sangue e antropologia biblica nella patristica,* ed. Francesco Vattioni, 1:529–46. Rome: Pia Unione Preziosissimo Sangue, 1981.

———. "La simbologia ecclesiologica di Pier Crisologo." In *Sangue e antropologia biblica nella patristica,* ed. Francesco Vattioni, 1:547–62. Rome: Pia Unione Preziosissimo Sangue, 1981.

Studer, Basil. "Peter Chrysologus." In *Patrology*, Vol. 4: *The Golden Age of Latin Patristic Literature From the Council of Nicea to the Council of Chalcedon,* ed. A. di Berardino, 575–77. Trans. P. Solari. Westminster, MD: Christian Classics, 1986.

Wilkins, M. *Word-Order in Selected Sermons of the Fifth and Sixth Centuries.* Washington, D.C.: Catholic University of America, 1940.

Zangara, Vincenza, "I silenzi nella predicazione di Pietro Crisologo." *Rivista di Storia e Letteratura Religiosa* 32 (1996): 225–68.

Zattoni, Girolamo. "Cronologia crisologhiana." In *Scritti Storici e Ravennati,* 309–18. Ravenna: Tonini, 1975.

INTRODUCTION

INTRODUCTION

1. The ecclesiastical history of Ravenna before the episcopate of Peter Chrysologus

Peter Chrysologus was bishop of Ravenna in the fifth century. The two principal sources for the early history of the church in Ravenna are his sermons and the ninth-century *Liber Pontificalis* of the priest Agnellus. In his zeal for his native city, Agnellus gives us in his chronicle of the lives of the bishops of Ravenna what amounts to a combination of history, legend, reflection on artefacts, and creative writing, all wrapped up into one. By emphasizing the church of Ravenna's antiquity and by recounting marvelous and miraculous events involving the bishops of that see, Agnellus aims to bolster Ravenna's prestige in an era when it was no longer as independent from Rome as it had been in the past few centuries.[1] The reliability of Agnellus as a historical source is debated by scholars.[2] On the whole, when Agnellus supplies information about buildings, artefacts, and geography that he has seen or to which he has had access he can be generally trusted, but otherwise caution seems to be in order, as is warranted by his own words:

1. To examine the whole question of Ravenna's autocephaly would take us far afield and into an era well after that of Peter Chrysologus. For more on this topic, see M. Mazzotti, "L'autocefalia della Chiesa di Ravenna (excursus storico)," in *ACCR*, 391–401, and Arnaldo Momigliano, "The Origins of Ecclesiastical Historiography," in *The Classical Foundations of Modern Historiography* (Berkeley: University of California Press, 1990), 132–37.

2. See G. Zattoni, "Cronologia crisologhiana," in *Scritti Storici e Ravennati* (Ravenna: Tonini, 1975), 309–10, in which the author criticizes the contradictions, anachronisms, trivialities, and legends that Agnellus relates. More favorably disposed is G. Cortesi, "Andrea Agnello e il 'Liber Pontificalis Ecclesiae Ravennatis,'" *Corso di Cultura sull'Arte Ravennate e Bizantina* 28 (1981): 42, where Agnellus's reliance upon various literary, architectural, and archaeological sources is emphasized.

When I have not found any history [of some bishops] or what kind of life they had led, with no information coming from any aged and venerable people, from any building, or from any source at all, so that there would be no gap in the series of the holy bishops as one after the other held this see, I have composed their life, through your prayers and the help of God.[3]

A certain St. Apollinaris was claimed to have introduced Christianity to Ravenna. The story went that he was from Antioch, followed St. Peter to Rome, knew Greek and Latin, and was ordained a bishop by Peter and sent to Ravenna. Some twenty-eight years later he was martyred during the reign of Vespasian.[4] Apollinaris was said to have baptized multitudes in the river and in the sea and to have performed miracles. That Apollinaris was not an invention of Agnellus is evident from *Sermon* 128, which Peter Chrysologus preached on the feast of this first bishop and martyr of Ravenna, and from the sixth-century church in his name at Ravenna's seaport, Classis.

It is doubtful, however, that there is much basis in historical fact for such an early beginning of Christianity in Ravenna. One scholar states that there is no evidence from archaeology and literature that Christianity took root in Ravenna before the late second or early third century.[5] The first bishop of Ravenna to whom any date can be assigned, apart from what Agnellus provides, is Severus, the twelfth bishop in Agnellus's list. Severus's name is listed among those present for the Council of Sardica in 343.[6] On the assumption, then, that Agnellus is using a reliable list of the bishops of Ravenna, unless the early bishops had exceptionally long episcopates, this would put Apollinaris at approximately the beginning of the third century.[7]

3. *Agnelli qui et Andreas Liber Pontificalis Ecclesiae Ravennatis*, ed. O. Holder-Egger, in *Scriptores Rerum Langobardicarum et Italicarum*, ed. G. Waitz (Hannover: Impensis bibliopolii Hahniani, 1878), 32 (subsequently referred to as: Agnellus, *Liber Pontificalis*).

4. Agnellus, *Liber Pontificalis* 1–2.

5. R. Farioli, *Ravenna Romana e Bizantina* (Ravenna: Longo, 1977), 18.

6. In addition, Agnellus, *Liber Pontificalis* 13, makes mention of Severus's presence at this council.

7. See F. Lanzoni, *Le diocesi d'Italia dalle origini al principio del Secolo VII (An. 604)*, Studi e Testi 35 (Faenza: Stabilimento Grafico F. Lega, 1927), 738.

As mentioned above, Peter Chrysologus delivered a sermon on St. Apollinaris. Chrysologus says nothing about Apollinaris being commissioned by St. Peter to found the church in Ravenna, nor does he claim that his see originated in the first century.[8] Chrysologus asserts that Apollinaris deserves the title "martyr," even though he did not die immediately from the wounds inflicted upon him. Apollinaris was a confessor on several occasions, but inasmuch as the newly established church of Ravenna was so dependent on his episcopal leadership, her fervent prayers managed to postpone his actual martyrdom.[9] As Chrysologus puts it: "Therefore, the enemy did not make him a martyr, since he did not inflict death, but he proved him to be a martyr, because he did not remove his faith."[10] Chrysologus calls Apollinaris the first bishop and the only native of Ravenna to be martyred, and says that he exemplified the Greek etymology of his name in having "lost" his life.[11] At the end of this sermon, Chrysologus refers to the burial place of Apollinaris, located where he is preaching. He calls Apollinaris a good shepherd standing at hand in the midst of his flock.[12] Perhaps the artist

8. Lanzoni, 739–40, makes a convincing argument from silence that Peter Chrysologus had no knowledge of the supposed Petrine mission of Apollinaris related by Agnellus. Chrysologus refers to St. Peter and the other apostles frequently in his sermons, but with no mention of the church of Ravenna. Bishops from other places in the fourth through sixth centuries emphasized their descent from Peter or another apostle, but Chrysologus did not. Also, in his *Sermon* 175, where Chrysologus defends his church's authority to consecrate the bishop of a suffragan see, he does not mention Ravenna's connection with St. Peter. All of this, together with the absence of any artistic depiction of Apollinaris's association with St. Peter, implies that the *Passio Apollinaris*, which was a source used by Agnellus, postdated Chrysologus.

9. *Sermon* 128.2.

10. *Sermon* 128.1.

11. Ibid. Venantius Fortunatus in his *Carmen* 8.3.167 in MGH.AA, ser. 1, vol. 4, ed. F. Leo (Berlin: Weidmann, 1881), mentions that the martyr Vitalis is buried in Ravenna, and in his *Vita Sancti Martini* 4.680–85 says that both Vitalis and an Ursicinus are buried there. Ambrose in his *Exhortatio Virginitatis* 1.1–8 (PL 16.351–54) tells of the transfer of the remains of a Vitalis and an Agricola from Bologna to Milan. It is unknown whether this is the same Vitalis who was thought to be buried in Ravenna in Venantius's day. There is a church in Ravenna dedicated to Saint Vitalis, dating to the sixth century. Apollinaris, however, seems to be the first martyr native to Ravenna.

12. *Sermon* 128.3.

who portrayed Apollinaris in the apse mosaic of Sant'Apollinare in Classe, believed to be built over the saint's remains, took his inspiration from Chrysologus's sermon.[13] Agnellus states that the first Christians congregated outside the city walls at Classis, the port of Ravenna, and that Bishop Probus, the seventh bishop, built the first basilica in Classis, where many of the early bishops of Ravenna were buried.[14] He goes on to say that all of the bishops from Apollinaris to Chrysologus were of eastern extraction.[15] The church of Ravenna began to expand under Chrysologus's immediate predecessor, Ursus. According to Agnellus, Bishop Ursus served for twenty-eight years and erected a new cathedral within the city walls.[16] Its baptistery, as renovated by Chrysologus's immediate successor, Neon, survives. That this was the first church constructed within Ravenna's walls confirms that Classis, and not Ravenna proper, was the residence of most Christians until the imperial court moved there in the early fifth century.

A major contributor to the church's growth in Ravenna was the Empress Galla Placidia, who reigned during the minority of her son Valentinian III following the death of the Emperor Honorius in 423. Her support for the church consisted primarily of a large-scale building program. She built a church to the Holy Cross, a monastic church in honor of St. Zacharias, and another to St. John the Evangelist in thanksgiving for her narrow escape from death when crossing the Aegean.[17] Her mausoleum survives, and it is thought to have originally been dedi-

---

13. Such is the suggestion of Otto G. von Simson, *Sacred Fortress: Byzantine Art and Statecraft in Ravenna* (Princeton, NJ: Princeton University Press, 1987), 53–54. Similarly, the baptistery built by Ursus is decorated with a mosaic dating from the time of Chrysologus's successor, Neon. This mosaic depicts the baptism of Christ and portrays the River Jordan personified and holding a towel in submission to Christ. Spiro K. Kostof, *The Orthodox Baptistery of Ravenna* (New Haven: Yale, 1965), 87, contends that the artist seems to have had Chrysologus's *Sermon* 160.5 in mind.

14. Agnellus, *Liber Pontificalis* 8.   15. Ibid., 24.
16. Ibid., 23.

17. Ibid., 42. The reliability of Agnellus's account in this instance is confirmed by an inscription from a wall in the Church of Saint John the Evangelist. See H. Dessau, ed., *Inscriptiones Latinae Selectae*, vol. 1 (Berlin: Weidmann, 1892), 818.1.

cated to St. Lawrence, who seems to have been a saint of importance to the Christians of Ravenna. *Sermon* 135, falsely attributed to Chrysologus, deals with Lawrence's martyrdom.[18] In an
account sent to St. Augustine in 425, we read: "Of the ten of us,
our second brother merited being healed, as we have heard, at
the shrine of the glorious martyr Lawrence, a shrine that was
recently located at Ravenna."[19] In Galla's mausoleum is a depiction of Lawrence bearing the cross as a trophy of victory. If she
herself did not build this edifice, she certainly embellished it
and wanted to associate herself in death with this martyr.

Galla Placidia was the daughter of Theodosius the Great and
the half-sister of Honorius. She had been widowed twice before
her reign in 424. Having been taken from Rome as a hostage
by the Goths, she married Alaric's brother Athaulf and after he
died was wed to Constantius III. She was regent for her son
Valentinian III and died on November 27, 450.[20] Galla's reign
as empress and Chrysologus's as bishop were virtually coterminous.

2. *The life and episcopate of Peter Chrysologus*

The difficulty in ascertaining significant dates in Chrysologus's chronology, especially regarding his birth and death,
stems in large part from the conflicting data Agnellus imparts.
Agnellus discusses him under the names of Peter I and Peter II,
the eighteenth and the twenty-second bishops of Ravenna, re-
spectively. It is the latter to whom he gives the title Chrysologus.[21] In actual fact there was a Peter II in the twenty-second

18. Concerning the authenticity of this sermon, see A. Olivar, *Los sermones de
san Pedro Crisólogo: Estudio crítico* (Montserrat: Abadía de Montserrat, 1962),
199–200.

19. Augustine, *Sermon* 322 (PL 38.1444). Agnellus, *Liber Pontificalis* 34–35,
also refers to Honorius's involvement in the establishment of this shrine.

20. A helpful book about Galla, her political and religious enterprises, and
the history of her era, is S. I. Oost, *Galla Placidia Augusta* (Chicago and London:
University of Chicago, 1968).

21. Meaning "golden word," found for the first time in Agnellus, *Liber Pontificalis* 47. Agnellus implies that the Church of Ravenna gave Peter this appella-
tion during his lifetime because of his great eloquence. But in the principal

place in the series of bishops, but he was bishop during the time of Theodoric in the late fifth and early sixth centuries. One must therefore rely upon other sources, in particular Chrysologus's own writings, in order to assemble his biography.[22] Peter Chrysologus was born ca. 380 in Imola (Forum Cornelii). Agnellus gives this as the place of birth for Peter II. Chrysologus too mentions his native Imola in *Sermon* 165, given at the consecration of his suffragan Bishop Proiectus of Imola.[23] He states, "And so my love for its name compels me to satisfy with desire the desires of the church of Cornelius, and with greater love to consecrate the venerable Proiectus as bishop."[24] In this sermon, Chrysologus also refers to an earlier bishop of Imola who himself was called Cornelius. This Cornelius was a spiritual father to Chrysologus, educated him in the Gospel, and consecrated him at the altar for some sacred ministry.

Imola was also the place where Chrysologus died and was buried. Knowing that the end was near, he went to Imola to the Basilica of Saint Cassian to offer a golden bowl, a silver paten, and gold diadems embellished with precious gems.[25] He breathed his last there and was buried next to the basilica.[26] Ag-

---

collection of Chrysologus's sermons, dating from the beginning of the eighth century, there is no reference to this title in the preface. It is therefore more likely that Peter was given the designation "Chrysologus" between the middle of the eighth and the beginning of the ninth century when Agnellus composed his history. The title was likely intended to indicate that while the east had its Chrysostom, the west had its Chrysologus. See Ruggero Benericetti, *Il Cristo nei sermoni di S. Pier Crisologo* (Cesena: Centro studi e ricerche sulla antica provincia ecclesiastica Ravennate, 1995), 65–66.

22. I shall follow in large part the chronology drawn up by A. Olivar, *Los sermones*, 227–31.

23. Imola had been previously under the jurisdiction of the Bishop of Milan. In 379 Ambrose of Milan wrote his *Letter* 2 (FOTC 26.88) to a certain Constantius, conferring upon him the temporary care of the church at Forum Cornelii in addition to his other episcopal responsibilities until a new bishop could be named.

24. Peter Chrysologus, *Sermon* 165 (see FOTC 17.271).

25. Agnellus, *Liber Pontificalis* 52. There is a mosaic of Cassian in the Archbishop's Chapel, built by Peter II during Theodoric's reign. Prudentius, *The Book of the Martyrs' Crowns* 9 (FOTC 43.182–89), describes the martyrdom of Cassian at Imola.

26. Agnellus, *Liber Pontificalis* 52.

nellus certainly saw Chrysologus's tomb at Imola and presumably had at hand an inventory of the offerings Chrysologus brought to the martyr's shrine. Chrysologus desired to be buried next to the great martyr of his home town. If he had been buried at Ravenna there would certainly have been some memorial to him there, but there was not.[27]

Around the year 426, Chrysologus was consecrated bishop of Ravenna by Celestine I, the bishop of Rome. Agnellus claims that he was consecrated by Sixtus III, Celestine's successor, who began his episcopate in 432.[28] Agnellus has the wrong bishop of Rome; from other sources it is fairly evident that Chrysologus was bishop before 431. Confidence can, however, be placed in Agnellus's assertion that Peter was consecrated by the bishop of Rome. Agnellus is not pro-Roman in his views and, as he writes, he looks wistfully back to periods when Ravenna was relatively independent of the see of Rome, so he would not have stated that the bishop of Ravenna was ordained by the bishop of Rome if he were not satisfied that this was the case. Second, the masterful work by Franco Sottocornola on the liturgy of Ravenna in Chrysologus's era makes the point that Ravenna was very much under Rome's influence insofar as its liturgical practice was concerned.[29] Both factors indicate the close ties between the churches of Rome and Ravenna.

Chrysologus's *Sermon* 130 appears to be his first sermon after

27. See Jean-Charles Picard, *Le souvenir des evêques* (Rome: École Francaise, 1988), 147–48. Those who argue against Chrysologus being from Imola would find it unlikely that he could have received such oratorical training in a small locale like Imola, and would situate him in Classis, from where the Ravenna Christians took their origin. Although there is no Bishop Cornelius listed among the bishops of Ravenna, some claim that Cornelius and Ursus were the same person, citing in support two letters of Pliny the Younger (4.9 and 5.20) addressed to a Cornelius Ursus. See, for example, G. Lucchesi, "Stato attuale degli studi sui santi dell'antica provincia ravennate," in *ACCR*, 51–80, and Augusto Benelli, "Note sulla vita e l'episcopato di Pietro Crisologo," in *In Verbis Verum Amare*, ed. P. Serra Zanetti (Firenze: La Nuova Italia, 1980), 63–79. But the association of Chrysologus with Imola in Agnellus's treatment, in his own *Sermon* 165, and insofar as his tomb is believed to be there, seem more compelling arguments to me.

28. Agnellus, *Liber Pontificalis* 49.

29. Franco Sottocornola, *L'anno liturgico nei sermoni di Pietro Crisologo* (Cesena: Centro studi e ricerche sulla antica provincia ecclesiastica Ravennate, 1973).

being consecrated a bishop. It was delivered before Galla
Placidia and the imperial court when he took possession of the
see.[30] Apparently there was an extended period of time during
which the see of Ravenna was vacant. The new bishop states,
"Just as a lengthy anticipation of some great thing that was
promised enkindles the spirit and wearies the mind, the awaited fulfillment of the promise stirs up all the senses and everything inside a person."[31] It is also in this sermon that Chrysologus refers to the Empress in very glowing terms. Earlier in this
sermon he spoke about the importance of a bishop complying
with kings and working with those holding power. He then goes
on to describe Galla as a pious Christian and likens her to the
Church in her intimacy with the Trinity. Chrysologus states:

Also present is the mother of the Christian, eternal, and faithful Empire herself, who, by following and imitating the blessed Church in
her faith, her works of mercy, her holiness, and in her reverence for
the Trinity, has been found worthy of bringing to birth, embracing,
and possessing an august trinity. This is how the Trinity rewards those
who are fervent in their love and zeal for him. She has been found
worthy of giving honor to herself and rejoicing that the grace of God
has made for her an object of devotion like him.[32]

Chrysologus's allusion here to the notion of the *pax deorum*—
that the ruler's reverence for God results in prosperity for the
Empire—is made even more explicit in another sermon delivered before the imperial family where he states:

Standing here is the most pious imperial family, serving the One, so
that they may reign over all; bowing their heads to God, so that all nations may bend their necks to them; offering gifts to God alone, so as
to obtain tribute from all peoples.[33]

30. A. Olivar, *Los sermones*, 197, believes instead that Chrysologus delivered
this sermon on the occasion of his consecrating a suffragan bishop.
    31. Peter Chrysologus, *Sermon* 130.1.
    32. *Sermon* 130.3. It is debatable who constitute this "trinity" of Galla's. I
hold that the members are her two children, Valentinian III and Honoria, and
the Eastern Emperor Theodosius II, Galla's nephew, whom, in a letter of hers to
Theodosius preserved in Leo the Great, *Letter* 56 (PL 54.859), Galla addresses
as "her ever-august son."
    33. *Sermon* 85b.3.

In light of Galla's disposition to bestow largesse upon the Church, her strong support of orthodox Christianity,[34] and, as noted below, her involvement in raising the see of Ravenna to metropolitan status, it is only natural that Chrysologus would not share the combative attitude of an Ambrose or a Chrysostom toward the imperial leader.

Some time before 431, Ravenna was elevated to the rank of metropolitan. In *Sermon* 136, Chrysologus is a simple bishop in the presence of a metropolitan *(antistes)* named Adelphius, presumably the individual who was bishop of Aquileia from 426 to 436.[35] In *Letter* 112 to Domnus of Antioch in 431, Theodoret of Cyrus refers to another letter he had sent to western bishops, and he mentions specifically Milan, Aquileia, and Ravenna.[36] Most probably these were the three Italian sees that, in addition to Rome, were of metropolitan standing.

The best indications that Ravenna rose to metropolitan status during Chrysologus's episcopate are the sermons he preached when he was exercising his privilege as metropolitan to consecrate bishops of suffragan sees. Chrysologus delivered *Sermon* 175 on the occasion of his first consecration of a suffragan, Marcellinus of Voghenza.[37] He remarks, "The holy church of Ravenna, in order to give birth to her first child, has made a journey, faced struggles, and experienced hardships."[38] Later in the sermon, he elaborates upon these struggles and hardships:

34. See her letter, cited in n. 32 above, where Galla tries to convince her nephew Theodosius II to convene a synod to deal with Monophysitism. S. I. Oost, *Galla Placidia Augusta,* passim, treats the whole question of Galla's religious views and piety.

35. *Sermon* 136.1. One scholar has suggested that this meeting between Chrysologus and Adelphius took place in order to prepare for Ravenna's promotion to metropolitan rank. See F. Lanzoni, *Le diocesi,* 752. A. Olivar, in his *monitum* to *Sermon* 136 in the CCL edition, p. 824, remarks that Chrysologus's excessive adulation for Adelphius in this sermon is characteristic of a young rather than a mature orator. It is therefore likely that this sermon was preached very early in Chrysologus's episcopate.

36. See SC 111.46–57.

37. A. Olivar, "La consagración del Obispo Marcelino de Voghenza," *RSCI* 22 (1968): 87–93, studies this sermon in detail and ascertains its date as October 31, 431. Chrysologus's *Sermon* 130a was also delivered on the occasion of his consecrating a new bishop of a suffragan see.

38. *Sermon* 175.1.

"The Lord [at His birth] managed to comply with the edict of Caesar, and a pagan one at that; yet a certain servant is still irreverently offering resistance to the decree of blessed Peter and the decree of the Christian leader."[39] From what Chrysologus has said, it is clear that the bishop of Rome ("blessed Peter") Celestine I and the head of state ("the Christian leader") Galla Placidia both issued decrees granting metropolitan privileges to the church of Ravenna. It was quite logical that Ravenna should have been made a metropolitan in light of the city's new political stature. Ravenna's growth and prestige as an imperial center warranted a correspondingly similar augmentation of its ecclesiastical status. Yet a "certain servant" opposed Ravenna's promotion. This opposition most probably came from the bishop of Milan.

The elevation of Ravenna came at the expense of Milan, and perhaps also of Aquileia. Voghenza could have been formerly Milan's suffragan see. Certainly Imola, which now was under Ravenna's jurisdiction, had previously belonged to Milan.[40] It is not at all peculiar that the bishop of Milan should have felt resentful about Ravenna's new prestige. Milan surely suffered a decline after the imperial court moved from there to Ravenna in the early fifth century. Milan's hold on some of the churches of Gaul was lost in 417 when Zosimus, bishop of Rome, elevated Patroclus, bishop of Arles, to a metropolitan and a papal vicar for the south of Gaul.[41] This promotion of Patroclus allowed Zosimus to secure a counterweight to the Gallic influence of the bishop of Milan.[42] Patroclus was also supported by Galla Placidia, whose deceased husband Constantius was Patroclus's former patron. He had been given the authority to convene

39. *Sermon* 175.3.

40. See Chrysologus's *Sermon* 165 (FOTC 17.270–71) and n. 23, above.

41. This served as well to bring the ecclesiastical structure of southern Gaul into line with the new imperial administrative structure, since the praetorian prefecture had moved from Trier to Arles around 395. See Ralph W. Mathisen, *Ecclesiastical Factionalism and Religious Controversy in Fifth-Century Gaul* (Washington, D.C.: The Catholic University of America Press, 1989), 18–19 and 49–50. Similarly, when the civil administration moved to Ravenna its ecclesiastical rank improved.

42. Ibid., 50.

church councils, depose offending bishops, and ordain succes-
sors in their place.[43] Hence, when another bishop of Rome and
the same Galla Placidia gave another see, such as Ravenna, privileges to the detriment of Milan, the bishop of Milan resisted.

In the middle of the 440s Germanus of Auxerre visited
Ravenna, met with Peter and Galla Placidia and eventually died
there. In the *Life of St. Germanus*, written around 480 by Constantius of Lyons, we read that "Bishop Peter directed the
Church of Christ according to the rule of the Apostles," and
"the Empress Placidia with her son Valentinian . . . loved the
Catholic faith to such an extent that, although they had authority over all, with deep humility they were obedient to the servants of God."[44] When Germanus died, Chrysologus and Galla
competed to obtain Germanus's relics: "The Empire takes one
portion and the episcopate claims the other; . . . The Empress
acquired the container with the relics; Bishop Peter took possession of the cloak with the hairshirt within."[45] The presence
of both Chrysologus and Galla in this account is another example of the amicable relationship between church and state in
Ravenna during this period.

Having been consecrated and, if Agnellus is to be believed,
actually chosen by the bishop of Rome for the see of Ravenna,
and having received a decree from the Pope elevating his see to
metropolitan status, Chrysologus is understandably loyal to the
see of Rome. In one sermon where Chrysologus describes St.
Peter during one of Christ's resurrection appearances, he says
that Peter "plunged into the sea, so that the one who had received the primacy of rank might be the first to return."[46] Even
more significant is Chrysologus's letter to Eutyches. He writes:

We exhort you, however, in all affairs, honorable brother, to follow
obediently these directives that have been written by the very blessed
Pope of the city of Rome, since blessed Peter, who lives and presides in
his own see, presents the true faith to those who seek it. For, out of a

43. Ibid., 72.
44. Constantius of Lyons, *Vita Germani episcopi Autissiodorensis* 35 in SC 112.
45. Ibid., 43.
46. *Sermon* 78.7.

desire for peace and for the faith, we are unable to hear cases apart from the consent of the bishop of the city of Rome.[47]

This letter is all that is extant of Chrysologus's correspondence. It was written in 449,[48] the same year that Leo wrote his Tome to Flavian, and that other bishops from the east appealed to Rome.

The only other possible source describing Peter's life is *Sermon* 107, found under his name but judged to be spurious.[49] This sermon refers to a Peter who had been a monk[50] and became a venerable priest of God, who gathers great numbers to the faith, corrects those engulfed by the waves of errors, sows precepts of righteousness, teaches heavenly doctrines, unlocks the mysteries of Scripture, and to whom people flock in massive numbers to hear.[51] One cannot prove that this sermon is praising Chrysologus, but such a possibility cannot be entirely eliminated.

As with much of the chronology of Chrysologus's life, there are scholarly debates about the date of his death. The *terminus ante quem* is 458, the year in which Leo wrote to Bishop Neon, Chrysologus's successor.[52] If we rely upon Agnellus's dates for the deaths of his Peter I and Peter II, we arrive at December 3, 450. Agnellus says that Peter I died when the Emperor Valentinian began to reign for himself,[53] that is, after his mother Galla Placidia died. She died on November 27, 450, and Chrysologus succumbed less than a week later.[54]

47. *Epistula ad Eutychen* in *Acta Conciliorum Oecumenicorum II*, ed. E. Schwartz, II, vol. 3, pt. 1 (Berlin: de Gruyter, 1935), 6. For more on this letter, including its authenticity, see Olivar, *Los sermones*, 87–94.

48. See A. Olivar, "Pietro Crisologo, arcivescovo di Ravenna, Dottore della Chiesa, santo," in *BSS* 10:685–91.

49. See A. Olivar, *Los sermones*, 97–100. The text of the sermon is in CCL 24A.665–66.

50. *Sermon* 107.2.

51. *Sermon* 107.3–4.

52. Leo the Great, *Letter* 166 (PL 54.1191–96).

53. Agnellus, *Liber Pontificalis* 26.

54. In his account of Peter II (the one whom Agnellus calls "Chrysologus") Agnellus gives December 3 as the date of death. This could well have been the date on Chrysologus's tomb in Imola. The date that Agnellus gives for the death of Peter I is July 31. See *Liber Pontificalis* 26 and 52.

3. Chrysologus on his own times

One can glimpse the society in which Chrysologus lived from his sermons' references to the events and issues of his day. Some of the images he uses reveal the various activities and professions found in Ravenna. These include agriculture (e.g., *Sermon* 7.5–6), seafaring (7a.1), the law courts (8.5), the battlefield (14.1), medicine (44.1), and commercial contracts (62.3).

Chrysologus refers a number of times to the barbarian invasions. When speaking about Christ calming the storm at sea and after mentioning that the rulers are now Christians and no longer persecutors, thereby securing tranquility for Christian believers,[55] Chrysologus describes a new harsh north wind that carries along with it wild peoples wreaking havoc wherever it goes.[56] He interprets these invasions as God's punishment for the people's sins, yet they do not repent. In *Sermon* 21, Chrysologus also uses the analogy of a storm to depict his era, but without as clear a reference to the invaders.

In another sermon he states that the world is wearied by extreme old age, weighed down by afflictions and diseases, attesting to the proximity of its end.[57] The Vandals had laid waste to North Africa in the 430s, the Huns in the late 440s created disturbances to the north, and in the middle 440s there was a series of epidemics.[58] Elsewhere Chrysologus remarks that famine and pestilence have spread everywhere.[59] It is no surprise, therefore, that he should have occasionally struck a note of pessimism in the face of such invasions and diseases.

Chrysologus encourages his congregation to deal in a constructive manner with the disturbances caused by the barbarians. As the Magi offered gifts to the infant Jesus, so too Christians are now called upon to make their contributions so that their bishop might liberate the "large number of captives." "Let us support our neighbors in their tribulations," Chrysologus urges, "so that we may be freed from our tribulations."[60]

---

55. *Sermon* 20.2 (FOTC 17.62).
57. *Sermon* 167.3.
59. *Sermon* 45.7.

56. *Sermon* 20.4 (FOTC 17.63–64).
58. A. Olivar, *Los sermones*, 235.
60. *Sermon* 103.7.

In another place, Chrysologus laments the captivity of Christians throughout the world, while celebrating the casting of Christ's nets among the various tribes and nations.[61] Also, in elaborating upon Christ's commission to preach the Gospel throughout the whole world, Chrysologus has Christ mention the very fierce nations that will come to acknowledge him.[62] Thus, the crisis created by the barbarian invasions is not only a chastisement sent by God, but also an opportunity to exercise charity towards one's Christian neighbors held in captivity and to evangelize these new peoples.

Chrysologus did not think it impossible that Christians of his day might face persecution and martyrdom. He does not specify if such violence would occur at the hands of the invading tribes or from some other quarter. He speaks about dying gloriously for the sake of innocence.[63] In another sermon, Chrysologus contrasts the tongue of the blasphemer that brings condemnation with the tongue of the martyr that receives the crown.[64] Yet, if Christians merit being martyred they owe it all to God and not to themselves. Martyrdom is a grace, a gift from God.[65] He does not want Christians to run to martyrdom. Those who rashly seek to become martyrs are in fact following the devil's admonition. The same devil who tempted Christ to hurl himself from the pinnacle of the Temple continues to tempt others to cast themselves down. Referring presumably to overzealous Circumcellions of a past epoch, Chrysologus says,

[The devil] seeks a fall, he orders crashes, and with such advice he creates martyrs throughout Africa by saying: "If you wish to be a martyr, cast yourself down," so that he may push those from on high to death, not so that he may lift and raise those from below to the crown.[66]

When Chrysologus speaks about the proper Christian behavior during persecution, one has the sense that it is the present prospect of martyrdom that motivates his remarks. His most extended treatment of this topic is found in one of his sermons

61. *Sermon* 47.3–4 (FOTC 17.101–2).   62. *Sermon* 83.3 (FOTC 17.135).
63. *Sermon* 113.6.   64. *Sermon* 177.7.
65. *Sermon* 152.9 (FOTC 17.258–59).   66. *Sermon* 13.5.

on the flight of Jesus, Mary, and Joseph into Egypt in which he finds warrant for justifying the flight of Christians in times of persecution.[67] That he still viewed martyrdom as a possibility may have come not only from invading tribes, but also from pagan, heretical, and other elements subversive to orthodox Christian doctrine and practice.

Chrysologus holds in some disdain the worldly knowledge and rhetoric espoused by certain philosophical schools. He singles out the Epicureans as the foremost example of those given to self-indulgent and sinful pleasure.[68] In his description of John the Baptist acting in the power of Elijah, Chrysologus resists any interpretation that would suggest the notion of transmigration of souls.[69] He opposes philosophy in general because, in his view, philosophy teaches polytheism and does not lead a person to the one true God.[70]

In *Sermons* 155 and 155a, Chrysologus rails against Christians participating in the festivities surrounding the Kalends of January.[71] Both the connection with paganism and the excessive revelry that was fostered by these celebrations roused his pastoral ire. There was also another reason for his opposition: Christian participation in these rituals allowed this element of paganism to survive. At a time when, as he alleges, pagans were converting to Christianity in Ravenna in large numbers,[72] Christians were helping paganism survive by taking part in New Year's spectacles

67. *Sermon* 151.6. The Scriptural references are Mt 10.23, Mt 5.44, and Acts 9.36. See also *Sermon* 150.11.

68. *Sermon* 5.4–5 (FOTC 17.47–48). This does not mean, however, that Chrysologus perceived any Epicurean opposition to Christianity. Rather, it was an apologetic convention to attack Epicureans as representing the nadir to which pagan philosophy could sink.

69. *Sermon* 88.6 (FOTC 17.142).

70. *Sermon* 44.6 (FOTC 17.98).

71. For studies on the treatment of Chrysologus and other Fathers on the Kalends of January, see Michel Meslin, *La fête des kalendes de janvier dans l'empire romain*, Collection Latomus, vol. 115 (Brussels, 1970), esp. 95–129; and Robert Markus, *The End of Ancient Christianity* (Cambridge: Cambridge University Press, 1990), 103–6.

72. *Sermons* 56–62a on the Creed are addressed to people forsaking pagan idolatry and coming over to Christianity. Because of their numbers, Chrysologus is forced to shorten the period of catechesis in order to receive them into the Church more quickly.

that commemorated the pagan deities. With somewhat less ve-
hemence Chrysologus also alludes to the theater,[73] which Salvian lamented was a popular pastime among the citizens of
Ravenna even while barbarians were creating havoc nearby.[74]

Magic, astrology, and divination seem to have exercised an
attraction in Ravenna, and Chrysologus spoke against them, as
had many Christian leaders before him. He warns his congregation, "[L]et us not be ensnared by augury, let us not be deceived by divination, let us not be captivated by fortune-telling,
let us not be deluded by palm reading, let us not be seduced by
death, let us not be enticed by reeking odors."[75] These are
means employed by the devil to deceive human beings.[76]
Chrysologus's sermons on the adoration of the Magi provide
him with an occasion to attack astrology. That a star guided the
Magi to Christ shows that the stars are under the control of the
Creator and exercise no control over the Creator or over creation but serve merely as signs.[77] Hence the narrative of the
Magi does not confirm the power of magic but dissolves it.[78]

4. Chrysologus's theological opponents

Besides his relatively infrequent allusions to some pagan
practices and ideas, as noted above, Chrysologus engages in a
more sustained confrontation with Judaism. In general his anti-
Jewish rhetoric is drawn from the New Testament and the subsequent Christian *adversus Iudaeos* tradition. Chrysologus customarily presents Judaism so as to make Christianity shine all
the brighter by contrast. Nevertheless, there are several occasions where he exhorts his Christian congregation to follow the
praiseworthy example of certain Jews. The Pharisee has one
commendable trait: he is called the "Catholic of the Jews" because he believes in the resurrection of the dead.[79] In urging

---

73. *Sermons* 71.5 and 173.7.
74. Salvian of Marseille, *The Governance of God* 6.9 (FOTC 3.167).
75. *Sermon* 18.9.
76. *Sermon* 71.5.
77. *Sermons* 156.6–10 (FOTC 17.267–70) and 157.2.
78. *Sermon* 156.10 (FOTC 17.270).
79. *Sermon* 95.2 (FOTC 17.148).

his own congregation to be generous, Chrysologus points with admiration to the Jewish practice of tithing.[80] The Jews are also portrayed in a positive light when compared with gentiles. Chrysologus emphasizes the difficulties faced by Mary and Joseph as they made their way to the land of Egypt, a place of sacrilege, idols, and demons, a place inhabited by gentiles, who have nothing in common with Jews and who transgress the Law, which the Jews cherish.[81] On one occasion Chrysologus gives a backhanded compliment to the Jews. Because he finds his flock to be so enamored of temporal goods and the ways of the world, he chastises them: "Therefore, we are more obstinate than the Jews, we who pursue a fleeting world."[82]

The Jewish population in Ravenna and Classis was minimal before the early fifth century, but increased significantly with the arrival of the imperial court. Many may have emigrated there from the older communities at Milan and Aquileia. Jews came to Ravenna, a center of commerce and now the residence of the emperor, as soldiers, public servants, lawyers, and merchants of luxury items.[83] Thus, the influx of Jews began approximately only two decades before Peter Chrysologus became bishop.

Although one scholar claims that Chrysologus was actively engaged against numerous Jews in Ravenna,[84] the textual evidence does not bear this out. His involvement seems to have been slight. He may be reflecting his own personal experience with Jews of his day when he refers to the "unhappy and detestable wickedness of the Jewish mind, always more ready to argue than to believe."[85] Chrysologus deals with two theological objections from Jewish circles: first, that angels, and not the

80. See *Sermon* 103.6.
81. See *Sermon* 151.2.
82. *Sermon* 167.4.
83. Lellia Cracco Ruggini, "Ebrei e orientali nell'Italia settentrionale fra il IV e il VI secolo d. Cr.," *Studia et Documenta Historiae et Iuris* 25 (1959): 227–29.
84. See Gottfried Böhmer, *Petrus Chrysologus Erzbischof von Ravenna als Prediger* (Paderborn: Schöningh, 1919), 4 and 6.
85. *Sermon* 49.3. In *Sermons* 29.5, 30.4, and 95.2 (FOTC 17.148), for example, Chrysologus appeals to Jews, as though present, to put faith in Christ and in the Church.

Son, were God's fellow workers in creation,[86] and, second, that Jesus was not virginally conceived, but was illegitimate.[87] Despite Chrysologus's arguments, since all his catechumens seem to have been gentiles, his pleas to the Jews seem to have been ineffective in converting them to the Christian faith. Contact between Chrysologus and the Jews does not appear to have been frequent, since there are no indications that he knew any of them personally, or was familiar with their doctrines or way of life.

Chrysologus also spoke out against various heretical groups. Whereas persecution racks the Church from without, heresy inflicts internal damage. He remarks that there were almost as many heresies as there are questions concerning the divine Law.[88] As noted above, Chrysologus seems to have been aware of the Circumcellion sect of the Donatists and their desire for martyrdom.[89] He also opposes those, presumably the Manichees, who think that evil is something created by God, that sin is attributable to nature, and that evil is a substance or a nature and not merely an accident.[90]

Furthermore, Chrysologus attacks a docetic view of Christ. With regard to Christ's birth, "it is a heresy that makes the false assertion that Christ took on a body of air, and did not have flesh, but concocts the claim that he merely pretended to be a

86. *Sermon* 131.12. The Biblical text in question is Gn 1.26. For examples of Jewish interpretation, see Philo, *De Fuga et Inventione* 68–70, in *Les Oeuvres de Philon d'Alexandrie,* vol. 17, ed. and trans. E. Starobinski-Safran (Paris: Cerf, 1970) in which God's assistants are the *dynameis.* See also *The Talmud of Babylonia: An American Translation, XXIIIB: Tractate Sanhedrin, Chapters 4–8,* trans. Jacob Neusner, Brown Judaic Studies, no. 84 (Chico, CA: Scholars Press, 1984), chap. 4 [38B]:X: "Said R. Judah said Rab, 'When the Holy One, blessed be he, proposed to create man, he created a group of ministering angels. He said to them, "Shall we make man in our image?"'"

87. *Sermon* 148a.3. Regarding the charge of adultery against Mary, see the pagan Celsus as spokesperson for this Jewish allegation in Origen, *Contra Celsum,* trans. with intro. and notes by H. Chadwick (Cambridge: Cambridge University Press, 1953), I.28 and 32. See also Chadwick's note 3, p. 31.

88. *Sermon* 21.4.

89. See *Sermon* 13.5, n. 12.

90. See, for example, *Sermons* 11.2 (FOTC 17.57), 52.2–3, 96.6 (FOTC 17.155), 111.2 (FOTC 17.176), and 113.4. Chrysologus's contemporary Leo the Great indicates that Manichaeism was still thriving in Rome at this time. See the introduction to the English translation of Leo's sermons in FOTC 93.9, trans. J. P. Freeland and A. J. Conway (1996).

man."[91] It is likewise erroneous to assert that "he did not undergo death in order to conquer it, but had merely pretended to die in order to delude."[92] Against Helvidius and Jovinian, Chrysologus emphasizes Mary's perpetual virginity.[93] He also opposes Nestorianism. In another sermon, after quoting Matthew 1.20—"What has been born in her is from the Holy Spirit"—Chrysologus goes on the offensive, "Let them come and hear, those who have exerted their energy in clouding over the purity of the Latin language with a Greek whirlwind, uttering the blasphemous *anthropotokos* and *Christotokos*, in order to do away with *theotokos*."[94] In the first section of his letter to Eutyches, Chrysologus mentions Origen and Nestorius as examples of those who erred by rashly investigating Christ's origin.[95] He gives no details, however, that suggest any familiarity with Eutyches's Monophysite Christology.

The heresy to which Chrysologus gives the greatest attention is Arianism. One logical reason for his concern is that Arianism had taken root in Ravenna, especially among the administrative and military organization, among the troops and their families. The Goths, who were Arians, formed a considerable portion of the imperial army.[96] Arius and Photinus, he says, not only discredit the Son, but by denying his coeternity with the Father also restrict the Father, since there was a time before the origin of the Son when he would not have been Father.[97] He chides the Arians for putting more stock in excessive and rash disputation than in faith, and for imagining the divine begetting in human terms.[98] The classic rebuttal to Arianism, to dis-

91. *Sermon* 144.4.
92. *Sermon* 58.6.
93. Chrysologus does not mention Helvidius and Jovinian by name. See H. Koch, "Petrus Chrysologus," in *PRE* 38:1369. See also *Sermons* 60.7 and 117.3, 5 (FOTC 17.200–201), where Chrysologus says that, since they are formed from earth, human beings are born from and with concupiscence, reminiscent of Augustine in his quarrels with Pelagius and Julian of Eclanum.
94. *Sermon* 145.6 (see FOTC 17.235–36).
95. *Letter to Eutyches* (FOTC 17.285–87).
96. See G. Montanari, "Elementi per una ricerca storico-teologica sull' 'arianesimo' nella città di Ravenna," in *ACCR,* 47–48.
97. *Sermon* 109.4 (FOTC 17.174).
98. See, for example, *Sermons* 23.2, 24.3, 60.4, 84.10, 88.5 (FOTC 17.141–42), and 144.7. *Sermon* 142.13 could be referring to either Arians or Nestorians.

tinguish the Word as pre-existent from the Word incarnate, is utilized by Chrysologus when he states, "But whatever inferiority the Son has, whatever he receives, whatever he does not know, comes from my body, not from his substance."[99]

Chrysologus also objects to those rigorists who say that priests do not have the power to forgive sins. After quoting John 20.22–33 concerning the risen Lord's bestowal of the Holy Spirit for the forgiveness of sins, he continues:

Where are those who declare that sins cannot be forgiven human beings by human beings? Where are those who oppress people such that once they fall because of the Devil's influence, they are never to arise? Where are those who out of their mean spirit take away and refuse a cure for their infirmities and medicine for their wounds?[100]

5. Chrysologus on relations between the Church and society

In addition to denouncing the debauchery surrounding the Kalends of January, Chrysologus also decries the excessive revelry of some on the feast of the birth of John the Baptist. It is for him a bitter irony that the way Christians observe John's birth resembles the debauchery at Herod's birthday banquet that occasioned John's death. Chrysologus insists that he does not oppose celebrating *per se*, but rather the kind of merrymaking that is extravagant, indecent, without regard for the poor, and with no reference to Christ.[101]

In many sermons, Chrysologus expresses his concern about the contrast between the rich and the poor in Ravenna. He frequently reminds the rich of their obligation to aid the less fortunate around them. When Chrysologus preaches on Luke 3.11 where the person with two coats is instructed to give one

99. *Sermon* 62.8: "my body" refers to the human nature shared by Chrysologus, and, indeed, by all humanity with Christ, by virtue of his Incarnation.

100. *Sermon* 84.7. *Sermon* 83.4 (FOTC 17.136) also encourages Christians to have confidence in forgiveness and not to despair, although there is no mention of the role of the priest in the penitential process here. *Sermon* 34.3 refers to a silent confession before God alone as wiping out sin.

101. *Sermon* 127.10.

to the person with none and the person with a surplus of food to act similarly, this gap between rich and poor in his congregation prompts him to say, "And if the one who does not give one of his two coats is guilty, what about the one who refuses one yet has a closet full of them? The result of locking up his clothes and withholding his bread is that the poor person dies of hunger and perishes from the cold."[102]

In this same sermon, Chrysologus warns tax collectors not to demand more than what is required, not to defraud anyone, and not to confiscate the goods of the downtrodden and the oppressed. Likewise, he admonishes soldiers not to terrorize anyone by extortion, nor spread false accusation.[103] That he felt compelled to address these issues means that such practices may have been fairly widespread.[104]

In another sermon, after he rails against drunkenness among members of the clergy,[105] Chrysologus directs those in positions of secular authority on the right use of their power. All those with any civil jurisdiction need to heed Romans 13.1: "There is no power except from God." He reminds kings, generals, soldiers, governors of provinces or cities, and judges that they all will one day render an account of their service before God. They are urged to exercise restraint in the use of the power entrusted to them, to be conscientious in their duties, and to secure justice while also showing mercy. In the matter of levying taxes, the amount collected must be enough to satisfy the legitimate needs of the military while not overburdening the taxpayer.[106] Since Chrysologus felt obliged to specify how one ought to exercise properly his or her position of authority, it is likely that there were persons of influence in the congregation, and that there were abuses of power that warranted such remarks.

Finally, Chrysologus alludes to a law from the Theodosian

102. *Sermon* 137.9.
103. *Sermon* 137.10–11.
104. Of course, it is possible that such remarks were merely a dramatic rendering of Lk 3.10–14, the text upon which Chrysologus was preaching, or his own reflections upon past events, and did not indicate contemporary ills.
105. *Sermon* 26.3–4.
106. *Sermon* 26.5.

Code (4.14.1) promulgated in 424, stipulating that property disputes must not be protracted for a period longer than thirty years. Chrysologus's point is that although in such secular matters the statute of limitations is thirty years, people still wrongfully engage in Christological debates so many centuries after Christ's birth.[107]

6. *Chrysologus as exegete*

Like other early Christian exegetes, Chrysologus considers the Bible to be a unified whole. He maintains that the divine teaching contained therein has different manners of expression, but is "one in its spirit and meaning."[108] He falls squarely within the tradition of finding multiple levels of meaning in a given Scriptural text. In contrast to interpreters like Origen and Ambrose, however, since Chrysologus's extant works deal primarily with the New Testament, he does not usually have to resolve the problem of relating the two dispensations nor have to explain Old Testament passages that are contradictory or "unworthy of God." Thus, the reader of Chrysologus's sermons does not sense that he employs the allegorical method of interpretation primarily to resolve difficulties that a literal reading of certain Biblical texts presents. One exception, however, is found in a sermon where he is dealing with the resurrection account that tells of the women arriving at the tomb of Jesus early in the morning after the sun had risen. How, he asks, could it be early in the morning if the sun had already risen? Was the evangelist unaware of what he was saying? Chrysologus's response is that there is no error, the truth is being spoken, but the apparent contradiction reveals a higher truth: the risen sun denotes the resurrected Christ.[109] His customary use of the alle-

---

107. See *Sermon* 145.10 (FOTC 17.237) and *Letter to Eutyches* 1 (FOTC 17.285).

108. See, for example, *Sermon* 116.1 (FOTC 17.194). A very helpful article about Chrysologus's exegesis is A. Olivar's "Els principis exegètics de sant Pere Crisòleg," in *Miscellanea Biblica B. Ubach*, ed. Romualdo M. Dìaz (Montserrat: Abadía de Montserrat, 1953), 413–37.

109. *Sermon* 82.2, and Olivar, "Els principis," 436.

gorical method, though, is to draw his listeners ever more deeply into the divine mysteries concealed within the Bible. Normally the literal meaning of a text is evident and accessible. Yet Chrysologus's love and reverence for the Biblical text encourage him, and through him his congregation, to delve more deeply. There is, he believes, an inestimable wealth in the Scriptures. If each word of Scripture had a book written about it, even then the mystery it contains would not be fully elucidated.[110] In a similar vein he states that not only each letter, but even all the "dots of the *i*" *(apices)* in the Gospel have profound meanings.[111]

Chrysologus admits that to arrive at the spiritual or deeper sense of a passage is often hard work. Yet that is in itself beneficial. If it were easy to grasp the meaning of every part of Scripture, one's mind would grow slack and one's ingenuity would remain unchallenged. Furthermore, if there were no significance to Scripture beyond the literal meaning, there would be equal access for all, the believer and unbeliever, the reverent and irreverent alike. A true understanding of Scripture comes only after "working up a sweat" *(sudantis fructus)*. In addition, after such labor one is made humble before Scripture's bounty and realizes that he is the recipient of a gift rather than the master of an intellectual conquest.[112]

Jesus' own pedagogy is the basis for Chrysologus's contention that only the reverent believer is capable of gaining access to the hidden meaning of Scripture. Christ's parables seemed enigmatic to most of his hearers; it was only to the believers that the mystery of the kingdom was made known. Since believers would have a saving knowledge that the unbelievers would not, Chrysologus states that the confusion, obscurity, and blindness of the unbelievers would, by contrast, increase the glory of the believers.[113]

---

110. *Sermon* 64.1.
111. *Sermon* 146.4 (FOTC 17.240). This and the previous reference are highlighted in Olivar, "Els principis," 416.
112. See *Sermon* 96.1 (FOTC 17.152): what is acquired is *accepta* rather than *possessa*, *inventa* rather than *subiecta*.
113. See *Sermon* 132.2 (FOTC 17.216): *infidelium poena fidelium redundet ad gloriam*.

Thus, an attitude of faith and respectful awe before the Scriptures is one necessary tool for proper interpretation. Chrysologus uses other resources to understand a given text. One way to clarify the meaning of a given Gospel passage is to look at its parallels in the other Gospels.[114] The etymologies of some words also add to the meaning of Scripture.[115] These tools were necessary mainly for establishing the sense of a passage on the literal level.

The usual distinction Chrysologus makes is between the literal[116] and the allegorical[117] meaning of Scripture. On occasion, however, he uncovers a moral dimension as well. The merchant who searches for the pearl of great price in Matthew 13.45–46 represents the person who shows mercy and seeks virtue.[118] The woman in the Gospel who is stooped over and the tax-collector who is weighed down signify those who are burdened by their sins.[119]

In other sermons Chrysologus interprets certain animals mentioned in the Scriptures as symbols of vices.[120] The swine in the parable of the Prodigal Son stand for those who live for their belly and wallow in their sins.[121] It is no coincidence that Jesus calls Herod a "fox" because, like a fox, he is full of craftiness, pretense, trickery, and deceit.[122] The raven represents one

114. See, for example, *Sermons* 66.1, 79.1, and 82.1, indicated in Olivar, "Els principis," 418.

115. He does this in *Sermons* 142.2 and 144.5, for example. In *Sermon* 128.1 he provides an etymology for the name "Apollinaris."

116. For the "literal" level he employs such terms as *historicus sensus* (*Sermon* 5.1, FOTC 17.43), *facies lectionis* (*Sermon* 95.1, FOTC 17.147), and *species lectionis* (*Sermon* 156.2, FOTC 17.265).

117. See A. Olivar, "Els principis," 421–22. Terms such as *sensus (sensus in littera latet), interna, altior* or *caelestis intelligentia,* and *profunda* make it apparent that for Chrysologus this is the deeper and more significant level of interpretation.

118. *Sermon* 47.2 (FOTC 17.100).

119. *Sermon* 105.4.

120. Chrysologus is following the tradition of the early Christian interpretation of the *Physiologus,* an anonymous work written between the second and fourth centuries, that assigns moral or allegorical meanings to many animals, the inspiration for medieval bestiaries. For an English translation, see *Physiologus,* trans. M. J. Curley (Austin: University of Texas Press, 1979).

121. *Sermon* 2.5 (FOTC 17.34).

122. *Sermon* 19.3.

who is bloodthirsty, cruel, and full of anger.[123] In his treatment of the clothing and food of John the Baptist, Chrysologus interprets the ugliness and crookedness of the camel as signifying those who are deformed and twisted out of shape by their sins. On a more positive note, the locust symbolizes one who flies from sin to repentance.[124] Elsewhere Peter says that kites, eagles, and vultures are images of vile and ravenous sins that lay waste to human minds and hearts.[125]

With regard to the Bible's even deeper, allegorical sense, Chrysologus's confidence that the word of Scripture can be a vehicle for a more profound level of meaning is based on Christ himself. As God incarnate Christ was a human vehicle of divine presence and revelation. Christ's incarnation, then, justifies allegorical exegesis. "Christ our God," Chrysologus remarks, "enters the temporal order."[126] Therefore, through the human, the earthly, and the physical realm, the spiritual realm can be made known and represented. By virtue of his incarnation, Christ "recommends heavenly goods by means of earthly examples, he gives a knowledge of future blessings from present ones, and he represents invisible matters with visible evidence."[127] In Christ and in the Scriptures heavenly mysteries are communicated through earthly realities.

According to Chrysologus, Scriptural exegesis was a cooperative venture between the preacher and the congregation, each bearing certain responsibilities.[128] Those who are preachers need the grace of divine inspiration in order to interpret the text correctly. When it comes time to give the allegorical meaning of a text Chrysologus asks his congregation to pray that Christ may shine the light of his word on him.[129] The preacher needs this divine assistance, because the Scriptures improperly interpreted will not merely fail to be of any benefit for salva-

123. *Sermon* 163.5.
124. *Sermon* 167.8–9.
125. *Sermon* 171.4 and 6.
126. *Sermon* 47.1 (see FOTC 17.99).
127. Ibid. (see FOTC 17.99–100).
128. Chrysologus's frequent use of the first-person plural conveys this idea and is thus more than merely a rhetorical device.
129. See, e.g., *Sermon* 64.1.

tion, but can even do severe harm.[130] In addition to providing
their prayer, the listeners also contribute by being keenly attentive.[131] Chrysologus likens the deep, divine meaning that is hidden in the human language of Scripture to gold that is buried
in the earth. The preciousness of what is concealed is certainly
worth the intensity of the effort to uncover it.[132]

Chrysologus also believed that official Church teaching, particularly the Church's faith in the equal divinity of the Father
and the Son,[133] was necessary to provide the parameters for interpreting the Scriptures.[134] Those with heterodox teachings
read into the Bible whatever they wanted. He states, "The one
who has set his course on error always hears what he wants
rather than what is."[135] In the same way that medicine properly
administered brings health and improperly taken brings harm,
so too if someone ingests the word of God rashly without following the dosage and instructions of the Church, damage will
result.[136]

Chrysologus implies that the exegesis and understanding of
Scripture is a gradual process that cannot be rushed. In his
preaching he never considers too much Scripture at one time
and on occasion devotes several consecutive homilies to the
same few verses. He wants Scripture to trickle slowly into one's
understanding, and not inundate it. Almost always he deals

130. See, e.g., *Sermon* 52.1.

131. See, e.g., *Sermon* 120.1 (FOTC 17.203). In *Sermon* 2.5 (FOTC 17.33)
Chrysologus notes that his listeners are not sufficiently attentive.

132. See, e.g., *Sermon* 139.1.

133. Following the lead of pro-Nicene writers a century before, Chrysologus
follows the rule that in reading a Biblical text concerning Christ, one must dis-
tinguish what refers to Christ's divinity from what refers to his humanity. See,
e.g., *Sermons* 65.5 and 144.7.

134. Chrysologus would agree with the following comment in a recent work
on Scriptural exegesis regarding both the limitations and the possibilities provided by Church teaching or "the Rule of faith": "[T]he Rule of faith is a negative rather than a positive principle. That is, it excludes incorrect interpretations but does not require a correct one. Of a given passage there may be many
interpretations that are valid because they do not contradict the Rule of
faith. . . ." R. A. Greer and J. L Kugel, *Early Biblical Interpretation* (Philadelphia:
Westminster, 1986), 197.

135. *Sermon* 131.5.

136. See, e.g., *Sermon* 156.1 (FOTC 17.265).

with the literal, narrative sense of the text first and then treats the allegorical or figurative sense.[137] He does this in three different ways: he may treat each verse individually, first literally, then allegorically;[138] he may devote one sermon to a particular Scriptural text and deal with the literal meaning in the first half of the sermon, and the figurative in the second half;[139] or he may deliver one or several sermons on the literal meaning of a passage, and then in a subsequent sermon or sermons consider the allegorical meaning.[140]

For Chrysologus, as for many patristic exegetes, Old Testament people, things, and events prefigured, or were types of, New Testament ones.[141] In addition, he found both in Christ's deeds and in the people and events of the New Testament typology for ecclesial or heavenly realities.[142] Chrysologus viewed salvation history as a continuum in which the Old Testament, the New Testament (that is, the earthly ministry of Jesus and the first generation of His followers), the Church, and, ultimately, the full manifestation of the kingdom are intimately linked. That he saw each as growing from and connected to its predecessor is clear from a sermon he delivered on the mustard seed:

---

137. *Sermon* 63.1, on the raising of Lazarus, is a good example: "[B]efore penetrating the depths of such a deed, let us consider just the external dimension of this resurrection." An exception to his customary practice, however, is found in *Sermon* 50.2, where he moves from the spiritual to the historical sense.

138. See, e.g., *Sermon* 9.

139. See, e.g., *Sermon* 18.

140. See *Sermons* 1–5 (1–4: literal; 5: allegorical) (FOTC 17.25–51).

141. Several such examples of OT typology are cited in Olivar, "Els principis," 429–30: Jonah as a type of Christ (*Sermon* 37.1); the Ninevites as a type of gentile believers (*Sermon* 37.5); the twelve Patriarchs and the twelve tribes of Israel as types of the twelve Apostles (*Sermon* 170.4, FOTC 17.279).

142. Several such examples of NT typology are noted in Olivar, "Els principis," 430: the woman suffering from hemorrhages (Mt 9.18–26 and Mk 5.21–43) as a type of the Church coming from the gentiles, and the daughter of the synagogue leader as a type of the synagogue (*Sermons* 35.4–5 and 36.3 [FOTC 17.78–79]); Jesus' resurrection as a type of the resurrection of all believers (*Sermon* 79.1); the sinful woman (Lk 7.36–50) as a type of the Church, and the house of Simon the Pharisee as a type of the synagogue (*Sermons* 93.7 and 95.4 [FOTC 17.147, 149–50]).

And so Christ sowed this mustard seed in his garden, that is, as a promise of his kingdom, which took root in the Patriarchs, was born in the
prophets, grew in the apostles, and in the Church produced a great
tree and sprouted manifold branches abounding in spiritual gifts.[143]

7. *Chrysologus as preacher and rhetorician*

Aside from his letter to Eutyches, the surviving literary corpus of Peter Chrysologus is comprised of 183 authentic sermons.[144] It is evident then that the liturgical assembly was the
locus for his exposition of Scripture. Chrysologus was acquaint-
ed with the classical tradition. He had some knowledge of
Greek inasmuch as he used Greek words that were not merely
stock theological terms.[145] In *Sermon* 5, Chrysologus manifests
an awareness of certain philosophical schools. We also find several references throughout his sermons to Latin classical authors such as Cicero, Horace, Ovid, Seneca, and Virgil.[146] As
mentioned above, he uses images from the occupations in
which the people of Ravenna were employed. On the one
hand, his sermons use some colloquial terminology of later
Latin, and Chrysologus himself acknowledges the importance
of using ordinary speech.[147] On the other hand, however, his

143. *Sermon* 98.6 (see FOTC 17.160).
144. The principal collection of Chrysologus's sermons is the Felician collection, arranged by Felix, an eighth-century bishop of Ravenna. It contains 176
sermons attributed to Peter. Of these, eight are judged to be spurious: 53, 107,
119, 129, 135, 138, 149, and 159. Fifteen other sermons are preserved outside
the Felician collection. In the CCL edition these are: *Sermons* 7bis, 62bis, 72bis,
72ter, 85bis, 85ter, 99bis, 130bis, 140bis, 140ter, 148bis, 155bis, 177, 178, and
179. In this translation "bis" is designated by "a" and "ter" by "b." Hence 72bis is
72a, and 72 ter is 72b. For a detailed study of the textual history and authenticity of Chrysologus's sermons, and for the basis of his critical edition of these sermons in the CCL, volumes 24, 24A, and 24B, see A. Olivar, *Los sermones de san
Pedro Crisólogo: Estudio crítico* (Montserrat: Abadía de Montserrat, 1962).
145. See, for example, *Sermon* 128.1, where he gives the Greek etymology for
Apollinaris. Other references are in D. L. Baldisserri, *San Pier Crisologo, Arcivescovo di Ravenna* (Imola: Stabilimento Tipografico Imolese, 1920), 79.
146. See H. Koch, "Petrus Chrysologus," in *PRE* 38:1369–71. See also the index in CCL 24B.1157–70. The references in *Sermon* 5 can be found in FOTC
17.47–48.
147. See J. Del Ton, "De Sancti Petri Chrysologi Eloquentia," *Latinitas* 6
(1958): 182. See also *Sermon* 43.1 (FOTC 17.90).

sermons are highly rhetorical. In a study that compares five preachers in Latin during the fifth and sixth centuries, Chrysologus is found to be the one most concerned with stylistic effects.[148] Chrysologus frequently employs strings of synonyms, chiasmus, repetition of the same word for emphasis, rhyme, assonance, antithesis, and the prefix *per* to intensify a word's meaning.[149]

Chrysologus is very eager to engage his congregation. He does this by using some of the techniques just mentioned, especially apostrophe. That is, in order to elicit and maintain his listeners' attention he often directs his remarks to one specific person, as it were. Thus, he uses such expressions as *Iudaee*, *Pharisaee*, and *haeretice*, as though such people were present. In a similar fashion he converses with some of the individuals of the Scriptural passage under discussion, calling out to Dives, Herod, Martha, or one of the apostles. His two customary forms of addressing his congregation as a body are *homo* and *fratres*. To prevent their thoughts from wandering, Chrysologus asks a multitude of questions of the text he treats, questions that were likely to surface in his listeners' minds, and he introduces possible objections by an expression like *sed dicit* or *dicis*.

Scholars debate over whether the sermons as we possess them are as Chrysologus preached them or whether they are merely summary notes of a stenographer. Directly related to this issue is the question of the length of his sermons. The sermons themselves suggest that they are not mere abridgements. Individual sermons frequently repeat the same Scriptural quotation, at times with slightly different wording. Also, Chrysologus on occasion ends a sermon by mentioning that he is bringing his remarks to a close so as not to violate his custom of

148. M. Wilkins, *Word Order in Selected Sermons of the Fifth and Sixth Centuries* (Washington, D.C.: Catholic University of America, 1940), 156.

149. See Del Ton, 177–89, and J. H. Baxter, "The Homilies of St Peter Chrysologus," *Journal of Theological Studies* 22 (1920–21): 250–58, for a fuller treatment of Chrysologus's oratorical skill. Especially noteworthy is Bogusław Kochaniewicz, *La Vergine Maria nei sermoni di San Pietro Crisologo* (Rome: Pontifical Theological Faculty "Marianum," 1998), 47–53, which indicates the wide variety of rhetorical devices Chrysologus employs in his preaching and furnishes examples dealing with Mariological themes for each rhetorical category.

maintaining brevity in preaching and of not wearying his listeners.[150] That there is a disparity in some of the renderings of an identical verse of Scripture in the same sermon and that there are references to particular circumstances while Chrysologus is preaching, such as the congregation's attentiveness or silence, or on one occasion to his inability to continue his sermon,[151] make clear that the texts we possess were written after he preached them.

Because of the highly stylized nature of Chrysologus's sermons, Alejandro Olivar is of the opinion that he wrote them down and memorized them before preaching and improvised occasionally according to the circumstances, such as those just mentioned. The text of the sermons in the form they have come down to us, however, is the work of stenographers who transcribed what they heard Chrysologus preach. Unlike some other patristic preachers, Chrysologus did not correct their work.[152]

The average length of Chrysologus's sermons was approximately a quarter of an hour.[153] Several sermons that are the last

150. See, e.g., *Sermons* 2.6 and 96.7 (FOTC 17.34, 156).

151. *Sermon* 35.5. In *Sermon* 86.1 and 7 Chrysologus refers to his earlier loss of speech and to his congregation's reaction at that time.

152. See A. Olivar, "Preparación e improvisación en la predicación patristica," in *Kyriakon: Festschrift J. Quasten,* ed. P. Granfield and J. A. Jungmann, 2:755–56 (Münster: Verlag Aschendorff, 1970), and idem, *La predicación cristiana antigua* (Barcelona: Herder, 1991), 620–21, where he holds that Chrysologus edited the text as recorded by the stenographers. His revised view, that Chrysologus undertook no such editing, is found in Pedro Crisólogo, *Homilías Escogidas,* intro. and notes by A. Olivar, trans. J. Garitaonandia (Madrid: Editorial Ciudad Nueva, 1998), 37.

153. In support of this view, see F. Lanzoni, *Le diocesi,* 752; R. D. A. Paganotto, *L'apporto dei Sermoni di San Pier Crisologo alla storia della cura pastorale a Ravenna nel secolo V* (Rome: Pontifical Gregorian University, 1969), 48; A. Olivar, "La duración de la predicación antigua," *Liturgica* 3 (1966): 178 and 184; and F. Sottocornola, *L'anno liturgico,* 154. For a contrary opinion, see D. L. Baldisserri, *San Pier Crisologo,* 71; R. J. Deferrari, "St. Augustine's Method of Composing and Delivering Sermons," *American Journal of Philology* 43 (1922): 212; and Del Ton, "De Sancti Petri Chrysologi Eloquentia," 182. The crux of the matter is how one translates *horae ipsius vix momentum* (*Sermon* 112.1), the amount of time during which Chrysologus says he preaches. The latter scholars take it to mean the period of one hour (as does G. Ganss, the translator of FOTC 17.180). The former group, to whose view I subscribe, render it "hardly a moment out of the hour itself," which perhaps implies that the entire liturgy lasted for about an

in a series on a particular Scriptural passage and in which Chrysologus gives his allegorical interpretation are longer than fifteen minutes.[154] Likewise, some that were preached on the occasion of an episcopal consecration, when the new bishop would have the last word, and others on a saint's feast day, when perhaps the martyrology would be read, are considerably shorter.

Of his 183 sermons, the vast majority (134) are on a Gospel text. Twelve are on a letter of Paul, six on the Psalms, fourteen directed to the catechumens (eight on the Creed and six on the Lord's Prayer),[155] six on fasting, two on the Kalends of January, four on a saint's feast day, three on the occasion of his consecration of a suffragan bishop, one on his taking possession of the see of Ravenna, and one in praise of a fellow bishop. All, apart from the ones given to the catechumens, appear to have been delivered in the context of a Eucharistic liturgy, and most of the rest were delivered during the Sunday liturgy, except for those on certain saints' days and several of the ones preached during Lent or the Christmas season.[156]

It appears that Chrysologus customarily used a passage from Paul, a Psalm, and a Gospel text in his liturgy. It is possible that he could have preached after each of the three readings, for after making reference in a sermon to a "threefold order of preaching," he goes on to say,

For the psalm relaxes our minds from constant labor, the authority of the Gospel refreshes them and rouses them to labor once again, and the Apostle's vigor does not permit our understanding to be displaced or to wander from the straight and narrow.[157]

hour, and the sermon for a mere fraction of that time, that is, approximately 15 minutes.

154. Occasionally when Chrysologus takes up and expands upon the theme of a previous sermon about which he still had more to say, he considers this subsequent sermon as the payment of a debt he owed to his people. See, for example, *Sermon* 126.1.

155. As Sottocornola points out in *L'anno liturgico*, 140, there are indications even in these sermons of the presence of the wider community, although the primary focus is on the catechumens.

156. On the frequency of the Eucharist in Ravenna, see *Sermon* 33.5, n. 13.

157. *Sermon* 115.1 (see FOTC 17.190).

If, in fact, Chrysologus delivered three sermons at each liturgy, it is more understandable why most of his sermons are brief, at least according to patristic standards![158]

158. The passage cited, however, could merely refer to the three different readings proclaimed from Scripture and not to three separate sermons. Furthermore, since the vast majority of Chrysologus's sermons that survive are on the Gospels, it is unlikely that such a disproportionate number on the Psalms and on Paul would be lost to us. It seems preferable to suppose that his usual preaching dealt with the Gospel of the day, and that only from time to time he chose instead to remark on one of the other Scripture texts read at the liturgy. On one occasion (*Sermon* 120.9 [FOTC 17.208]), however, after Chrysologus had preached on a text from Paul's Letter to the Romans, he felt compelled to give another sermon on the Gospel passage of the day as well.

SELECTED SERMONS
VOLUME 2

SERMON 7

On Quinquagesima[1]

HEN GOD CHANGED HIMSELF from Lord into Father,[2] he wanted to rule by love rather than power, and he preferred to be loved rather than to be feared;[3] he warned us with fatherly affection not to lose anything from a very noble endeavor. Thus the evangelist states: *When you fast, do not become sad like the hypocrites; for they disfigure their faces in order to show people they are fasting. I tell you truly: they have received their reward* (Mt 6.16).

1. It is likely that this sermon, which treats Mt 6.16–23, was delivered at the beginning of Lent. See Franco Sottocornola, *L'anno liturgico nei sermoni di Pietro Crisologo* (Cesena: Centro studi e ricerche sulla antica provincia ecclesiastica Ravennate, 1973), 66 and 431. There is some debate about whether the season of *Quinquagesima*, anticipating the Lenten fast, was actually the practice in Ravenna at this time. The titles are the creation of a later editor and not of Chrysologus himself. It is likely that *Quinquagesima* is a scribal interpolation, here and at *Sermon* 7a, in place of *Quadragesima* ("Lent"), used at *Sermon* 8.1 (see n. 1 there). Convincing in his argumentation is Franco Sottocornola in his *L'anno liturgico*, 202–4. Quinquagesima did not make its appearance formally in the West until the sixth century. Because Chrysologus elsewhere (e.g., *Sermons* 11.4 and 166.9 [FOTC 17.58 and 275]) insists on the fast of forty days for Lent and emphasizes the Biblical symbolism for the forty-day period and never draws out the symbolism for the fifty days in this or *Sermon* 7a, the only sermon that contains *Quinquagesima* in the body of the text, it is unlikely that these two sermons are evidence for an early appearance of Quinquagesima in Ravenna. Like *Sermon* 7a, then, this sermon also was delivered at the beginning of Lent. For another example of the term *Quinquagesima*, however, probably referring to fourth/fifth century Christians in Italy who wanted to begin the Lenten fast early, see Maximus of Turin, *Sermon* 50.1 (CCL 23.197). For more on this topic, see D. J. Froger, "Les anticipations du jeune Quadragésimal," *Mélanges de science religieuse* 3 (1946): 207–34.

2. See *Sermon* 5.2, where Christ is referred to as the Father of Christians (FOTC 17.44–45, although this English translation does not clearly bring out this point). For another likely example from an earlier writer, see Melito of Sardis, *On Pascha* 9 in OECT, trans. S. G. Hall (Oxford: Clarendon, 1979), 6–7.

3. While this is a favorite theme in Chrysologus's sermons, it is found earlier, for example, in Ambrose, *Letter* 74.10 (FOTC 26.409).

Hypocrisy is a subtle evil, a secret illness, a hidden poison; it is an adulteration of virtue and a worm that consumes sanctity. All things hostile mount their assault with their own strength, fight with their own arms, and attack openly. They are guarded against as easily as they are seen. Hypocrisy pretends to be free of danger, feigns prosperity, deceives carefully, and in its cruel craft it lops off the virtues with virtue as its sword; it kills fasting by fasting, by praying it makes praying empty, and it debases mercy by mercy. Hypocrisy, like a fever, boils up within while being cold without.[4] What dropsy is for the body, hypocrisy is for the soul. That is, dropsy gets thirsty by drinking, and, even in its drunken state, hypocrisy is still thirsty.[5]

2. *Do not become sad like the hypocrites; for they disfigure their faces in order to show people they are fasting.* Hypocrisy, while it desires to captivate the eye, becomes itself captive to the eye. *For they disfigure their faces.* And if faces are disfigured, what will be left to adorn the body? Thus it is with reason that the Lord said: *If the light in you is darkness, how pervasive is that darkness?* (v.23) Hypocrite, although your face is unwashed, your skin is dirty, your expression is sad, your appearance disfigured: you have thereby found praise from people, but from God you have lost the benefit of your fast.

Hypocrite, you have toiled by fasting, only to have the toil of your fast gain you nothing. Hypocrite, you have entered the waters of abstinence, you have ridden the waves of self-denial, you have swum the sea of fasting, and in the very harbor of fasting you have been shipwrecked! You have gained no profit, but you have purchased vanity, since you have made merely a human business out of what God has lent you. This is why you are going to render an account to God, since you have collected interest from people off your wretched fraud.[6]

3. Brothers, the disease must be avoided, the pestilence evaded which creates sickness out of remedies, which causes ill-

4. Literally, "serves a hot drink in a cold cup."

5. There is a wordplay here between *hydrops* and *hypocrisis*.

6. On the issue of usury in the early Church, see Robert P. Maloney, "The Teaching of the Fathers on Usury: An Historical Study on the Development of Christian Thinking," *Vigiliae Christianae* 27 (1973): 241–65.

ness to result from medicine, which turns holiness into sin, which changes atonement into guilt, and which generates division out of reconciliation. Whoever flees hypocrisy conquers; whoever runs into it does not escape. Let us flee hypocrisy, let us flee it, my brothers. May ours be the fast of simplicity; may it be holy from our innocence, pure from our purity, sincere from our sincerity. May it be hidden from people, unknown to the devil, but known to God. Whoever does not hide his treasure flaunts it; virtues that are flaunted will not remain. Just as virtues desert those who flaunt them, so they work hard at shielding those who shield them.[7] Therefore, fasting, which is the first virtue against vices, should be placed in the fortress of our heart, since, so long as it presides within us, vices will not be able to disturb us from without.

4. In order for a Christian to be able to possess it, this is what Christ urges when he says, *When you fast, anoint your head and wash your face, in order not to be seen fasting by others, but only by your Father who is hidden; and your Father who sees what is hidden will repay you* (vv.17–18). When he says, *Anoint your head and wash your face*, the master is not enjoining his servants to have the hair of their heads saturated with seductive ointment, nor does he want their faces to gleam with habitual washings, but he does want a Christian to hide the fact that he is fasting by looking as he does when he is eating, since he does not want Christian fasting to be characterized by an artificial sadness. But let us resume what we have begun.

5. *Anoint your head and wash your face* (v.17). He is not hereby endorsing sensuous appearances, but is prohibiting looks that are pretended. A face downcast in sadness professes a hunger against one's will, not a voluntary fast. If a person is willing, why the sadness? If unwilling, why the fast? One deserves to live in such pain who creates for himself a vice out of virtue, a lie out of truth, a loss out of gain, a sin out of forgiveness. If the farmer does not push the plow, if he does not dig a furrow, if he does not cut down the briars, if he does not root out the grass, if he does not place seeds in the earth, he deceives himself, not the

---

7. *Custodire custodes:* see Juvenal, *Satire* 6.347–48: *Quis custodiet ipsos custodes?*

earth; he does no harm to the earth, but he produces no harvest for himself. And if the one who deceives the earth with his fraudulent and empty hand so deprives, so cheats, and so attacks himself, what will one do, what will he have, what will he find who lies to God with his flesh starving but brimming over with hypocrisy?

6. And since we have made mention of the farmer, let him know that he engages in an empty labor and he will have nothing if he pushes the plow of fasting, plucks out the weeds of gluttony, and roots out the briars of luxury, but sows no seeds of mercy. This is what the Lord wanted to reveal when during his teaching on fasting he added these words: *Do not lay up for yourselves treasures on earth, where moth and rust consume and where robbers break in and steal; but lay up for yourselves treasures in heaven, where neither moth nor rust consumes, where thieves do not break in and steal* (vv.19–20).

How fatherly, how deeply rooted in love, what a far-seeing counsel of charity! He wants you to lose nothing, he who wants your property to be stored in heavenly treasure chests. How securely does one sleep who has deserved to have God as guardian of his goods! How liberated from care is he, how much anxiety has he cast aside, how tranquil is he, what arrogance from his slaves does he avoid by entrusting his goods to be kept safe by his Father. Paternal affection preserves goods in a way that servile fear cannot. The Father who gives his own goods to his sons does not embezzle what the sons have entrusted. He does not know what a father is nor that he is a son who does not believe his father.

Door-bolts do not shut moths out but shut them in. They produce them rather than repel them. Things kept in storage invite rust rather than prevent it. For what takes its origin from the thing itself is unavoidable. Where there is need, thieves cannot but be present. Therefore, whoever deposits his goods amidst moths, rust, and thieves exposes his goods instead of protecting them. Just as a moth originates from clothes, rust from metal, and a thief from need, so avarice arises out of wealth, covetousness out of acquisition, greed out of having possessions.

So let whoever wants to conquer avarice, to stamp out covetousness, to extinguish the burning fire of greed, give away his wealth, and not store it up. Brothers, let us send our treasure chests ahead of us to heaven.[8] The poor are the transports who in their lap can carry to the heavens what is ours. Let no one have any hesitations about the qualifications of these porters. Safe this is, safe this transportation through which our goods are carried to God with God as the guarantor.[9]

8. See also *Sermon* 29.1.
9. Leo the Great speaks in a similar fashion in his *Sermon* 17.2 (FOTC 93.64–65).

SERMON 7A

On the Fast of Quinquagesima[1]

S WE ARE ABOUT to undertake the customary sacred fast of Quinquagesima,[2] we must realize that what soap does for human bodies, this is what fasting supplies to Christian souls: it cleanses the filth off the senses, it washes away the offenses of the mind, it removes the crimes of the heart, it removes the blemishes from the heart, and with marvelous splendor it leads the entire human being to the luster of chastity. And just as spring curbs and reins in all the violent storms, clears up the sky's complexion, gives peace to the earth, and calls forth and rouses to living vigor the whole body of the world, which had been buried in the death of winter; so too does fasting quiet every conflict, restore peace to one's limbs, enkindle souls lulled to sleep and deadened by the chill of negligence, and bring virtue to life and thaw it out entirely.

Fasting, brothers, is the rudder of human life, it governs the whole ship of our body, it lifts the heart to the heights, it hoists the sails on the mast with the ropes of abstinence, it makes ready the oars of our souls, and with the sail of sincerity unfurled it evokes and invites the full blast of the heavenly Spirit;[3] and so amidst those tidal waves of the world, those perils of life, it directs and conveys the vessel of our flesh to the perfect resting place of the divine harbor.[4]

1. For attestation concerning the authenticity of this sermon, see A. Olivar, *Los sermones de San Pedro Crisólogo: Estudio crítico* (Montserrat: Abadía de Montserrat, 1962), 320–21.

2. See *Sermon* 7, n. 1.

3. *Spiritus* means "spirit," "breath," and "wind." Chrysologus probably has all three meanings in mind here.

4. See *Sermons* 8.1, 21.1, and 41.1 for other examples of the analogy of the ship to describe the human body.

2. The Apostle cries out, "The night has passed, day has drawn near; let us cast off the works of darkness and equip ourselves with the armor of light; let us proceed honorably as in daylight; not in debauchery and drunkenness, not in license and lust, not in strife and jealousy, but put on the Lord Jesus Christ and have no concern for the desires of the flesh."[5] The night has passed; day has drawn near. Day is a symbol of life; night is an image of death. Night leads into darkness; day brings back to light. The one is always burying; the other is always raising up. You see the fools. If only the sleeper knew he was sleeping! Their rest is restless, stressful their leisure, laborious . . .[6]

5. Rom 13.12–14.
6. The text breaks off here.

SERMON 8

A Second on the Same[1]

HEN A PRUDENT CAPTAIN casts off from the coast, when he enters the deep to journey across the sea, he puts aside his concerns for his home, his country, his wife, his children; and he is so totally consumed in mind, body, and emotion with the tasks of sailing that he is able to overcome the perilous waves and, victorious over danger, enter the quarters of a profitable port. So we too, my brothers, having set out along the route of abstinence, on the sea of fasting, on the journey of Lent, let us cast the ship of our body off from the coast of the world, let us renounce our concerns for our earthly country, let us fully unfurl the sails of our mind on the mast of the cross; let us secure the safe passage of our vessel with the ropes of the virtues, with the oars of wisdom, with the rudders of discipline; and having set forth from the land let us gaze upon the sky, so that by the guidance of the signs of heaven along the clear and narrow paths of our hidden journey[2] we might hold our course unobstructed.

And so with Christ as our pilot and the Holy Spirit providing the wind, when the foam of the pleasures has been overcome, the waves of the vices have been conquered, the storms of misdeeds weathered, the rocks of sin evaded, and when we have steered clear of the vessels of all the offenses, then let us

1. Although a later editor has placed this sermon immediately after *Sermon 7*: "On Quinquagesima," the term *Quadragesima* ("Lent") is used in the first paragraph and indicates that this sermon was actually delivered during Lent, probably at the very beginning of that season. See *Sermon 7*, n. 1.

2. According to Chrysologus the paths are clear *(liquidos)* and narrow in that they comprise the penitential practices of prayer, fasting, and almsgiving, which are externally visible. The journey, however, is hidden because it is directed toward and governed by the unseen God. *Liquidos* refers to both the clearness of the path and, in conjunction with his sea-faring analogy, its liquidity.

enter the port of Easter, life's reward, the joys of the resurrection.

2. However, since we shall be making our journey across a watery surface, through salty eddies, and through uncharted, barren regions, and so must bring along all the food and drink we need, it will be beneficial for us to include in our supply of provisions an abundance of mercy. Brothers, when fasting is not fed on the food of compassion it gets hungry; when it is not given to drink from the cup of mercy it gets thirsty. Fasting gets cold and gives up when the coat of almsgiving does not cover it, when the clothing of kindness does not protect it.[3]

Brothers, what spring is for the earth, this we know is what mercy is for fasting: just as the spring breeze makes all the seeds in the fields bloom, so does mercy bring to flower all the seeds of fasting, and it makes fasting in all its vigor bear fruit unto the heavenly harvest. What oil is for the lamp, this is what compassion is for fasting: just as the density of oil fuels the light of the lamp and by its regulated flow makes it shed comforting light all night long, so compassion makes fasting glow, and self-restraint shine in all its luster.

What the sun is for the day, this is what we consider almsgiving to be for fasting: just as the sunbeam makes the day brighter and scatters all the dark clouds, so almsgiving sanctifies the sacredness of fasting and by the light of compassion drives out all death that comes from desire. And in short, what the soul is for the body,[4] this is how generosity is regarded for fasting: for just as the soul by leaving the body kills the body, so too the departure of generosity is the death of fasting.

3. Certainly fasting is the death of vices, the life of virtues. Fasting is the peace of the body, the glory of the bodily members, the embellishment of life. Fasting is strength for minds, vigor for souls. Fasting is the safeguard of charity, the bulwark of chastity, the fortress of sanctity. Fasting is the school of

3. On the prominence of this theme in Chrysologus's preaching, see Mario Spinelli, "Il ruolo sociale del digiuno in Pier Crisologo," *Vetera Christianorum* 18 (1981): 143–56.

4. Reading *quod est anima corpori* (mss. S and T) rather than Olivar's *quod animae corpus est* in the CCL text. See *Sermon* 41.3.

morals, the teaching of teachings, the discipline of disciplines. Fasting is the saving companion along the churchly journey. Fasting is the invincible commander of the Christian army. But among these virtues fasting thrives, conquers, and triumphs only when it defends itself with mercy as its general.

Mercy and compassion are the wings of fasting, by means of which it is lifted up and carried to heaven, without which it lies prostrate and writhes on earth. Fasting without mercy makes an idol out of hunger and is no image of holiness. Without compassion fasting is an opportunity for avarice; it is no commitment to self-restraint. That is no self-restraint which fattens up the purse as fast as it slims down the body. Fasting without mercy is not true, but imagined.[5] But where there is mercy there is the truth, as the prophet attests when he says, "Mercy and truth have met."[6] Fasting without mercy is not virtue, but hypocrisy, as the Lord says: "But when you fast, do not act like the hypocrites; they disfigure their faces so that they may be seen by human beings to be fasting."[7]

4. Whoever does not fast for the poor person, is playing tricks on God. Whoever does not give away his lunch when he fasts, but instead stores it away, is proven to fast for the purpose of avarice, not for Christ. Therefore, when we fast, brothers, let us store away our lunch in the hand of the poor person, so that the hand of the poor person may save for us what our belly had been about to consume.[8] The hand of the poor person is the bosom of Abraham,[9] where whatever the poor person receives, he immediately stores away. The treasure-house of heaven is the hand of the poor person: he stores away in heaven what he receives, so that it does not perish on earth. "Store up for yourselves," he says, "treasures in heaven."[10] The hand of the poor person is Christ's treasury, since whatever the poor person receives, Christ receives.

Therefore, O man, give the earth to the poor so that you

---

5. *Non est veritas, sed figura.*   6. Ps 84.11 LXX; Ps 85.10.

7. Mt 6.16.

8. See *Sermon* 29.1 on the same theme.

9. See Lk 16.22.

10. Mt 6.20.

may receive heaven; give a coin that you may receive the kingdom; give a morsel so that you may receive it all. Give to the poor so that you may give to yourself, since whatever you give to the poor you will have; what you do not give to the poor another will have.[11]

5. God proclaims: "I desire mercy."[12] Whoever refuses to give God what God wants, wants God to refuse to give him what he desires. "I desire mercy." O man, God asks not for his own sake but for yours. "I desire mercy." God asks for human mercy so that he may bestow divine mercy. The mercy that is in heaven is what one attains by means of earthly mercy. "Lord," [Scripture] says, "Your mercy is in heaven."[13]

When you are about to plead your case before the judgment-seat of God, take mercy as your advocate, by means of which you can be freed. Whoever is certain about having mercy as his defense is assured of pardon, and will have no doubt about forgiveness. Mercy not only preempts the proceedings and anticipates the judge's every move, but it also overturns the verdict and releases those condemned. The Ninevites[14] attest to this: they were already subjected to judgment, sentenced to punishment, ready for execution, handed over to death. But mercy snatched them so forcefully, held them so tightly, and protected them so well that God preferred that the sentence be overturned rather than deny anything to mercy.

Certainly also at that time fasting was helping their case: it sprinkled the ashes, it spread the sackcloth, it gave groans, and shed tears; and what it was unable to excuse with words it tempered with signs of sorrow. But it would have been powerless to revoke the sentence, unless mercy had come to help by its pleading.

6. Mercy both frees sinners and restores saints; since, if mercy had not been present, when David committed adultery he would have lost the gift of prophecy;[15] when Peter made his denial he would have lost the primacy of the order of Apostles;[16]

---

11. On the same theme, see the conclusion of *Sermon* 43.
12. Hos 6.6.   13. Ps 35.6 LXX; Ps 36.5.
14. See Jon 3.5–10.   15. See 2 Sm 11.4.
16. See Mt 16.18–19 and 26.68–75.

and when Paul committed blasphemy, he would have remained
a persecutor. Paul admits this when he says, "I was a blasphemer, a persecutor, and a violent man, but I have obtained mercy."[17] Brothers, let us procure mercy through our acts of mercy
toward the poor, so that we can be free of punishment and sure
of salvation. "Blessed are the merciful," [Scripture] says, "since
they will obtain mercy."[18] In vain does he hope for mercy there
who has done nothing merciful here. The one who does something merciful runs toward the reward; the one who does nothing merciful rushes down to punishment.

17. 1 Tm 1.13.
18. Mt 5.7.

SERMON 9

A Third on the Same <and on the Gospel: "See to it that you do not perform your righteousness before human beings">[1]

OD DEALS WITH US, he deals with us in this world that we not lose anything in the future world, as is clear from the very beginning of the reading: *See to it,* it says, *that you do not perform your righteousness before human beings, in order to be seen by them; otherwise you will have no recompense in the presence of your Father, who is in heaven* (Mt 6.1). So God deals with us, he deals with us in this world so that we may lose nothing in the future world.

2. *Do not perform your righteousness before human beings.* And how is it that what is done for human beings is not done before human beings? Hidden righteousness goes unperceived. But what can be secret about a public act? Only one who can conceal the rays of the sun will be able to hide the gleam of righteousness![2] Righteousness, the light of reality, is not veiled by attempts to keep it obscured. When a righteous act is done and shines forth, it illumines all people by its example.

And why is it that God does not want done before human beings an action through which human affairs gain stature? *See to it that you do not perform your righteousness before human beings.* So what about this? "So let your light shine before human beings that they see your good works and give glory to your Father who is in heaven."[3] How is it that he wants to conceal the righteousness whose works he wants to shine so brightly?

Brothers, this heavenly precept means to remove boastfulness, take away ostentation, do away with vanity, uproot empty

---

1. Mt 6.1–4. This is another sermon delivered during Lent. See *Sermon* 7, n.
1. Angle brackets indicate text restored by A. Olivar in his edition.
2. I emend the text to be a declarative statement rather than a question.
3. Mt 5.16.

glory; and so it does not mean to conceal righteousness. Righteousness, which in and of itself redounds to its own glory, does not require the audience of a crowd, public praises of people, the plaudits of human beings, worldly glory. Born from God, it looks to heaven and acts before God's eyes; mingled with heavenly virtues, it always looks to be given glory only by God. But this is the righteousness that is from God.

That righteousness, however, which is hypocrisy is not righteousness: it is deceptive to the eye, it is false in appearance, it mocks those who see it, it lies to those who hear it, it seduces the crowds, it leads people astray, it sells its reputation, it buys applause, it is done for the world, not for God; it grabs its recompense in the present, it does not look for any reward in the future; blind itself it blinds the eyes; without sight itself it desires to be seen. In the face of such blindness Christ begins in the present instruction as follows: *See to it;* that is, "Do not desire to be seen."[4] *See to it that you do not perform your righteousness before human beings.* Why? *In order not to be seen by them.* And if you are seen, what then? *You will have no recompense in the presence of your Father, who is in heaven.*

Brothers, the Lord is not passing judgment here, but merely giving an explanation; he is exposing deceptive thoughts, he is laying bare the minds' secrets, he is pointing out the measure of righteous retribution for those who unrighteously flaunt their righteousness. The righteousness that hires itself out to human eyes cannot expect a divine recompense from the Father. It wanted to be seen, and it has been seen; it wanted to please human beings, and it has pleased them. It has the recompense that it wanted; it will not have the reward that it had no desire to have. But let us hear from what follows the reason why these preliminary remarks have been made.

3. *When you give alms, do not blow the trumpet in front of you as the hypocrites do* (v.2). A "trumpet" is appropriate because this kind of almsgiving is militaristic, not civil; it is given not to show mercy but to make a din; it serves discord rather than provid-

4. Chrysologus is engaging in wordplay: *adtendite* versus *gestiatis adtendi*. His point is: "You, pay attention, rather than striving to have others pay attention to you."

ing compassion; it is a carnival of ostentatiousness and not the
way modesty conducts its business. Whoever shows off his almsgiving offers insult. *But you*, he says, *when you give alms, do not
blow the trumpet in front of you as the hypocrites do in the synagogues
and on the streets, so that they may receive glory from human beings. I
tell you truly, they have received their recompense.*

You have heard how he censures almsgiving where people
congregate, on the streets, at crossroads, as not given for the relief of the poor, but advertised to procure the favor of human
beings, in order to indicate that they do not bestow mercy
freely, but they sell it. We must flee from hypocrisy, brothers, we
must flee from it; since it is a slave to praise, it does not relieve
the shame of the poor, but it makes it worse; out of the groaning of the needy it seeks a pompous and boastful display of itself; it inflates its own glory from the agony of the poor; from
the misery of the beggar it spreads the fame of its own ostentatiousness.

4. But you the listener say: "So then, where people congregate, on the streets, at crossroads, mercy is to be denied, food is
not to be offered?" Clearly both everywhere and at all times
mercy is to be rendered, food is to be offered, nakedness is to
be covered, but in the manner in which the Author of mercy
has taught, so that acts of mercy not be made known on earth,
but in heaven; not publicized before human beings, but before
God. On the streets and at crossroads compassion keeps the secret to itself; on the other hand, there is a street, there is a
crossroad when the hypocrite does nothing secret in secret.
Brothers, in giving such an admonition God is not finding fault
with positions but with dispositions; not with deeds, but with
the motivation; with the intention, not with the giver.

He accuses the one who gives bountifully for his own reputation, not for the hunger of the poor.[5] He judges not where or
when you give, but how you give; since God measures deeds according to the heart, not according to the hand, he also deter-
mines the quality from the motivation, not from the place of

5. There is a wordplay between the *famam* of the hypocrite and the *famem* of
the poor person.

one's actions. He wants acts of mercy to be done before him alone who alone is both the rewarder and witness of mercy. And what does he say? "I was hungry, and you gave me to eat."[6] He wants charity to be given to himself in the poor person; and he who wants it to be given to himself, wants to be indebted for what has been given; and he who wants to be indebted for what has been given wants the givers to lose nothing. God asks for only a little and will pay the highest returns.

Therefore, O man, if you lend to God in the poor person,[7] you do not need human beings to give testimony. Faith does not look for eyewitnesses. The one who does not give without intermediaries calls into question the trustworthiness of the recipient. The one who divulges the loans he has given scorches the debtor with shame. Therefore, O man, what you are going to give to God, give secretly, so that what you give may not be onerous but honorable.[8] For this reason your Benefactor has come to you in the poor person, so that you may have no doubts that he will return what he has received, since he has freely allowed you to possess something to give.

5. But how private a matter is the poverty in the poor person, inasmuch as he wants your generosity to be kept secret, he himself reveals when he says: *But when you give alms, do not let your left know what your right is doing, so that your almsgiving may take place secretly; and your Father who sees what is hidden may repay you openly* (vv.3–4). Don't you realize how much he wants no one else to know since he wants a certain part of you not to know you yourself, who do the deed? *Do not let your left know what your right is doing.* Just as we have virtues on our right side, so too we have our portion of the vices on our left. Therefore, just as the work of the right is what the silent giver does, what the noisy giver does is the hypocrisy of the left.

Hypocrisy, deceit, pretense, fraud, lying, boasting, haughti-

6. Mt 25.35.

7. See Prv 19.17. This terminology of "lending to God" through almsgiving is found throughout the writings of Cyprian of Carthage, e.g., *The Dress of Virgins* 11; *The Lapsed* 35; *The Lord's Prayer* 33; *Works and Almsgiving* 15 and 16 (all found in FOTC 36.40, 87, 156, and 241–42).

8. This renders the wordplay *oneris . . . honoris.*

ness, and bragging pursue us and threaten us from the left. So, whenever we have the opportunity for goodness, compassion, and mercy, do not let the left side know this. The left is that which always wages spiritual battles against us and takes pains that the virtues do not come into effect; heartlessness sees to it that there be no compassion; greed fights so that almsgiving may not conquer; avarice rages so that mercy may not gain strength; so that innocence, purity, simplicity, and sanctity may not reign, hypocrisy alone strikes, hypocrisy that Christ excludes from us with this kind of proclamation: *But when you give alms, do not let your left know what your right is doing.*

Brothers, in this world let us flee from those things that come from the left, if we desire in the future to stand on the right and hear: "Come, blessed of my Father; receive the kingdom that has been prepared for you from the beginning of the world."[9] O man, while on earth give to the poor those things that you want to abide with you in heaven. O man, campaign here alongside the poor if you want to reign there with Christ.

9. Mt 25.34.

SERMON 10

On the Twenty-eighth Psalm[1]

LL WHO LIGHTEN AND RELIEVE the arduous rigors of their labors show that music has been given to us as a natural solace for toil. Hence, sailors overcome the perils of the sea by singing; in this fashion they transport immense burdens with the comfort of songs; hence, the sound of music enables travelers to climb steep hills; hence, a melody leading the way even rouses soldiers to undergo the bitterness of warfare; and in short, any task, however hard and laborious, a sweet song masters and brings to completion. So let us, brothers, join the divine songs to the fasting of Lent, so that the heavenly symphony may temper and lighten the burden of abstinence.

Blessed David prompts us to do this: from the times when his shepherd's pipe soothed his dear sheep and delighted them as they grazed, he learned how to overcome the harshness of warfare with a song; with a song he succeeded in leading his people to safety; with a song he was able to summon the nations, to rally the Jews, to put the demons to flight, to rouse the sons of God to obey their heavenly Father, as his melody sounded so inviting.

2. *Bring to the Lord*, he says, *you sons of God* (v.1). Do you suppose that with these words he is addressing heavenly powers or

1. LXX numbering. In Hebrew, this is Ps 29. F. Sottocornola in his *L'anno liturgico*, 66–67, and 77, finds noteworthy that this sermon was delivered during Lent yet contains in section 5 a plea to members of the congregation to urge their relatives and others for whom they were responsible to come forward to prepare to be baptized at Easter. With apparently such a brief time available for catechesis, it is no wonder that in some of his sermons on the Creed *(traditio symboli)* to those soon to be baptized Chrysologus laments the lack of sufficient time to provide adequate instruction. See the opening remarks in *Sermons* 56, 58, 60, and 61 (this last sermon is found in FOTC 17.110–14).

that he is turning human beings into sons of God and raising earthly flesh up to the heavenly nature? *Bring to the Lord, you sons of God.* It is to human beings, brothers, to human beings that the prophet is speaking here, about whom he chants elsewhere as follows: "I have said: you are all gods and sons of the Most High."[2] We have heard, my brothers, how high God's graciousness has brought us, and how high the celestial paternity has exalted us. Let us believe that we are sons of God, let us prove equal to our lineage, let us live for heaven, let us represent our Father by our resemblance so that we do not destroy with our vices what we have attained through grace.

Bring to the Lord, you sons of God. Bring. You see that our heavenly Father declares his love by his generosity, he manifests his affection by what he has given and his charity by his gifts. And truly, brothers, whoever does not compliantly obey the Author of his life, whoever does not unite with him through worship,[3] whoever does not honor him with gifts does not know that he is his son, is heartless, denies his nature, and is ungrateful to his Father. *Bring to the Lord, you sons of God.* Let us see what it is that the prophet advises here and encourages us to bring to so great a Father.

3. *Bring to the Lord, you sons of God, bring to the Lord sons of rams.* This is all that he desires, all that he seeks. *Bring to the Lord sons of rams.* The divine progeny is urged to bring to the Divine Father the offspring of sheep, the common offshoot of an earthly animal, young animals spread out along the roadside, creatures dispersed throughout the fields. Is it perhaps that what the Creator of all now seeks are the Jews' victims, bloody sacrifices, offerings bleating under the knife?

Then what about the passage that said: "I shall not accept from your house calves, nor goats from your herds; all the beasts of the forests are mine, the wild animals on the mountains and the oxen; I know all the birds of the sky, and every

2. Ps 81 (82).6.
3. From *devincire* ("to bind"), *devincit cultu* means literally "binds [God] by worship." What Chrysologus means is that through the worship of God one puts God quite literally "in a bind" by placing God in one's debt. Alternately, *devincit* could be a form of *devincere* ("to conquer"), yielding the meaning of "win [God] over by worship."

creature of the field is my possession. If I hunger, I shall not tell you; for mine is the whole earth and its fullness"?[4] If he rejected those, what are the sons of rams that he demands to be brought to him?

Abraham makes this clear: "Take your beloved son, and you will offer him to me as a holocaust."[5] Abraham the ram was mature in uprightness, aged in faith, perfect in sacrifice, ready for the holocaust; he was bringing the son of the ram; he was immolating his own son, or rather himself in his son; he was sanctifying his mind, he was making his faith fertile, in order that the same one be victim and officiant, priest and sacrifice. The suffering there was entirely the father's, yes, the father's, where the son did not know that he was going to be sacrificed, the son was present but unaware, the son was being tied up to be able to receive martyrdom from his father's suffering, to receive a reward from his father's loss, and to gain the crown from his father's struggle.

In the end his father's right hand was stayed, his father's sword removed, since it was not the son's death that was being sought, but it was the father's love that was being tested; the son's blood was not desired, since the victim was present in its entirety in the father's love, as the Scripture teaches when it says: "Now I know that you love the Lord your God, because for my sake you did not spare your beloved son."[6]

4. We have said that Abraham was the ram, so as to show that Isaac was the son of the ram, and to make abundantly clear who are the sons of rams that the prophet wants us to bring to the Lord. *Bring to the Lord sons of rams.* The Christian now is being urged to bring sons of the fathers, of the patriarchs, prophets, apostles, martyrs, and confessors, since the Lord's flock is free to graze in the pasture of faith, since the heavenly Shepherd wants his own sheep to be brought to the Lord's sheepfold, so that they not be scattered throughout the pagan wilderness and devoured by attacking wolves. But let us now speak more plainly about what the divine word urges.

---

4. Ps 49 (50).9–12.   5. Gn 22.2.
6. Gn 22.12.

5. *Bring to the Lord sons of rams.* Bring to the Lord those who
are to be baptized; bring those whom faith and not flesh conceives; bring those whom the grace of God and not earthly nature generates; bring lambs whom innocence provides, not
those who are as dull as cattle. Bring, yes, bring those whom necessity prevents from coming of their own accord, or age hin-
ders, or ignorance detains, or vices restrain, or sins delay, or appearance deceives, or poverty tricks and confuses. Entice the
willing, compel the unwilling. Gain for yourselves a reward
from the need of another.

If a master has a slave who is a catechumen, let him bring
him forward so that he might now have a fellow believer. Let a
father offer his son and not hinder him, so that upon the one
whom he has provided life in the present he may also confer
life in the future. Let the husband lead his wife to faith, so that
what is one in the flesh may not be divided in spirit. Let a
friend draw a friend to salvation, so that he may ground human
love on divine grace. Let the citizen usher the foreigner, the
head of the household usher the guest to God's table, so that
with no cost to himself he may be generous from God's abundance.[7]

Compel the unwilling. Let no one say, "He is unwilling," because even Abraham bound his son so that he could offer him;[8]
and angels clutched Lot by the hand and lifted him up in order
to rescue him from the flames;[9] and the Lord girded Peter with
the help of his strength so that he would go to the martyrdom
for which he was unwilling, when he said: "Another will gird
you, and lead you where you do not wish."[10] And our heavenly
Father not only receives the willing, but also draws the unwilling, since his Son says: "No one comes to me, unless my Father
draws him."[11] How does one believe that he is a Christian if he
does not lead to Christ the aged and the old? Or how does one

7. The term Chrysologus uses for "generous" is *humanus.* Both here and in
the previous section, where he speaks about grounding human love on divine
grace, Chrysologus is making a subtle theological point: "God's abundance,"
namely grace, enhances rather than detracts from the human.

8. See Gn 22.9.   9. See Gn 19.16.
10. Jn 21.18.   11. Jn 6.44.

consider his home to be the sheepfold of God when he does not give the grazing offspring,[12] the bleating lamb of God?

6.[13] [I beseech and entreat you, my dearest brothers, through our Lord that all of you keep watch in this regard, seeing to it that no one in these days be left in exile from the grace of God and divine generation; that what God is going to confer upon others through his grace may grow and overflow unto your joy. We are human beings living in a time of uncertainty, and we do not know what the next day may bring.[14] So let us take care, dearly beloved, that if slaves or sons, spouses or parents are overtaken by death, they may not be deprived of the present life and fail to come to the future one.]

12. The Latin is *pascuale germen,* which also means "Paschal offering," that is, one who is brought to new life through the conferral of baptism at Easter.

13. A. Olivar (CCL 24.71 n.) in his critical text of Chrysologus's sermons is of the opinion that this final paragraph of *Sermon* 10 is inauthentic because the style and vocabulary are markedly different from what is found in his authentic corpus.

14. See Prv 27.1.

SERMON 12

A Second on Lent <and on the Gospel: "Jesus was led into the desert">[1]

INCE WE SEE THAT THE SPRINGTIME of the fast and the season of spiritual warfare have arrived, as soldiers of Christ, after ridding ourselves of any listlessness of body and soul, let us set forth to the field of the virtues, so that the limbs that have been softened by the leisure of the winter may be strengthened by the military training[2] of heaven. We have given a year to our body, let us give some days to our soul. We have spent time and time again on ourselves; let us devote a portion of time to the Creator; let us who have lived entirely for the world live for a little while for God.

Let us put to the side our concerns at home and remain in the camp of the Church; let us keep vigil in the battle line of Christ and not seek the slumber of our beds. Let us join ourselves to the valiant and be far from embraces; may the love of victories hold us fast, may the coaxing of children not summon us, may the voice of God resound in our ears, and the din of our family not disturb our hearing. May a sparse amount of food be consumed from the rations of heaven, may an abundance of earthly excess not be sought, may our drinking be measured in cups of sobriety, and drunkenness not weaken our strength. Concerning our pay, let the poor person, our fellow soldier, receive whatever excess there is; let there be no deadly extravagance to cause any devastation. In time of conflict whoever has fed the hungry and enfeebled will receive help himself.

1. Mt 4.1–11. The extended title is reconstructed from *Sermon* 11 (see CCL 24.72). Because of the references in *Sermons* 12 and 13 to the temptation of Jesus as recorded in the Gospel of Matthew, it is likely that Chrysologus delivered them on the first Sunday of Lent. See F. Sottocornola, *L'anno liturgico*, 64, 67, and 200.

2. In March, coterminous with Lent, military exercises began again after being suspended all winter. See 2 Sm 11.1 and F. Sottocornola, *L'anno liturgico*, 210.

2. Thus fortified, brothers, thus prepared, let us declare war on our sins, let us undertake the battle against our offenses, let us announce our engagement against our vices, being sure of victory since no earthly enemy will be able to conquer heavenly arms, no worldly adversary will be able to withstand the Divine King, and no sudden assault will be able to overcome those who are firm in faith and ready for combat. The devil will not succeed with his surprise attacks in throwing the careful, the vigilant, and the sober into confusion. Certainly not daring to contend in open warfare with us who have been armed in such a way, may he not attempt to attack us with trickery, but may our mind persevere in gazing heavenward, so that it may crush and deflect the deceitful snares of the devil and the hidden snares of the flesh.

3. Certainly on his own the devil is wicked; nevertheless, he becomes more so when he is called forth. Listen to the apostle when he says: "The devil like a roaring lion goes about in search of someone to devour."[3] The devil starves while we fast since he always gorges himself on our failings. He brings our eating to the point of gluttony and extends our drinking to intoxication, so that he might make our mind mindless and render our flesh besmirched; so that our body, which is the abode of our mind, the vessel of our soul, the protection of our spirit, the school of the virtues, and the temple of God, he might reduce to a stage show of wickedness, a public spectacle of vice, and a theater of pleasure.

He feels full, he experiences pleasure, he is glutted with feasting when superfluousness slackens us, lust excites us, extravagance seizes us, ambition drives us, anger agitates us, fury swells us, envy enkindles us, desire inflames us, cares disturb us, quarrels vex us, greed overtakes us, business profits constrain us, obligations bind us, money bags weigh us down, gold crushes us; when the virtues die, the vices live, pleasure overflows, honor vanishes, mercy is scarce, avarice abounds, confusion reigns, order is vanquished, and discipline is overthrown.

These are the things, yes, these are the things that fight

3. 1 Pt 5.8.

against the soldier of Christ; these are the troops of Satan,
these the legions of the devil; these are the things that have be-
sieged the world with tombs, have vanquished peoples, have
devastated the nations, have led the whole earth into captivity.
These are the things that no mortal being on his own can withstand; and therefore God came to conquer them; he the very
King of heaven, he himself descended, he the one and only victor came, establishing the fast of Lent in preparation for battle,
in order that the four tenfold days[4] of fasting might fortify with
an impregnable wall all four corners of the world.

4. Fasting, brothers, we know is the citadel of God, the camp
of Christ, the bulwark of the spirit, the standard of faith, the
sign of chastity, and the trophy of sanctity. Adam preserved this
in paradise, but gluttony dislodged him from paradise.[5] Noah
guarded this in the ark, while drunkenness submerged the
world.[6] Through fasting Lot extinguished the fire of Sodom,
but through drunkenness he was burnt by the fire of incest.[7]
Fasting made Moses shine with a divine light, when feasting
and drinking plunged the people of Israel into the darkness of
the error of idolatry.[8] Fasting transported Elijah to heaven,
while drunkenness cast the godless Ahab down to hell.[9] Fasting
made John the greater among those born of women, while intoxication rendered the sovereign Herod a murderer at the order of a woman.[10]

5. The fast of Lent, brothers, has revealed and exposed the
old tricks of the devil. For the devil, who had despised Christ
when he ate, and had considered him to be human when he
drank, when he saw him fasting, he suspected that he was God,
and he confessed that he was the Son of God. *If you are the Son
of God*, he said, *tell these rocks to become bread* (Mt 4.3). By saying
this the devil wants to manifest the man, not God; he does not

4. A similar wordplay on *Quadragesima, quattuor decadae*, and *quadrat(ur)am* is
found in *Sermon* 11.4 (FOTC 17.58).
5. See Gn 3.6, 23–24.
6. Gn 6–8, which describes the events associated with the flood, says nothing
about Noah's fasting or the world's drunkenness.
7. See Gn 19.30–38.   8. See Ex 24.18, 32.4–6, 34.28–35.
9. See 2 Kgs 2:11.   10. See Mt 11.11, 14.1–12.

want to provide food, but he wants to cut short the fast. *If you are the Son of God, tell these rocks to become bread.* After fasting it is not divine strength but human infirmity that requires bread; God is not so wearied by hunger that he devotes the power he has to provide food for himself.

6. And so, from what follows the devil reveals what it is that he is attempting. *If you are the Son of God, cast yourself down* (v.6). It is clear enough that he wants to test the man, for whom he provides not ascent, but downfall. The human condition finds ascent difficult, but falling easy. *If you are the Son of God, cast yourself down.* You are in error, devil, and you have no knowledge about tempting; God is unable to fall.

7. Then *he showed him all the kingdoms of the world* (v.8), and pointing out from a very high mountain all the glitter of this age he said the following: *I shall give all these things to you, if you fall down in homage before me* (v.9). This is the very one who was calling Christ earlier the Son of God. *If you fall down in homage before me.* Oh, the boldness of the devil! He says to God: "Adore me."

But at a later time he perceived God by his powers, the Judge by his punishments, the Intercessor by his rewards, the very one he was now interrogating; for by the name of Christ, by the name of him who was fasting he began to be cast out from the bodies that he had possessed, and in his terror he began to give glory to the one he had haughtily and cunningly proposed to injure. Christ conquered by fasting in order to bestow upon us in this manner the strength to conquer and the way to conquer: "This kind," he says, "is not cast out except by fasting and prayer."[11] So let us fast, brothers, if we wish to imitate Christ, and if we wish to overcome the crafty tricks of the devil.

11. Mt 17.21.

SERMON 13

A Third on Lent <and on the Gospel: "Jesus was led into the desert">[1]

ERE IS THE SEASON in which the soldier goes off to the field,[2] and the Christian returns to fasting. Here is the season in which the idleness of the flesh, the list-lessness of the mind, the concern for the belly and all the usual sloth and self-indulgence must be cleared away. Here is the season in which soul and body must be strengthened and trained to bear heavenly arms. Here is the season to be trained in courage for our struggle, with Christ at our side and the angels at hand. Now is the season in which gluttony vies with fasting, sobriety with drunkenness, chastity with promiscuity, faith with faithlessness, reverence with irreverence, patience with rage, greed with generosity, mercy with avarice, humility with haughtiness, holiness with guilt, while Christ presents the prize.

Therefore, while God awaits, while the heavenly trumpet already resounds, while the company of angels is eager for action, if anyone is caught up in the bedroom's delights, weakened by its downy softness, and languid in bed with nuptial pleasure, and neglects to come to train in the virtues, he loses the reward of the struggle, the glory of virtue, the prize of the contest, the crown of righteousness, and will in the future also be given a severe beating for the crime of desertion.

2. Today, my brothers, Christ our King has addressed his fellow soldiers from the tribunal of the Gospel, he has declared war on his enemy, he has promised rewards for those who will fight, he has reported the reasons for the warfare, he has revealed the enemies' deceptions and objectives, and he has pointed out in a solemn decree where, when, and how we must

---

1. Mt 4.3–10. See *Sermon* 12, n. 1.
2. See Sermon 12, n. 2.

do battle. And although he could obtain victory by himself, nevertheless, because of us and our trepidation he has ordered that all the help from on high be available.

Therefore, whoever has had no desire to hear these things and who has despised knowing the many such commands of our King, you be the judges as to whether he has not deprived himself of the sacraments of our army[3] and has once again made himself an exile from heavenly companionship. But you, my brothers, who wish to follow in this Lenten fast the pattern of the Lord's fasting, you who are about to fight, as we have said earlier, against the troops of vices, against the battle line of sins, against the hideous forms of desire, against countless legions of demons all spread out and filling the air, assure yourselves of triumphs out of the very temptations that followed upon the Lord's fast.

3. For when the Lord undertook the fast of forty days[4] with that tireless example of his strength, straightaway the devil went out to meet him and to fight him with treachery, because he was unable to oppose with force one who was fasting. For to the extent that he has dominion over those who eat and drink excessively, to that same extent does he fear those who pray, and to that same extent does he flee from those who fast, as the Lord says: "He is not cast out except by fasting and prayer."[5] But by what deception the devil dared to tempt him, let us hear:

4. *If you are the Son of God, tell these stones to become bread* (Mt 4.3). You have heard what the enemy himself thinks and judges about fasting. *If you are the Son of God.* You see that he now believes him to be not the Son of Man but the Son of God since he had observed that he was free from slavery to the belly. He realized, yes, the devil realized that fasting precedes all the virtues. He had seen John exchange urban comforts for a

3. Chrysologus is using *sacramentum* in two senses: the more ancient meaning of "military oath" to fit his analogy from warfare, and the more properly Christian meaning of "sacrament." For more on this topic, see F. I. Dölger, "*Militiae sacramenta* bei Petrus Chrysologus," in *Antike und Christentum* 5 (1936): 150–51.

4. *Quadragesima,* the term for "Lent."

5. Mt 17.21.

dwelling in the desert wilderness, scorn the softness of the flesh by the harshness of his dress, curb every worldly excess by food that grew in the wild, and, what is characteristic of God alone, forgive human sins;[6] and nevertheless, the devil did not say to him: *If you are the Son of God.* But only when he sees the Lord continually fasting does he proclaim: *If you are the Son of God.*

The devil errs when he directs against the Lord the wickedness and arguments of his cunning. *If you are the Son of God, tell these stones to become bread.* Why is it that while Christ was fasting the devil looks for all the characteristics of divinity solely in the promise of bread, and the one whom he perceives to be the Son of God by the sign of constant fasting, he desires to be manifested as the Son of God from the promise of bread, from the care for the belly? *If you are the Son of God, tell these stones to become bread.* Why did he say, not, "If you are the Son of God, tell human beings or angels or whatever to become something else"; but, *Tell these stones to become bread?*

He seeks the sign of bread who shudders at the sign of fasting. He seeks the sign of bread so that he may avoid the sign of fasting that so frightens him. The wicked comforter proposes bread in order to adulterate virtue, in order to break the resolve of the one fasting. But let us see what the "Bread that came down from heaven"[7] had to say about bread. *Not on bread alone does the human being live, but on every word of God* (v.4). How true it is that the Word of God lives on the word of God! How true it is that the Bread does not need bread! What a sign of divinity that he changes stones into human beings since from stones he raises up children for Abraham as proof of his majesty![8]

5. And since the impudent enemy does not know that he has been conquered once, to augment the victor's triumph, *he set the Lord on the pinnacle of the temple and said: "If you are the Son of God, cast yourself down"* (vv.5–6) What a sign! *Cast yourself down.* It would have been more appropriate for him to say: "If you are the Son of God, go up to heaven," since it is a characteristic of

6. See Mt 3.1–6   7. Jn 6.58.
8. See Mt 3.9.

the human being, to be sure, to fall to the depths, but it is a characteristic of God to ascend to the heights. *If you are the Son of God, cast yourself down.* This is the way he persuades his own; this is the way he always provides for his own; he lifts his own so high that from the heights he more forcefully casts them down to ruin.[9] *If you are the Son of God, cast yourself down.* With his admonitions the devil reveals his true self.

Cast yourself down. He seeks a fall, he orders crashes, and with such advice he creates martyrs throughout Africa[10] by saying: "If you wish to be a martyr, cast yourself down," so that he may push those from on high to death, not so that he may lift and raise those from below to the crown. And just as the devil reveals his true self by his admonitions, so too does the Lord show himself by his response. He says: *You shall not tempt the Lord your God* (v.7). By saying these things he wanted it to be understood that he certainly is Lord, that he certainly is God, since not merely from the pinnacle of the temple did he plunge to the earth, but he cast himself from the heavens all the way down to the underworld, not to be a model of those who fall, but to be the resurrection of the dead.

6. Observe, brothers, whether the cruel enemy, although often conquered, can submit to the Man: he hears and perceives that he is the Lord God, and yet still does not refrain from tempting him. *He placed him on a very high mountain, and he showed him all the kingdoms of the world and their glory, and said to him: "All these I shall give to you, if you fall down in homage before me"* (vv.8–9). He says this not as one who can give, but as one who can deceive; not to grant what he promises, but to steal by his promises the very things that are already possessed.

All these I shall give to you (v.9). He offers to God what belongs to God; he promises to the Creator what belongs to the Cre-

9. For similar language see Maximus of Turin, *Sermons* 1.3 and 31.3 (CCL 23), which recount the headlong fall of Simon Magus as recorded in the *Acts of Peter* 32 (3) (*NTApo* 2:316).

10. This reference to the Circumcellions, a radical sect often allied with the Donatists, is consonant with descriptions of them in Augustine's writings, such as *De haeresibus* 69.4 (CCL 46.332); *Contra Gaudentium* I.27.30 and 37.49 (CSEL 53.228, 249); *Tractates on the Gospel of John* 11.15 (FOTC 79.26–27) and 51.10 (FOTC 88.276–77); *The City of God* 1.26 (FOTC 8.60).

ator; he tries to persuade the One who is to be adored by all to adore him, and made blind by his daring he admits to the Judge even before the time of judgment how he used to deceive simple people. To him the Lord responds not so much by the testimony of the Law as by the power of his divinity: *You shall adore the Lord your God* (v.10). You shall adore him the Lord your God, to whom all creatures bend the knee, not only in heaven and on earth, but even under the earth.[11] Therefore, screaming and wailing in hell you will adore him whom now you rashly invite to adore you, you rebel.

7. And so having been rebuffed by the Lord so many times and in such a fashion, the devil with all his fury now prowls about around us, the Lord's servants; and just as Christ addresses and arms his soldiers, so too does the devil do the same with his servants. So the devil says: "This season with its observance of fasting is now weakening us severely; through gluttony, through intoxication, through drunkenness, through excess we are unable to tempt human beings. Incite quarrels, sow seeds of discord, excite hatred, rouse anger, inspire lies, extract false oaths, prompt blasphemies, provoke frivolous talk, stir up deception, enkindle avarice, and arrange for dishonest profit, so that what the belly now does not pay for excess, the purse at any rate may lock up and keep for punishment. Take care above all else that mercy, almsgiving, or kindness not destroy our past labors, nullify our present ones, nor prevent any in the future."

8. But inasmuch as we, my brothers, both acknowledge the warnings of our King and hear what the devil has commanded his own, let us carry out our fasts without a quarrel, without a din, without anger, without deception, and without pretense, but with all mercy, charity, and piety. Then the Lord, who has rejected the bloody oblations of beasts but has asked for the sacrifice of a contrite spirit and a humbled heart,[12] will be appeased and well-disposed and receive our fast, offered in peaceful silence.

11. See Phil 2.10.
12. See Ps 50.19 LXX; Ps 51.17.

SERMON 14

On the Fortieth Psalm[1]

OR THOSE EXPERIENCED IN BATTLES the military trumpet signals discipline, but for those who are inexperienced it gives only a terrifying sound. The trumpet, the commander of wars, gives strength to her own, but gives fear to the enemy. The one who wages war without a trumpet is not a soldier; he is driven by fury, not by the battle; he does not act courageously, but perilously; he is looking to perish, not to conquer. We have said this so that the soldier of Christ might understand why a refrain has been provided from heaven. Stationed in the battlefield of the world we fight with the devil, we stand our ground against the vices. And so whenever the prophet's blare sounds in our ears, it makes us cautious in periods of peace, brave in deployment, and invincible in battle.

2. For today the blessed psalmist prompts our understanding through the heavenly acclamation: *Blessed is the one who has understanding for the needy and the poor* (v.2[1]a). And what is there to understand where poverty is evident? It is the power of understanding if deep matters should be examined, if what is hidden should be perceived, if what is covered should be laid bare; however, what is apparent to the eyes, what is out in the open, and what is self-evident are not things to be understood, but to be seen. When someone is shivering in his nakedness, emaciated by hunger, parched with thirst, weary with exhaustion, pale from want, who has to struggle to understand that

1. LXX numbering. In Hebrew, this is Ps 41. According to F. Sottocornola, *L'anno liturgico*, 68 and 76, the exhortation to acts of mercy in this sermon, together with the theme of spiritual warfare, suggests that this was delivered during Lent, when such topics were prominent in Chrysologus's preaching; his other sermons on the Psalms are all Lenten.

the person is in need? And if there is no struggle to understand this, what benefit does a person with understanding enjoy? Let us pray, brothers, that the very one who so clearly points out that he is to be understood in the poor person[2] may allow us to understand what we must.

3. That the very one who arrays the sky is naked in the poor person, that the Fullness of the universe hungers in the hungry, and that the Fountain of fountains thirsts in the thirsty, how is this anything but something great and blessed to understand? That poverty encompasses him whom the heavens cannot contain; that he who enriches the world is in need in the needy person; that the Giver of all things seeks a crumb of bread and a cup of water; that, out of love for the poor, God so humbles himself not merely to be mindful of the pauper, but even to be the pauper himself: the very one whom God grants to behold this, does behold it.

4. But how he either transfuses the poor person into himself or fuses himself into the poor person, let him now tell us: "I hungered," he said, "and you gave me to eat."[3] He did not say: "The poor person hungered, and you gave him to eat," but "I hungered, and you gave me to eat." He declares that what the poor man has received has been given to him; he says that he eats what the poor man consumes; he affirms that what the poor person drinks is poured into him. Oh, what results love for the poor produces! God is glorified in heaven from what causes shame to the poor person on earth; and he deems as an honor for himself what is considered the poor person's disgrace.

It would have been sufficient for him to have said: "You gave me to eat," and "You gave me to drink," but he prefaces it with: "I was hungry, I was thirsty,"[4] because it would have been a paltry love for the poor to have assumed[5] the poor person, and not

---

2. See Mt 25.40.   3. Mt 25.35.
4. Ibid.

5. From *suscipere*. Chrysologus is making a Christological statement here. In the Person of Jesus the Word assumed or took upon himself a poor man with all liabilities and sufferings entailed in being poor. For numerous examples of Chrysologus's use of this verb with reference to Christ's assuming of humanity,

also to assume what the poor person suffers; and certainly love is shown to be true only through suffering. True is the love that has made its own the distresses of the one in distress. It is extraordinary that the food of the poor is tasty to God: he who has no hunger for the goods of all creation prophesies that in the kingdom of heaven before all the angels in the company of the resurrected, he was nourished on the food of the poor.

That Abel suffered, that Noah preserved the world, that Abraham maintained faith, that Moses brought the Law, that Peter was crucified upside down,[6] about all of this God is silent, and declares this alone: that the poor person ate. In heaven the subsistence of the hungry person ranks first; the offerings made to the poor person are the first consideration in heaven. Distribution to the poor is the first thing written in the divine registers. Blessed is the one whose name is read by God every time the poor person's account is recited in heaven.

5. But let us hear also the fruit of this blessedness. *On the day of evil the Lord will free him* (v.2[1]b). The one who knows that he spends his life among the evils of the world should always bring along with him almsgiving as an aid, he should summon the throngs of the poor to come to his assistance, he should lavishly prolong his generosity in feeding the poor, and he should calm his fears by making frequent donations to the poor: he who fills the hand extended by a beggar knows no lack; the treasury is unable to be exhausted since a coin from it is all that is needed.

On the day of evil the Lord will free him. On the day of evil God will be present to free the one who frees the poor person from evils. God will hear crying out in distress the one who has heard the poor person when he was crying out. The one who enabled the poor person to have good days will not see the day of evil. But the one who comes to judgment day without a poor person as his advocate will see the day of evil. The case is dismissed when sins accuse one whom[7] a poor person excuses. Yet, the

---

see Ruggero Benericetti's *Il Cristo nei sermoni di S. Pier Crisologo* (Cesena: Centro studi e ricerche sulla antica provincia ecclesiastica Ravennate, 1995), 97–99.

6. See also *Sermon* 27.2 (FOTC 17.71).

7. Reading *quem* in PL 52.233 rather than *quam* in Olivar's CCL text.

one whom the poor person's hunger accuses cannot be excused.

6. *May the Lord,* it says, *preserve him and give him life* (v.3[2]a). The psalmist did not say: "He preserves and gives life," but said, *May he preserve and give life.* He said this so that these words would not be a declarative statement but a prayer. The one who has heard the prayers of the poor, now hears throughout the whole world the Church praying for him as follows: *May the Lord preserve him and give him life.* May he preserve him from suffering punishment; may he give him life so that he may rise from the dead and receive life. *And may he not deliver him over to the hands of his enemy* (v.3[2]b). Of what enemy? Certainly the devil: he is the very instigator of all enmities. He who treads under foot the very originator of enmities despises enemies.

7. *May the Lord help him on his bed of pain* (v.4[3]a). The prophet describes all the troubles of human frailty. But *may the Lord help him on his bed of pain.* What is the bed of our pain if not our body in which the soul lies and lies in pain, and is in pain that in its desire to return to heaven it is weighed down by the earthly nature of the body?[8] *You have changed his whole bed in his infirmity* (v.4[3]b). He does not change the just man in his bed, but in his bed the sick man is changed. Therefore it is the flesh that is changed and changes; it is that which is tossed about by adversities and changes in prosperity. The Lord then changes our bed when he turns adversity into prosperity for us.

8. And since his mind was being tossed about while transported in his bed, that is, in the bed of the body, the ill person himself who was being tossed about cries out: *I have said: "Lord, have mercy on me; heal my soul"* (v.5[4]). Because through its association with the flesh he realizes that he has contracted sickness of soul, he begs that his soul be healed; and he confidently asks for mercy since he has shown mercy to the poor person. Blessed is the one who by lending to the poor has furnished for himself the very Judge as his debtor.[9]

8. See Ambrose, *Expositio Evangelii secundum Lucam* 5.14 (CCL 14.139) as a possible source for this Platonic interpretation of this verse.

9. See, for example, *Sermon* 9.4 on a similar theme.

SERMON 15

On the Centurion[1]

YOU ARE ABOUT TO HEAR TODAY, brothers, how a centurion of a Roman cohort became a leader in the Christian army. And deservedly so because he began to teach before he believed. *Jesus came,* it says, *to Capernaum. A centurion came up to him and addressed him with this request: "Lord, a servant-boy of mine lies at home paralyzed and badly afflicted." And Jesus said to him: "I shall come and cure him." The centurion said in reply: "I am not worthy to have you come under my roof, but only speak the word, and my boy will be healed. I, however, am a man placed under authority, and I have soldiers under me, and I say to this one: 'Go,' and he goes; and to another: 'Come,' and he comes; and I say to my slave: 'Do this,' and he does it"* (vv.5–9).

You see that before he engaged in the task of discipleship the centurion had obtained a position as teacher; for he shows the manner of petition, he provides the standard for believing, he makes known reasons for faith, and he furnishes patterns of the virtues, although he has not yet begun the discipline of Christian learning.

2. *A centurion came up to him with a request of him.* This is a matter of being wise, not of making a request. *A servant-boy of mine lies at home.* As a master he pleads the case of the servant. Truly the centurion, who has changed his earthly pay into a profit one hundred times[2] as great in heaven, also has raised servitude in the earthly military up to divine dignity. *Lord, a servant-boy of mine lies at home.* He who calls him "Lord" faithfully confesses his own servitude. And how is it that this centurion who thus acknowledges his Lord has dared to declare that the ser-

---

1. Mt 8.5–13.
2. There is a wordplay here between *centurio* and *centenarium.*

70

vant is his own, as though unaware that the property of the slave belongs to the master? Or is he ignorant about ordinary things while teaching things so age-old and profound?

A servant-boy of mine: "I call him mine, because he is lying down; if he were yours, Lord, he would not be lying down. The prophet attests to this when he says: 'Come, now bless the Lord, all you servants of the Lord, who stand in the house of the Lord':[3] You who 'stand,' not 'lie down.' Your servants stand, the servants of human beings lie down. May my servant-boy who is lying down rise in order to be yours. He is mine because he is paralyzed; may he now be healed so as to be yours. He is mine because he is badly afflicted; so that he be yours, may he now be in no pain.

"Lord, it is not fitting for your servants to be subjected to evils. The pain of your servants is an injury to you. The force of evils should not take hold of your servants. Your servants, although they suffer evils, do not suffer them for punishment, but undergo them for crowns; for them adversities are not causes of distress, but causes of victory. Servants of human beings are the ones who suffer evils unwillingly, because their masters are unable to help them in their desperation. But you, O Lord, whom the powers serve, whom cures obey, to whom healing remedies submit, how will you regard him as your servant while you see that he is the slave of such diseases?

"Your goodness is known among the wicked, even the godless acknowledge your kindness, and outsiders proclaim your mercy: am I to say that he is yours, even though your benevolence does not seek him out as he lies ill? *He lies at home and is badly afflicted.* And so, the magnitude of the affliction does not allow me to bring him and present him to you, lest the infirmity of the servant, if made public, cause him both pain and shame."

3. The centurion moved the Judge by making so great and heartfelt an appeal, and he was so effective that the Lord of heaven himself willed to go to his servant. *I shall come,* said Christ, *and cure him.* Brothers, the centurion did not coerce the

3. Ps 133 (134).1.

Author of compassion to show compassion, nor did he compel
Christ to go to that for which Christ had come; but rather the
centurion is taught in this way to perceive and to understand
why Christ came to the servant in a servant, why God came to
man in a man. Assuredly he came to raise the prostrate, to set
back on their feet those who had been knocked down, to free
those in shackles,[4] and, since he himself is the most kind bearer
of his own creation, to carry those whom no one as yet was able
to bring and present. But let us now hear what response the
centurion made.

4. *Lord,* he says, *I am not worthy to have you come under my roof.*
He gave a response owing to his humility, and by his extraordinary awe he signified that this one was Lord. Who brings God
down to the house of his soul, to the secrecy of his heart, and to
the shelter of his conscience? Who brings God to the inner
sanctum of his mind, where all his intimate thoughts[5] dwell
hidden and jumbled and do not allow the temple of the human
heart to abide in silence and integrity without the din of vices?
And so he responds to the Master with fear: *Lord, I am not worthy to have you come under my roof.*

This is the same reason why when Peter recognized Christ as
the Creator of the universe, he exclaimed: "Leave me, Lord, for
I am a sinner."[6] Peter begs him to leave him in the same way
that the centurion asks him publicly not to come to him. Both
are concerned lest the unworthiness of the lodging result in an
insult to the guest. *I am not worthy to have you come under my roof.*
This would have been appropriate to say before God had entered the lodging of our flesh.[7]

But now why is the centurion so opposed to having Christ
enter his dwelling, since he now sees Christ abiding completely
within the dwelling of his own body? Brothers, the centurion
now saw in Christ the form of his own body, but he did not see

4. See Ps 145 (146).7–8.

5. *Familia cogitationum:* literally, "the family" or "the household of his
thoughts."

6. Lk 5.8.

7. For more on the idea of the *hospitium nostrae carnis,* see R. Benericetti, *Il
Cristo,* 91–95.

in him the passions of his own body. Christ was born in the flesh, but he was born from the Holy Spirit; he received flesh as his dwelling place, but from the Virgin's temple, so that there be both a true human body, on the one hand, and that he have none of the defilement of the human race, on the other. Correctly then does the centurion judge his own dwelling unworthy for Christ, since the dwelling of our body in which Christ was abiding was unique, in accordance with that statement of the prophet: "I kept watch, and I became like a solitary sparrow on the roof."[8]

5. *But only speak the word, and my boy will be healed.* This centurion, although he was without the Law, did nothing apart from the Law. He says: *Only speak*, since it had been said: "He spoke, and all things were made."[9] And if all things were accomplished by an utterance, how is the infirmity of one person not going to be cured by a single utterance? *Only say the word.* And what is said without a word? But the word that this man is requesting is not for use in conversation but for an act of power. It is the word about which it has been said: "He sent forth his word and healed them."[10]

Only say the word. This man believed that all powers abide in the word. Your word is healing, your word is life; when your word approaches, then pain immediately flees, and infirmity soon departs. It is the word in which Peter made an enormous catch when he lowered the nets, but without the word this ever-watchful fisherman both spent the night in ignorance and accomplished nothing. "Lord," he said, "laboring the whole night we have caught nothing, but at your word I shall lower the nets."[11] And as though what he[12] had declared about the word were not sufficient, as though what he requests could not be made evident in a word, he grounds it in reality and amplifies it with an example.

6. *For I also to be sure am a man placed under power, having soldiers under me, and I say to this one: "Go," and he goes; and to anoth-*

---

8. Ps 101.8 LXX; Ps 102.7.   9. Ps 148.5.
10. Ps 106 (107).20.   11. Lk 5.5.
12. I.e., the centurion.

*er: "Come," and he comes; and to my slave: "Do this," and he does it.
For I also am a man.* That is to say: "You are God." *Placed under
power* means "You yourself are the Power of powers." *Having soldiers under me* means "You have the virtues." *And I say to this one:
"Go," and he goes* signifies "say to the infirmity: 'Go,' and it
goes." *To another: "Come," and he comes* signifies "say to health:
'Come,' and it comes."

And to my slave: "Do this," and he does it means that "my boy
will be your slave when he receives healing. Let him hear, indeed let him hear: 'You have been made healthy, do not sin any
more!'[13] May he do righteous deeds, so that he may be freed
from the paralysis of all sins, and be able to sing with the
prophet: 'Turn back, my soul, to your rest, because the Lord
has done good things for you; for he has snatched my soul from
death, my eyes from tears, my feet from falling; I shall be acceptable before the Lord in the land of the living.'"[14]

7. Brothers, let whoever desires to reap fruit a hundredfold
imitate the centurion. So that we do not lightly pass over the
prudence of this centurion, may the words about him today suffice, since the mystery that he represents[15] is very great.

13. Jn 5.14.
14. Ps 114 (116).7–9.
15. Literally, "which is contained in his figure." Olivar, in *Los sermones*, 145,
thinks it possible that the next sermon Chrysologus preached was *Sermon* 102,
which is on the Lucan version of Jesus' encounter with the centurion (Lk
7.1–10). In fact, in *Sermon* 102.9 Chrysologus indicates that the centurion represents the Christian people. F. Sottocornola, *L'anno liturgico*, 68–69 and 102,
however, disagrees with Olivar and thinks that these two sermons were delivered
in different years, not sequentially.

SERMON 16

When Jesus Came to the Region of the Gerasenes[1]

HAT CHRIST CROSSES SEAS and visits places is not a matter of human desire, but is the cause of human salvation. Christ walks not in order to see places, but in order to meet human beings who had been perishing from various calamities. What would the One who had made the places see that was new in those places? Or what escaped the view of him who was everywhere? As man he was seen in places, but as God he saw everywhere. At any rate he saw even those who were without hope; he saw those upon whom he was going to bestow divine remedies. He was going about to cure those for whom a human cure had been lacking up until then, as is shown in today's reading.

2. *When Jesus had come,* it says, *across the sea to the region of the Gerasenes, two men possessed by demons met him; they were coming out of the tombs and were so very savage that no one was able to pass along that road* (Mt 8.28). It is clear that the Lord saw what evil, what danger was occurring in those places; and so he went there in order to help those who were so desperate, so afflicted, so miserable. *Two men possessed by demons, coming out of the tombs, met him.* The authors of death had made their abode in the tombs. Notice what cruelty, what fury, what rage the demons have against the human race: as short as the lifetime of human beings is, they cannot endure it, they are not content that human beings die, but they are eager to bury human beings alive; they commit themselves to the graves, so that they may drag human beings down to the grave; they feed on corpses, they are fattened on what is putrid, they are delighted by the stench, since they have complete pleasure at the death of human beings.

1. Mt 8.28–34.

3. But let us understand what trickery they scheme, what evils they contrive, whose cruelty makes no headway out in the open; what they do when they display riches is to sow the seeds of avarice; in order to spread pride they design ostentation; they promote individuality in order to exclude what has to do with life in common; in order to foster anger they incite lawsuits; in order to do violence to kindness they stir up alienation of affection; they invent philosophy in order to make human beings know nothing by seeking more; they fashion a multitude of gods so that the God who is one and true may not be known.[2]

Two men possessed by demons met him. Since a multitude of demons had come to two men, the Scripture means that a whole legion had come together as one.[3] But it does this to teach that one should be wary of demons but not afraid of them, and at the same time it shows how unique is the power of Christ, because merely by the name of Christ every multitude of demons is put to flight. *Two men possessed by demons met him.* They showed themselves, but not willingly; they came at the Ruler's command, not of their own accord; they were forced out against their will, running not on their own authority. In short, at the presence of Christ the men left the tombs, and in a complete reversal they now held captive those who had held them captive; they handed over to punishment the ones who had afflicted them with torments; they delivered over to judgment those who had up to now sentenced them to the graves.

4. *Two men possessed by demons met him, so very savage that no one was able to pass along that road.* You see that the demons had blocked the road for those who were coming to Christ; they had denied them access. For this is the concern of the demons, that human beings be unable to find the way back to God; for in no other way can they possess human beings, except by removing them from fellowship with their Creator. *Such that no one was able to pass along that road.* This is why Christ became the Way. *Such that no one was able to pass along that road*—that one,

2. For a similar sentiment about philosophy and polytheism see *Sermon* 44.6 (FOTC 17.98).
3. See Mk 5.9 and Lk 8.30.

not this one. "I am the Way,"[4] he says, so that the power of demons may not prevail in impeding those coming to the way through the Way, to God through God. It is not possible to attain to God except through God. But now let us hear what the demons shouted.

5. *What do you have to do with us, Son of God?* (v.29) That is to say: "Author of life, what do you have to do with the dead? Inhabitant of heaven, what do you have to do with graves? Fragrance of paradise, what do you have to do with a stench? We whom you have cast out of heaven, whom you have excluded from paradise, from whom you now take away cities, from whom you deny habitable regions, at least allow us to dwell in graves; even if we are worthy of such persecution, you are not worthy of such an affront."[5]

What do you have to do with us? What? Namely, what a judge has to do with a convict, what an avenger has to do with a criminal, what a king has to do with a deserter. *What do you have to do with us, Son of God?* This is what thieves say to the owner, what robbers say to the master; they hold the spoils, they carry the booty, and they ask the one who demands back what is his what he has to do with them. *What do you have to do with us, Son of God?* What? That you give back human beings, that you return the world to its Author, and, now that the Creator has come, that you realize that you no longer have any power over creatures.

6. *What do you have to do with us, Son of God? You have come ahead of time to torture us* (v.29). *What do you have to do with us?* And what do you have to do with human beings? *What do you have to do with us, Son of God?* They acknowledge, yes they acknowledge God, they admit that he is their Judge, they proclaim that they are liable to judgment, and they register a complaint about the time. *What do you have to do with us, Son of God? You have come ahead of time to torture us.*

They pit time against the Creator of time. *You have come ahead of time to torture us.* In this fashion they complain about

4. Jn 14.6.
5. Namely, such an affront to his divine glory by being so personally involved with the sordid and foul nature of demons and death.

time, as though they could accomplish with time the burying of the living in graves. *You have come ahead of time to torture us.* It is their premature cruelty that cuts off time, that anticipates death, that buries the living; and this cruelty is what complains about time, as if it ought to have time, and not to be punished as soon as it has arisen. The hardened wickedness of this world disputes about time. The wicked have little patience, and the good have a revenge that is slow in coming. What is long for the victims, is short for the perpetrators.

7. *There was*, it says, *not far from them a herd of many swine that was out to pasture. The demons, however, were pleading with him in these words: "If you cast us out, send us into the swine." He said to them: "Go." And they went out,* it says, *into the swine; and the whole herd went headlong into the sea, and were drowned* (vv.30–32). Undeserved subjection desires what is deserved: *Send us into the swine.* Wickedness begs to be sent from the tombs into swine, so as not to lose the stench, but to change it. *Send us into the swine.* The ones who fall from heaven seek filth; after their heavenly abodes they strive after the wallows of swine. *Send us into the herd.* The herd is sent into the herd, in order that the multitude of demons may be revealed, in order that it be evident that two men endured what a number of swine could not tolerate.

8. *He said to them: "Go."* The vile beast is handed over not for the will of the demons, but so that by such a deed it may be noted how the ones who desired the swine so as to destroy them rage in a human being and desire the deaths of human beings. Demons ardently seek to destroy, not to retain, all that is, that is done, that is accomplished, and that lives. Therefore, let no one suppose that a human being becomes like them; their enmity against the human race is age-old, their anger is constant, and their malice is resolute. The demons do not give in unless they are conquered, but they are not able to harm unless bidden. Therefore, the vile herd is handed over in order to make clear that to demons nothing is permitted against human beings, since it was decreed that they be permitted to enter swine. Therefore, either by our vices we bring it about that the demons receive power to harm us, or by our virtues we join with Christ in triumph, make the demons subject to us, and tread on their necks.

SERMON 17

A Second on the Same[1]

HAT THE LORD CAME across the waters of the sea into the region of the Gerasenes, and that as soon as he disembarked from the boat he was met by a man who came out of the tombs, who had an unclean spirit, who had a dwelling in the tombs, and who was bound by chains and shackles, we know from the words of today's Gospel: *Who had a dwelling in the tombs* (Mk 5.3). The author of death lies in the resting place of death, and in his eagerness for homicide he attempts to bury alive as though dead those whom he is not able to kill in his cruelty. He rages, he is furious, who in his bitterness exacts our destruction. For him it is a punishment that a human being is born; he is in agony that death comes so slowly. He strives to consign the life of a human being, as short as it is, to the frightful graves.

The enemy, who is disordered and perverse with regard to both the living and the dead, thrusts the living into graves, and serves food and pours wine for the dead, so that he may both kill off the living and disturb the dead.[2] The man was restrained and bound by chains and shackles, bound by the crime of another, and although innocent he was being tormented by the

---

1. Mk 5.1–13.

2. Despite efforts by Church leaders to eliminate such graveside feasting and drinking, there are numerous references to such activities perduring. See, for example, Tertullian's reference to people returning from these festivities "half tipsy," in *The Testimony of the Soul* 4 (FOTC 10.137–38, trans. R. Arbesmann); Augustine's remark that "drinking bouts and extravagant banquets in cemeteries are believed . . . to be . . . a solace to the dead," in *Letter* 22 (FOTC 12.55, trans. W. Parsons [1951]); and Augustine's remark that his mother Monica abandoned such practices when she came to Milan because Ambrose prohibited them since they "smattered of the superstitious ancestor-worship of non-believers," in *Confessions* 6.2.2 (FOTC 21.132, trans. V. Bourke [1953]).

wickedness of the inhabitant dwelling within him. The devil's guilt was responsible for the man's punishment, and that brigand enclosed within was feasting on the miseries of his prey; his wretched ill will does not reveal the one doing the deed but the one suffering it.

The Lord in his desire to relieve this affliction crosses the sea, that is, in the vessel of our body he crosses the boundary into this vacillating world, he reaches the shores littered with the shipwrecks of our salvation, and he floods with the splendor of his light the region covered in the gloomy darkness of ignorance. He is about to uncover the plots of the crafty enemy, and to put to flight with his Kingly power the very prince of spiritual wickedness with his legions, so that at long last he might liberate those whom the power of the enemy held captive for so long.

2. *Seeing Jesus*, it says, *from a distance, he ran up and did him homage, and shouting in a loud voice said: "What do you have to do with me, Son of the most high God? I beg you in God's name, do not torture me"* (vv.6–7). At the command of Christ the system of punishments has been altered; earlier an innocent man was being tormented by the terrorism of the devil; now the man runs free, but the devil pays the penalty.[3] The flesh is favorably disposed, but the unclean spirit lies powerless and prostrate. *He ran up and did him homage.* What is this, devil? The one whom you tried to make fall with your three temptations, whom by the promise of a kingdom you were trying to trick into worshiping you, now you all trembling and pitiful fall on your face and adore. Look how the one who was promising all the honors of a kingdom and glory is found dwelling in stinking graves amidst decomposing corpses. Thus, when this one promises, when this liar tricks people here above into consulting with him, he deceives them so successfully that he drags them with him down to hell.

What do you have to do with me, Son of the most high God? And now only as a flatterer, not as one who is devoted and obedient does he do homage, since he wants to avoid punishment and is

3. The attempt at a rhyme here is an effort to reproduce Chrysologus's word-play of *currit* and *incurrit.*

afraid of losing his prey. This unfortunate one actually believes that the One whom he was unable to overcome with temptation, or to influence with gifts, he can sway with flattery. But he is accustomed to release those in bondage, to liberate those in captivity, and to reestablish for himself the boundary lines, not recently drawn up but as originally constituted by him; to strike down the enemy by the unhindered exercise of his power, and not through deceitful conduct to pursue the hostile possessor of those who belong to him.

3. *And shouting in a loud voice he said: "What do you have to do with me, Son of the most high God? I beg you in the name of God not to torture me."* Look what human frailty does and suffers when it is subjected to such great torments of this kind! See how the devil using the voice of the man as his advocate, cries out as he is about to do in the man, and all the members of the man are in the service of their enemy for their own ruin. *What do you have to do with me, Son of the most high God?*

What do you have to do with me? That which a judge has to do with the one to be punished, what a king has to do with a deserter, what an owner has to do with a thief. *What do you have to do with me, Son of the most high God?* If you acknowledge the Son, certainly you are not ignorant of the heir; if you know the heir, why do you presume to steal the inheritance? *I beg you in the name of God not to torture me.* The renegade fears and makes pretense; he confesses the Son, but so that God may not be recognized, he schemes in his customary fashion: he begs God in the name of God so that he might make him appear to be someone else; so that he might deceive and trip up the audience that is present.

4. Jesus asks him: *What is your name?* (v.9) He asks: he is not ignorant, but he fulfills his role as Judge, he observes the order of a judicial examination. He asks the name in order to investigate the matter at hand, to make a judgment about the guilt, to sentence him for the crime, and to show beyond any doubt that he is God through the sentence that is given.[4] The devil answers: *Legion, because we are many* (v.9). And so, Christ's question dispels our ignorance and reveals for us what was hidden.

4. For other references in Chrysologus's sermons describing the action of Christ in juridical language, see R. Benericetti, *Il Cristo,* 235.

Legion has attacked one man. The soldier's sloth is evident, if he should desert the battle line, if he should retreat, if he should be terrified of fighting, when he considers that the one man held captive is stronger than an enemy of great number. Before the King what are they who have assembled in full regiment in order to capture one man who is not yet even a recruit? Where would they have been if they had already seen on that occasion the standard of the cross, the insignia of Christ?[5] Go, Christian, go forward free from care; a battalion so great and so numerous that has such fear of one who is unarmed, will flee far away if it should see, sense, or recognize one who is armed.

5. *The spirits implored him, saying: "Send us into the swine"* (v.12). See where Satan desires to relocate: from graves to pigs. Ever rotten to the core he searches for dwellings that are stinking and foul, he is delighted by filth and mire, since without fail he always feeds on the stench of crimes and the squalor of the vices. But so hellish and harsh is his odor that not even swine were sufficiently constituted to contain him. In a word, they preferred to drown in the sea and to perish in the waves than to endure his filthiness and tolerate his rottenness. Now what can demons appropriate for themselves, since they are not even able to affect swine unless divine authority permits it? Wretched is the one who abandons the Judge and seeks in vain the favor of the tormentor who has no power to begin or cease or diminish or increase his torturing, but everything that scoundrel does is by the authority and the decision of the Judge.

5. The "insignia" refer to the sign of the cross within each baptized Christian and visible to the demons. As the next sentence indicates, the baptized Christian, in contrast to the possessed man in this account, is "armed" with these *Christi signa.*

SERMON 18

On Simon Peter's Mother-in-law[1]

HE ATTENTIVE LISTENER TO TODAY'S READING
has learnt why the Lord of heaven entered the earthly
dwellings of his servants. But it is no marvel if he who
in his mercy had come to help all people did not disdain entering all places. *When Jesus had come,* it says, *to Peter's house, he saw
his mother-in-law lying in bed with a fever* (Mt 8.14). You see what it
was that moved Christ to enter the house of Peter: certainly it
was not the desire to have a meal but the illness of the one in
bed; not the need to eat, but the opportunity for healing;[2] a
work of divine power, not an extravagant human banquet. In
Peter's house not wine but tears were flowing; there the family
was not worrying about a banquet, but about the one who lay
ill; there a fever, not gluttony, was raging. So Christ entered
there not to take a meal, but to restore life. God seeks human
beings, not human things; he desires to give heavenly goods, he
does not long to obtain earthly goods. So Christ came to re-
trieve us, not to acquire what belongs to us.[3]

2. *When he had come,* it says, *to Peter's house, he saw his mother-in-
law lying in bed with a fever.* Entering Peter's house Christ saw
why he had come, he did not attend to the quality of the house,
nor the crowds of those coming to meet him, nor the proces-
sion of those gathering to greet him, nor the family members
surrounding him, and certainly not the elaborateness of the
furnishings, but he gazed intently at the groaning of the one
who was ill, he directed his attention to how high her fever was,
he noted how dangerous and desperate was her condition, and

---

1. Mt 8.14–16.
2. The Latin *salutis* carries the meaning of "salvation" as well as "healing."
3. *Recepturus nos, non nostra quaesiturus.*

immediately he stretched out his hand to exercise his divinity. Christ did not recline for human sustenance until the woman who was lying prostrate arose for divine purposes.[4]

3. *He held her hand*, it says, *and the fever left her* (v.15). You see how the fever leaves one whom Christ held; infirmity has no footing wherever the Author of salvation stands near; death has no access to the place where the Giver of life has entered. *He held her hand*, it says. What was the need to touch, when the power to command was present? But Christ held the hand of the woman to give life, since from the hand of a woman Adam had received death. He held her hand, so that what the hand of the presumptuous one[5] had lost, the hand of the Author would restore. He held her hand, so that the hand which had plucked a death sentence might receive pardon.

4. *And she arose*, it says, *and began to wait on him* (v.15). Did Christ need the service of the woman, and a woman at that who was well along in years, of a very old age, and having borne children? In Peter's house was there not a young slave, a servant, a relative, a neighbor, or at least his wife who could do the serving in place of her mother? And in short, didn't Peter consider it shameful for himself that an elderly woman, that his mother-in-law, should do for the Master what a disciple ought to have done? Brothers, Christ did not need human service from her upon whom he had exercised his divine power; but he allowed her to serve him as a proof that she had recovered her health. Christ puts diseases to flight in such a way that the next moment he restores one's former strength. Where skill works the cure, there no fatigue from the infirmity remains; where power cures, there debility leaves no trace.

5. But lest any of the spiritual meaning[6] in this reading be

4. The "divine purposes" in question are more clearly indicated in sections 4 and 7 of this sermon as a manifestation of a divine act of healing and as sanctified good works.

5. The Latin poet Sedulius in his *Paschale Carmen* 2.4 refers to Adam as *praesumptor* (CSEL 10.44). A. Olivar in CCL 24.108 is of the opinion that by "the presumptuous one" *(praesumentis)* Chrysologus is referring to Adam. It is more likely, in my view, that it instead refers to Eve who, according to Gn 3.6, plucked the fruit from the tree.

6. *Spiritalis intelligentiae.* This terminology for allegorical exegesis is also found in *Sermon* 50.2.

hidden, if we wish to know it, let us not go searching about the little flowers of the words. The one who seeks ripe fruit despises the charming things growing in the field. Violets, roses, lilies, and daffodils are pleasant flowers, but bread is even more pleasant. What the aroma is to our noses, this is what elegant speech is to the ears; what bread gives to life, this is what knowledge gives to salvation. The pleasure of eloquence must be set aside when the firmness of knowledge is put forward.

6. *When Jesus had come*, it says, *to Peter's house* (v.14). Christ came to Peter's house so that Peter's house would come to Christ. Christ came to Peter's house the moment when he entered the dwelling of our flesh. *When Jesus had come to Peter's house.* What is Peter's house? It is that about which the Lord says: "And you, house of Judah, you are not the least among the princes of Judah; from you," he says, "will come a leader to rule my people."[7] Furthermore the Apostle says: "From them came Christ according to the flesh, who is God, blessed for ever."[8]

7. *When he had come to Peter's house, he saw his mother-in-law lying in bed with a fever.* He saw the synagogue lying in the darkness of its lack of faith, prostrate under the burden of its sins, in a fever from its vices to the point of delirium; and so he held her hand, since not only with his word, but also with his hands does he accomplish the salvation of the Jewish people. Listen to the prophet: "But God our king before the ages accomplished salvation in the midst of the earth."[9] *He held her hand* (v.15), so that her hand would be cleansed of the blood of the prophets before receiving the sacrament administered by the Church. *And she arose and began to wait on him.* This is the reason why she who was lying prostrate was raised up, and was waiting on Christ, and now in good works sanctifying her hands, which earlier she was defiling by wicked works.

8. *As evening came*, it says, *they brought him many who were possessed by demons, and he cast the spirits out with a word* (v.16). How can this be understood in a human fashion, namely that with no regard for daylight, in the evening those eager for healing brought many who were badly afflicted for the restoration of

7. Mt 2.6. See Mi 5.2.   8. Rom 9.5.
9. Ps 73 (74).12.

their health? But in the evening is the time when the day of this age is drawing to a close, when the world is turning away from the light of time. The Restorer of light comes late in order to restore the eternal day to us gentiles who have come in the nighttime of the ages.

As evening came, however, they brought him many who were possessed by demons. In the evening, that is, in this last age the faithful and dedicated devotion of the apostles presents us gentiles to the Lord, and demons are expelled who used to rule over us by our worship of idols. Listen to the prophet: "All the gods of the gentiles are demons."[10] Ignorant of the one God we were paying homage to innumerable gods by sacrilegious and the most abject slavery. *And he cast the spirits out with a word*, since Christ came to us not with his flesh, but with his word.

When, therefore, faith came "by hearing, and hearing through the word,"[11] he freed us from slavery to demons, and he deposed the demons from their wicked tyranny and made them captive. This is the reason why the demons are tormented under our hands and at our orders, since they used to subject us to wood, enslave us to stone, and torture us daily with groundless fear through useless images.

9. Only now, brothers, take care that faithlessness does not call us back to enslavement to them; let us not be ensnared by augury, let us not be deceived by divination, let us not be captivated by fortune-telling, let us not be deluded by palm-reading, let us not be seduced by death, let us not be enticed by reeking odors;[12] instead, let us commit ourselves and our actions to the Lord, let us entrust ourselves to the Father, let us have faith in God, that as God he guides human history; and so as Father he directs the actions of his children, and as Lord he does not forsake the care of his family.

10. Ps 95 (96).5.
11. Rom 10.17.
12. For a similar litany of demonic activities, see *Sermon* 71.5.

SERMON 19

A Second on the Same <or> About the One Who Promised to
Follow Christ Wherever He Would Go[1]

 ODAY THE EVANGELIST BEGINS as follows: *Upon seeing the crowds around him, Jesus gave the order to go across the sea* (Mt 8.18). How often the slow-learning crowd pours out around the Lord, its conscience all stirred up and storm-tossed; it deserts a quiet place, heads for the waves, passes ports, and falls into shipwreck; striving for the heights, it sinks into the deep. Then Christ orders this sea turbulent with such crowds to be crossed. *Upon seeing the crowds around him,* it says, *Jesus gave the order to go across the sea:* not that he who had come for the salvation of human beings should run away from them, but, rather, he gives the foolish more time to return; he hopes that the wayward will return; he shows patience for pardon, since he does not want to execute judgment; he endures the obstinate, since he does not want to lose but to save what he has made.

2. *One of the scribes,* it says, *drew near him and said, "Master, I shall follow you wherever you go"* (v.19). The one who makes a rash promise falls down, he does not draw near.[2] Who promises that he is able to follow God into all things? It would have been more reasonable for him to have said: "I shall follow you wherever you bid"; certainly it would have been more humanly possible if he had said: "wherever you will." *I shall follow you wherever you go:* so says the one who ignores the difference between himself and God. So says the one who does not understand Christ to be God, but only the Master. *I shall follow you wherever you go.* Peter follows him through the sea; he follows, but he sinks;[3] he follows him to his passion, but he denies

---

1. Mt 8.18–22. 2. *Decidit, non accedit.*
3. Mt 14.28–31.

him.[4] And if Peter is so deficient, if even he falters to such an extent in these small matters, who is this one to make such a promise that he will follow the Lord into all things?

I shall follow you wherever you go. So this one says, as if he were able to undergo scourging with Christ, to submit to the ignominy of the cross for the sake of glory, to enter the stronghold of death, to put death to death through death, to penetrate the unfamiliar realm of hell, to burst the bonds of the underworld, through their own bodies[5] to call back souls now hardened by centuries and oblivious to the light, to shake the earth, to rend rocks, to open graves, to lead the buried out of the underworld, and to furnish witnesses to their resurrection. Let him still aim to go wherever Christ goes: let him sit upon the shoulders of angels, let him mount the heavens, let him take his seat beside the Father, let him reach the summit of all heavenly honors. Why does this foolish scribe, this haughty slave, promise that he will follow Christ into those places, follow the Lord into these regions?

3. But he receives from Christ an answer that such presumption deserves: *The foxes have lairs, the birds of the sky have nests; the Son of Man, however, has no place where he can lay his head* (v.20). What does this mean? The fox is weak in strength, strong in cunning, an inventor of trickery, a contriver of fraud, a master of pretense, lacking in simplicity, but full of deceit, one who preys on domestic birds,[6] and is hostile to its own household.

It is fitting that Christ has this [animal] symbolize Herod, the leader of the Jews, who forgot his ancient freedom, took a post subservient to Rome, achieved dominion through craftiness, ruled by cunning, had power by fraud, held authority by trickery, and was powerful through hypocrisy; and because he was unable to carry off booty from foreign nations, he devoured his own race, his native people, domestic birds, as it were. Christ shows this when he sends word to Herod: "Go, say

4. See Mt 26.33–35 and 69–75, and parallels.

5. The plural *propria corpora* refers to the bodies of Christ and the scribe, who is hypothetically accompanying Christ.

6. This rather odd remark is explained in the next sentence with reference to the tetrarch Herod Antipas.

to that fox."[7] Truly he is a fox since by trickery he seized a kingdom that he did not deserve either by his birth or by his manner of life. So here Herod set the lairs of his own wickedness
within the bodies of the scribes, which resulted not in the death
of Christ but in his own entrapment, and he did not leave a
place where Christ could lay his head, that is, God.[8]

4. *Foxes have lairs, and the birds of the sky have nests.* Here he
calls "birds" all the demons flying about in the air who have
also made the nests of their malice in the hearts of the scribes,
where they could sow all the seeds of their wickedness. This is
why when the devil inserted himself into the mind of Judas,[9]
the next moment he conceived what sprang from deceit and
produced the crime of betrayal. You see that Christ did not
drive away a scribe of good will, but he revealed his pretense,
and he loathed his presumption. Now why would Christ, the
Author of kindness, the Giver of salvation, prohibit that man
from coming if he so willed, especially since right afterwards he
would keep another disciple from leaving when he wanted to
go?

5. It says: *Another disciple said: "Lord, let me first go and bury my
father." But Jesus said to him: "Follow me, and let the dead bury their
dead"* (vv.21–22). Is Christ hereby denying the final act of devotion, is he forbidding the last service that is owed to one's parents? No, he is not denying the act of devotion, but he is placing obedience to God above human affections. He hears what
his disciple said: *Let me first go and bury my father.* This ought not
to have been first for him but second. One's earthly father must
be ranked after the heavenly Father. *Follow me, and let the dead
bury their dead.* That is to say: "Follow me into the shame of the
passion, so that you can attain with me to the glory of the resurrection."

Let the dead bury their dead. Why should a son of faith return
to a house of faithlessness? Why should an offspring of salva-

7. Lk 13.32.
8. Chrysologus's exegesis is clearly a bit strained here in his attempt to indicate that God is the head and governing principle of Christ, on the one hand,
and that God has no place in the life of Herod Antipas, on the other.
9. See Jn 13.27.

tion mourn the lost with those who are lost? What concern does a child of the resurrection have for the grave of his father? *Follow me, and let the dead bury their dead.* How do they bury their dead? Brothers, he himself has said: "I am the life."[10] What the soul is to the body is what Christ is to the soul. Without the soul the body does not live; the soul does not live without Christ. As soon as the soul leaves the body, stench, corruption, rottenness, the worm, ashes, horror, and everything that is loathsome to the sight take its place; when God leaves, immediately the stench of faithlessness, the corruption of sin, the rottenness of the vices, the worm of guilt, the ashes of vanities, and the horror of infidelity enter the soul, and there comes to pass in the living tomb of the body the death of the soul now buried.

Resembling this case was the one in which a corpse was being waked amid false and faithless rites, and by a service of irreverence an act of devotion was being attempted: "Jesus," it says, "upon entering the house of the leader saw the musicians."[11] Are not such people making a sacrilege out of devotion when they employ music for grief and outsiders' lamentations for the burial rites of their own? Where mourning is not genuine, there the song is bought and hired. It is not a skillful flute, but simple affection that mourns the dead. Therefore, Christ was willing to have his disciple not be absent from his father's funeral, but was unwilling to have him involved with profane mourning.

10. Jn 14.6.
11. Mt 9.23.

SERMON 21

When Christ Was Asleep in the Boat[1]

HENEVER CHRIST IS ASLEEP in our boat, and he is asleep in the body[2] with the slumber of our sloth,[3] the storm with whirling winds in full besets us, threatening waters surge, and while they repeatedly rise and fall with their waves of foam, they produce in the sailors a heightened fear of shipwrecks, as the present reading from the Evangelist has indicated: *And Jesus said to them that day as it was becoming late: "Let us cross to the opposite side." And dismissing the crowd they took him in the boat just as he was* (Mk 4.35–36).

And Jesus said to them that day. On what day? On that day, surely, when as Isaiah said, "He will rise up to shatter the earth";[4] on that day when all the brightness of the earthly light grows dim; on that day when night looms near and images spread of futile things that are best avoided. *As it was becoming late.* It is late at the moment when tumultuous events precede and announce to human senses the end times and the final hour. *Let us cross to the opposite side:* from the earthly to the heavenly, from the present to the future. And *opposite* is the correct word, because divine things are always opposite to human ones; while human affairs drag those subject to them into weakness, divine matters elevate those who follow them to strength.

And dismissing the crowd: the ones who dismiss the crowd are those who keep away from where the popular breeze blows and from the public that always wanders about wavering in its opinion; they are not delayed along their journey of virtue by an addiction to human adulation, but resolute and secure in their

1. Mk 4.35–41.
2. This likely refers to the Church as Christ's body.
3. Chrysologus employs the wordplay of *in navi et ignaviae*.
4. Is 2.19.

91

good conscience they pass through the unsteady waves of praise and detraction with Christ accompanying them.

2. *And they took him*, it says, *in the boat just as he was*. What is this? In one way Christ is in heaven, in another way Christ is contained in a boat; in one way he is perceived in the majesty of his Father, in another way, in the humble state of a man; in one way he is co-eternal with the Father, in another way he is seen in time, progressing through the stages of life; in one way he sleeps in our body, in another way he keeps vigil in the holiness of his Spirit.

They took him, it says, *in the boat just as he was*. It is the glory of faith to receive Christ just as he is and as he is contained in the boat, that is, in the Church, where alone we find salvation[5] by confessing that he is born, that he has grown, suffered, was crucified, and buried, that he ascended into heaven and has taken his seat at the right hand of the Father, from where he will come as Judge of the living and the dead. Whoever in this fashion confesses Christ and thus takes him in our boat, even if it is beaten by the blows of the waves; nevertheless, it is not submerged and overwhelmed by the perilous waters.[6]

3. *And a great storm came up*, it says, *and was casting[7] waves against the boat, so much so that the boat was being inundated* (v.37). *And a great storm came up*. The storm dared not to test the power of the Lord who was asleep, but rather to strike at the faith of his disciples, not to instill fear, but to show to its Creator as much deference as was deserved. *And he was there*, it says, *sleeping in the stern* (v.38). The ones who are awake flee to the one who is sleeping, and they believe that he can resist the raging elements, even though in the midst of their affliction they see him overcome with sleep; they think that the slumber coming

5. Of course, Chrysologus intends both meanings of *salus* here, namely "safety" in the face of the storms of life and "salvation" based on the credal affirmations that follow.

6. Other early Christians, such as Hippolytus, Augustine, and Bede, also made use of this image of the Church as a boat successfully weathering the storms it faces. See H. Rahner, "*Navicula Petri:* Zur Symbolgeschichte des römischen Primats," *ZKTh* 69 (1947): 1.

7. Reading *mittebat* instead of *mittebant*, which is a typographical error in Olivar's CCL text. See PL 52.258.

from his human condition is so deep that he will not be able to be awakened even by the crashing of the sea, the din of the waves, nor even by the very imminent threat of shipwreck.

And where is that affirmation: "Behold, the Guardian of Israel will neither slumber nor sleep?"[8] He does not sleep on his own account, nor does his majesty, which is free from weariness and unfamiliar with rest, fall asleep, but he does all this through me and for me, since he changes the appearance of his action and of his countenance as often as he denounces and reproves the inconstancy of our souls.

Listen to what the prophet says: "His eyelids examine the sons of humans."[9] You see in what fashion God's eyes are shut, so that he not see and punish those who go astray. "Turn your face," he says, "away from my sins."[10] And on the other hand they are open to spur on those running towards him, to rouse the weary, to look kindly on those who beseech him. So this sleep of the Lord tests the faith of his disciples, it discloses their doubt, and it reveals that they have little confidence, since they believe that the elements can rise up not only against them, but even against the Creator himself.

4. *That storm*, it says, *was casting waves against the boat:* since both from outside the waves of the pagans, that is, the turmoil of the persecutions, inundate and batter the Lord's boat, and from inside the swollen waves of the heretics rush upon it and rage furiously. Blessed Paul states that he has suffered through this storm when he says: "Quarrels outside, fears within."[11] *Such that the boat was being inundated.* With good reason the evangelist mentions that the boat was filled with foaming waves, since the Church suffers almost as many heresies as the number of questions we read concerning the divine Law.[12]

---

8. Ps 120 (121).4.   9. Ps 10.5 LXX; Ps 11.4.
10. Ps 50.11 LXX; Ps 51.9.   11. 2 Cor 7.5.
12. It is unclear what specifically Chrysologus had in mind in remarking about the numerous questions on the divine Law. Perhaps he was alluding to the many queries that divine revelation elicits from theologians. On this sort of point, see Origen's preface to his *Peri Archon* (SC 252.76–89). A. Olivar, *Los sermones*, 234–35, n. 15, suggests that the heresies in question may well be monophysitism or Nestorianism. It is also possible that Chrysologus could be referring to Arianism, given the Arian persuasion of some of the Goths who were

5. *And he was there,* it says, *sleeping in the stern on a cushion. They roused him and said to him: "Master, are you not concerned that we are perishing?" And arising he rebuked the wind and addressed the sea: "Be quiet and hush." And the wind died down, and everything became very calm* (vv.38–39). While the reading relates the deed, the present time recommends it as an example. Inasmuch as an exceedingly severe and violent storm is threatening, while from all sides a raging and destructive whirlwind blasts forth, the seas roar, the very islands are uprooted from their foundation, and every shore is beaten by the grim crash.[13]

But since we have said: Christ is asleep in our boat, let us approach him in faith rather than in body, and let us rouse him by a work of mercy rather than by a touch in desperation; let us wake him, not by excessive noise, but by the sound of spiritual canticles, not by restless grumbling, but by vigilant supplication. Let us give to God some time out of our life, so that this unprofitable sadness and miserable anxiety may not consume the whole day; so that ill-spent sleep and useless slumber may not waste away the entire night, but rather that a portion of the day and a portion of the night may be given over to the very Creator of time.

6. Stay awake, man, stay awake! You have an example—offer to your Creator what service the cock devotes to you his host, especially since he crows for your benefit, he rouses you for work, and announces that day draws near; how much more appropriate then is it for you with celestial hymns to rouse God to use his heavenly power for your salvation. Listen to the prophet as he says: "By night my spirit keeps watch for you my God."[14] And the psalmist: "With my hands at night in his presence I am not deceived."[15]

Indeed, the same psalmist instructs us to allot three periods

---

prevalent in the imperial army, or he could be referring more generally to all heresies, past and present. See Introduction, pp. 18–20.

13. Although Chrysologus is not as explicit here as he is in *Sermon* 20.4 (FOTC 17.63), this too seems to refer to the devastation wrought by the invading peoples from the north. See also A. Olivar, *Los sermones*, 234–35.

14. Is 26.9.

15. Ps 76.3 LXX; Ps 77.2.

a day to God when he says: "At evening, at morning, and at midday I shall speak what I have to say, and you will hearken to my voice."[16] For those three periods while Daniel was diligently beseeching God, not only did he obtain[17] foreknowledge of the future, but he also merited the freedom of his people held captive for so long.[18] So let us say what the prophet says: "Rise up, rise up, and do not reject us for ever."[19] Let us say with the apostles: *Master, are you not concerned that we are perishing?*

And truly he is the Master, not only because he made all the elements, but also because he guides and directs them as well. When he hears us, when he deems it the right time to awaken, the waters will be made level, the swollen waves and crests will be brought low, the winds will disperse, the squall will die out, and that storm that threatens, and a great storm at that, will be transformed into the greatest stillness.

16. Ps 54.18 LXX; Ps 55.17.
17. Reading the textual variant *impetravit* rather than the *impendit* of Olivar's CCL text.
18. See Dn 6.10.
19. Ps 43 (44).23.

SERMON 23

A Second on Tricesima[1] *<and on the Text: "Do not fear, little flock">*[2]

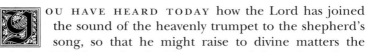OU HAVE HEARD TODAY how the Lord has joined the sound of the heavenly trumpet to the shepherd's song, so that he might raise to divine matters the minds of his sheep that had been stooped down for so long, and immediately lift them up to the heavenly kingdom. *Do not fear, little flock*, it says, *because it has conjointly pleased*[3] *your Father to give you the kingdom* (Lk 12.32). Humility has acquired what arrogance lost, and the little and meek flock has subdued every kind of savagery by its own gentleness. The little flock has conquered and crushed as many kinds of beasts as the nations were diverse that it put under the yoke of Christ.

The flock that was little and meek, endured being put to death, and for a long time submitted to being devoured, until the cruel pagans, filled up with blood and flesh, after partaking of the pleasant food of the Gospel and the streams of the divine fountain, would shun all sustenance coming from the world of their own kind, and after having deteriorated from being human to becoming beasts they would return from being beasts to becoming human. Moreover, that the prophets experienced

---

1. See Olivar's *monitum* in CCL 24.128. *Tricesima* refers to the thirtieth day before Easter, or the Second Sunday of Lent in some ancient liturgical texts. In a later era in Ravenna the Gospel text from Luke was read on the Second Sunday of Lent (a typographical error in the CCL *monitum* refers to the "Third" [*tertia*] Sunday of Lent). Although the titles of the sermons do not come from Chrysologus himself (see *Sermon* 7, n. 1), it is possible that this is a Lenten sermon. See also F. Sottocornola, *L'anno liturgico*, 394–95. *Sermons* 22, 23, and 25 are on the same Gospel text and were preached in three different years (see A. Olivar, *Los sermones*, 261, and F. Sottocornola, *L'anno liturgico*, 394).

2. Lk 12.32–33.

3. The significance that Chrysologus attaches to *complacuit* ("*conjointly* pleased") will be expounded in section 3 of this sermon.

this, that the apostles accomplished this, that the martyrs endured this, Scripture attests in that instance where it says: "On your account we are being slain all day long; we are considered as sheep for the slaughter."[4]

But for this flock of the new order to engage in battle, whereby the one who had been killed lives, the one who had fallen has conquered, and the one who loses his life finds it,[5] it imitated its King, that sheep, and it followed that Lamb who "as a sheep was led to slaughter and as a lamb before its shearer, did not open its mouth."[6] The one who is silent suffers willingly; he screams who is slaughtered unwillingly; one cannot bewail death if he has deigned to accept death and was not coerced. It is a mark of power when one willingly dies for many; when one is led to death unwillingly it is a matter of great distress: because the first arises out of contempt for death, the second out of one's natural condition.

So Christ is sheared like a sheep that is both willing and silent, in order to cover that nakedness that Adam first introduced. Just like a lamb he is killed so that by his sacrifice he may pardon the sin of the whole world. He lays down his life for the sheep[7] in order to carry out both the devotion and the care of the shepherd. For you, therefore, he has become King, for you Priest, for you Shepherd, for you Sacrifice, for you the Sheep, for you the Lamb, for you for whom he had made everything he has become everything; and he who for himself never, but for you so often is changed; for your sake he is shown in various forms, he who remains in the form of his unique majesty. And why should I say more? God gives himself to you as a man so that you can bear it, because you are unable to endure him as he is. But let us hear now what such a Shepherd promises his little flock.

2. *Do not fear, little flock*, it says, *because it has conjointly pleased your Father to give you the kingdom.* What abundant goodness! What exceptional devotion! What unspeakable affection! The Shepherd receives the sheep as partners in his wealth, and the

---

4. Ps 43 (44).22.   5. See Mt 10.39.
6. Is 53.7.   7. See Jn 10.11.

Lord grants the servants a share in his authority; the King admits the flock of the whole people to participate in the kingdom. In this manner does he make his gift, he whose wealth cannot be diminished, whose kingdom cannot be weakened, whose power cannot be lost by his generosity. But the Lord begins prudently by saying: *Do not fear, little flock, because it has conjointly pleased your Father to give you the kingdom.*

The one whose status is a servant is not able to hear the promise of a kingdom without fear, because the one who is hardly worthy of freedom is not strong enough to take up the insignia of sovereignty. Therefore, the Lord strengthens the minds of his servants with these words so that the unexpected news that the kingdom is promised them may not be their downfall. It is a crime for a servant to desire a kingdom, it is dangerous for him to hear such a thing, and it is reckless for him not to be fearful. But in Christ's regard really how great or how wondrous is it that he gives the kingdom to servants, and that he makes his servants sharers with him in his authority, since he washes the feet of his servants in order to serve his servants with unparalleled service?[8]

Let them come here, let them come who attack his power, and then let them argue about his benevolence when they are able to grasp, declare, and evaluate such great kindness. Let them no longer slander him if he should call himself while in our body less than the Father,[9] since not by word but by deed he subjects and submits himself to the feet of his dear servants when he washes their feet.[10] Come now, man, and spare yourself, because in order that you spare yourself, God washed your feet, he held them, and he embraced them! But let us return to what we began.

3. *Do not fear, little flock, because it has conjointly pleased your Father to give you the kingdom.* See that the one who gives speaks about the Father as doing the giving. Does he deny his own

8. *Ut extrema servis serviat servitute.*

9. See Jn 14.28. The slanderers at issue, of course, are the Arians. For other similar anti-Arian references in Chrysologus's sermons, see Introduction, p. 19, n. 98.

10. See Jn 13.1–11.

generosity by saying this? Far from it. He is not lessening his power, but he is revealing his affection; by saying this he is not making any distinction, but he is demonstrating that the Father's will is his also, and he is confirming their unity. However, since he said: *It has conjointly pleased,* and not simply: "It has pleased," he is teaching about the operation of the Trinity, because what it has pleased the Son to do for us has conjointly pleased the Trinity.[11] *Do not fear, little flock, because it has conjointly pleased your Father to give you the kingdom.* And so, after so generously imparting such a grace upon you, the Lord bids you who are about to reign to cast off the abject and scanty little property that is yours as a servant.

4. *Sell what you possess, and give alms* (v.33). Royal power does not permit common attire; majestic honor is conferred only with the diadem and the purple robe. Therefore the one who believes that he is consecrated king by God must cast off the dress of a slave. This is why the heavenly King ordered that the one who dared to enter the banquet of his Majesty with unsuitable clothing be bound and evicted head-first into the darkness outside, because the vileness of the guest casts insult on the host.[12] Also, the one who has just now been enriched with divine and royal wealth but clings to the property that he was free to own earlier is held captive by his misery and does not know that he is happy.

It is customary and indicates a healthy personality that one who has attained to a kingdom thereafter generously distributes what was his own private property to his parents, his neighbors, and needy citizens, so that he who has gained wealth and honor may not be beggarly in spirit. Therefore with such prudence and foresight the Lord orders us, who shall possess in the kingdom of heaven all the things that are in heaven and on earth, to sell, bestow, and give away things that are cheap and perishable.

5. But if you wish to preserve the value of your property, and

11. See R. Benericetti, *Il Cristo*, 89, n. 47, who interprets this passage as directed against Arian beliefs and as affirming the consubstantiality of Father and Son.

12. See Mt 22.11–13.

if perchance what is stashed away in your purses delight you, well then make purses for yourself of the kind that he has ordered, he who is now the guardian and custodian of your desire. In short, inasmuch as he realized that *Sell what you possess* was a hard saying, he immediately added: *Make for yourselves purses, and purses that do not wear out, an unfailing treasure in heaven* (v.33). Again you are saddened because you are forced to invest what you have in heaven. I beg you, put your trust in your God, you who put trust in your servant, and be more obliging to God than to a human being. But if you fear that the kindness of the bearer may spend some of it or distribute some of it, mark your purses with the seal of faith, so that you may sleep securely with such a guardian, because where he is there is no place for a thief. He will not be able to deny you your money, since he has conferred upon you all that is his and has enriched you with the honor and glory of his kingdom.

SERMON 24

A Third on the Same <or on the Scripture Text: "Let your loins be girt">[1]

O ONE IS UNAWARE THAT VIGILS are beneficial always and for all things, because in fact the more one stays awake, the more he lives; for what looks as much like death as the one who is asleep? What seems as full of life as one who is wide awake? We must make allowances to sleep so that the body might be restored, but not slackened; so that one might renew his strength, not enervate it. No one is unaware that vigils are beneficial always and for all things. What skill, what work, what condition, what power, what duty looks for advantages in life without burning the midnight oil?

This is why a king is in watchful readiness to guard against and escape the plots of a crafty enemy; why in the camp a soldier by vigilant alertness repels sudden assaults at night. Thus a sailor by keeping watch finds the unmarked routes of a sloshing journey; he enters uncharted paths, and with the trail all concealed he manages to reach the longed-for stopover of a profitable port. And so a shepherd adds nights to days, and denies himself the whole period of sleeping, so that there be no opportunity provided for wolves to grow fat from his flock thanks to his being asleep. Thus the expert traveler through the breezes of the night beats the heat of the sun, and more prudently stays in the house for the duration of the day.

---

1. Lk 12.35–38. A. Olivar in *Los sermones*, 260–61, is of the opinion that this sermon was preached after *Sermon* 22 (FOTC 17.65–69). F. Sottocornola in *L'anno liturgico*, 70–71, has, in my opinion, a more compelling argument that this sermon follows *Sermon* 23, because Arianism is a topic Chrysologus addresses in both, and because this sermon treats Lk 12.35–38 while *Sermon* 23 deals with vv. 32–33. *Sermon* 22, by contrast, covers the entirety of vv. 32–38, so it would have been redundant for Chrysologus to have preached *Sermon* 24 immediately afterwards on only the last four verses. It was perhaps preached during Lent (see *Sermon* 23, n. 1).

The prophet was aware of this when he cried to the Lord not only during the day but also the whole night long: "Lord, God of my salvation, I have cried day and night before you."[2] Why need I say more? The Lord himself spends the night in praying to God,[3] in order to free us by prayer before redeeming us by his passion. And if the Master keeps watch on behalf of the servants, rightly so does he thus command the servants to keep watch on their own behalf: *Let your loins be girt,* he says, *and lanterns be burning brightly in your hands, and be like servants waiting for their master to return from a wedding* (Lk 12.35–36).

2. *Let your loins be girt.* A new order of vigils, a new way of dressing is being ordered. *Let your loins be girt, and lanterns be burning brightly in your hands.* The watchful servants are given no advice about clothing, shoes, or the preparation for the meeting itself, but the entire concern is directed to the girding of the loins, the entire force of the command is focused on keeping the loins secured, with only the solace of lanterns added, without which the darkness of night is impenetrable, nor does the face of one who approaches become visible. *Let your loins be girt, and lanterns be burning brightly in your hands.* Certainly a belt is a proper indication of servitude in making servants unencumbered for their running about and in ensuring their compliance.

But it would have sufficed for him to have said: "Be girt." Why does he refer explicitly to the loins? Why does he who deserves such reverence give a command that makes particular mention of the loins? You seek to know why? Because in the loins is the entire source of the body; in the loins all the business of the flesh is stirred up; all human susceptibility to failure and to weakness resides in the loins.[4] From there comes what renders people ignorant of virtue, and what makes them more sluggish. Therefore, this is why the Lord makes foremost his command that our loins be girt by the belt of chastity, and why

---

2. Ps 87.2 LXX; Ps 88.1.

3. See Lk 6.12.

4. The Augustinian idea of concupiscence as an effect of the Fall and as most evident in sexual desire and activity is likely at the foundation of Chrysologus's remarks here.

he orders that the whole flaccid, soft, and loose part of our flesh be held fast by the unbroken waistband of virtue, so that with the flesh girded our mind may be rendered free, swift, and unimpeded to approach and meet the Lord.

Nevertheless, when you hear these things, O man, you must realize that the flesh does not hold you back from meeting God, because it is an inseparable companion for meeting him and for serving him, so long as you keep its burdens under control, lighten its loads, and as a well-prepared traveler you bind up its coverings[5] that dangle and curve. Why need I say more? You will have a wholesome companionship[6] if you are not idle and careless in regulating it.[7]

In what way, however, you ought to distribute its loads and moderate its legitimate burdens, the Apostle teaches as follows when he says: "Put to death your members that are earthly: fornication, impurity, lust, evil desire, and avarice, which is servitude to idols."[8] Therefore, the flesh must be constrained by the belt of continence, lest by becoming dissolute in vices and weighed down by every burden of sin it may not be able to press on in its journey to God and heaven.

Therefore, it was well that the Lord added: *Let your loins be girt, and lanterns be burning brightly in your hands.* Since a lantern is always carried at nighttime as a testimony to innocence, and just as darkness is always amicable to the vices, so the lantern is always the enemy of sin, the lantern is always the ally of good deeds. But in the hands of the holy ones the good deeds themselves are lanterns, as the Lord says: "Thus may your light shine before human beings, so that they may see your good deeds, and glorify your Father, who is in heaven."[9] And they really do carry their lanterns, they really do light their lamps with the

5. It is unclear whether these "coverings" refer to clothes or to the skin that covers the flesh.

6. The Latin is *contubernium*, which can connote one's "companionship," both with one's own flesh, and with another, presumably in marriage.

7. Chrysologus is being unusually vague in this section. It does appear that here he is speaking, albeit obscurely, about being restrained in exercising the sexual faculty within marriage.

8. Col 3.5.

9. Mt 5.16.

fuel of their deeds, with the oil of mercy, who, even though they keep concealed in terms of place, purpose, or inclination, yet by their deed, virtue, and merits gleam and shine throughout the whole world.

3. And because the Lord whom they await knew that delays are quite gloomy and disquieting, lest anyone be overcome by weariness, lest anyone be worn out by the delay, lest anyone succumb to the fatigue that comes from a long wait, to those who persevere he promises heavenly beatitude and heavenly service: *Blessed,* he says, *are those servants whom the Lord will find wide awake when he comes* (v.37).

And, so that the quality of this blessedness not be left in question, next he added: *I tell you truly, that he will gird himself, and have them take their places at table, and will cross over and serve them* (v.37). God will gird himself, and have his servants take their places at table, and will serve them. What an unheard-of change of events, what a terrifying diminishment of power, what a tremendous reversal of servitude! For a short time the servant stood girded in expectation of his Lord, and he bore[10] his faith, which sustained him in his brief period of toil; so that the Lord might repay him in the same fashion, divinity conceals itself in its very divinity!

He will gird himself and serve them. God ministers to the human being at table, and he ministers in heaven. The Lord serves the servant at dinner, and girded he serves his slaves; Christ performs ministry for the ministers, and he does it while established now in the glory of his Father. O man, you insult him; the Father still has what is conferred by him who showed you on earth extreme service by washing your feet,[11] and promises in addition the ultimate ministry in heaven. Believe, you heretic, and strive to render the same service to him: he prepares a feast for you in heaven, doing the serving himself, and you do not stop pouring out and producing on earth incessant blasphemies against him.[12]

10. Reading the variant *portavit* from several manuscripts instead of *portabit* of Olivar's CCL text.

11. See Jn 13.5.

12. An allusion to Arians, who claim that the Son is inferior to the Father. For

And he will make his crossovers: *And he will cross over and serve them.* From a position of authority he will cross over and move to a position of service to his faithful, but he will also cross over from being a merciful Father to the most severe Judge. *And he will cross over and serve them.* He will serve a banquet to those who confess him and wait for him; he will also serve you, but a sentence appropriate to your denial.

4. *And if he comes at the second or third watch of the night*, it says, *blessed are those servants whom the Lord will find wide awake when he comes* (v.38). *If he comes at the second or third watch.* The world knows numerous vigils, but the expectation of the Trinity knows only three. But why then did he begin at the second, and kept silent regarding the first one? Because the first vigil had already passed away with the dawning of the Lord's birth. The shepherds prove this since, while they keep watch over their flock, they are counted worthy of finding, seeing, and holding the Creator of their flock himself in the manger.[13]

But let us inquire into what are the second and third vigils. For just as the first vigil is that of his birth in the flesh, so the second vigil is when he returns and is raised to life again in our flesh. Accordingly, so that it might come to the Risen One, the world is aroused and keeps watch annually.[14] The third vigil is that expectation that comes completely to an end when he who is to come finally arrives, that just as he rose for us, so then we shall rise for him unto eternal life.

---

similar remarks against Arians in Chrysologus's preaching, see Introduction, p. 19, n. 98.

13. See Lk 2.8–20.

14. This appears to be an allusion to the Easter Vigil and perhaps, more remotely, to the Lenten season, possibly the season in which this sermon was preached.

SERMON 25

A Fourth on the Same <or on the Words: "Do not fear, little flock">[1]

ODAY YOU HAVE HEARD how the Lord consoled with soothing words of encouragement the flock of disciples[2] that began so small and insignificantly. *Do not fear, little flock*, he says, *because it has pleased your Father to give you the kingdom* (Lk 12.32). Hope removes anxieties, the outcome takes away doubts, it banishes and excludes every fear, since at the very start he promises the kingdom to the newborns: *Because it has pleased your Father to give you the kingdom.* Who sighs for food, clothing, ordinary wealth, and a common, plain, old hovel when he is certain about the kingdom and sure to wield power? He is his own worst enemy when after having been raised to the heights he casts himself down to the depths and sinks into poverty.

But it is appropriate to understand who this Father is, what he is like, and what is the kingdom that he promises to his children. Who this Father is you recognize from your prayer each day as you proclaim: "Our Father, who art in heaven."[3] You have certainly examined what he is like from the sheer magnitude of his works: he made the sky out of nothing,[4] he made the earth firm and distinct from the water, he weighed the mountains in scales,[5] and he enclosed the seas within their proper boundaries solely by the authority of his command.

But if you desire to know the kind of kingdom that he promises to his little ones, he himself makes it clear when he says:

1. Lk 12.32–33. This sermon may have been preached during Lent (see *Sermon* 23, n. 1).
2. Literally, "the evangelical flock" or "the flock in the Gospel."
3. Mt 6.9.
4. See *Sermon* 46.6 for another reference to *creatio ex nihilo*.
5. See Is 40.12.

"Let the little children come to me; for of such as these is the kingdom of heaven."[6] To be in heaven is a wondrous thing; to live in heaven is majestic. But how great it is to reign in heaven is beyond our mortal intelligence to judge. Nevertheless, O man, you have learnt that you are unable to make such a judgment from the following words of the Apostle: "What eye has not seen nor ear heard is what God has prepared for those who love him."[7]

And what you are uncertain about deserving, having, and possessing, you are now compelled to confess. What then does one who possesses heaven have to do with earth? What does one who has gained divine goods have to do with human ones? Unless of course you prefer groaning, you are fond of labors, you love dangers, you are delighted by the worst kind of death, or unless you like having evils inflicted rather than goods conferred upon you. But let us see what counsel such a Father gives to those about to reign.

2. *Sell what you possess, and give alms* (v.33). If you who are now wealthy believe that you are going to live and reign in heaven, then let those things that are yours go before you now to the place where you will be, where you will go, and where you will reign; by means of mercy tally up your vile riches; change what is human into what is divine. And so that none of you may be without means to transport the goods that you are sending along, the poor person has been pressed into service; the poor carry your burdens, and they carry them willingly, because they are not weighed down by such a load, but they are lightened. *Sell what you possess,* he says, *and give alms. Make for yourselves purses that do not wear out, an unfailing treasure in heaven, where neither a robber draws near nor a moth destroys* (v.33).

Make for yourselves purses that do not wear out. You see that this Father wants to enrich his children, not strip them bare. *Make for yourselves purses that do not wear out.* In a new manner, indeed in a heavenly manner, the one who heeds him purchases by selling, and stores up his goods by spending them; while he

6. Mt 19.14.
7. 1 Cor 2.9.

casts off, he acquires. How much he desires that money endure, that purses of riches last, that what is stored up remain, since he says: *Make for yourselves purses,* and purses *that do not wear out!*

Look how he teaches avarice, he who had begun by urging contempt. *Make for yourselves purses that do not wear out.* And he who was rebuking those who were storing up temporal goods, now thoroughly fans the flames of greed when he commands that purses that remain permanently be sought. O Christ, look how far your love for your people leads you! In order to win over a greedy person you have him hear what he desires, not what is fitting. You order purses; you want eternal treasures to be provided that will not run out, so that while the greedy person hastens after wealth, as is his custom, he may either grasp virtue, or be grasped by virtue. Truly you are a Father[8] who treat your own, your little ones, in this fashion. For we also do this to our children: when they ask us for harmful things, we bring them beneficial things that look like those harmful ones, deceiving them in their ignorance, but not betraying our affection.

You have said: *Make for yourselves purses that will not wear out, unfailing treasures in heaven, where a robber does not draw near* (v.33). And why is a purse provided where a robber does not rob? Why are there locks where innocence itself is the guard? What is a seal doing where there is no suspicion of fraud? If a purse is needed even in heaven, worry is not cast off, but merely changed. Lord, you have seen to it that in their treasure chests the greedy might have life, in their purses they might have faith; and so you want to provide purses in heaven that are incorruptible, so that the one who does not follow you to heaven, may at least follow his purses.

3. Greedy one, make purses for yourself, make them according to the orders of God, because the Divine Majesty looks favorably on your prayers. But make for yourself purses by making contributions, because whatever the poor person receives, our heavenly Father safeguards. And where does he store it? In

---

8. See *Sermon* 7.1 for another reference to Christ as "Father."

heaven. And lest perhaps you regret having lost the interest on it, as it were, you will receive one hundred-fold in heavenly interest whatever you send on to heaven with the poor person bearing it. Worldly interest pays one on a hundred, God receives one and pays out a hundred.

And still human beings do not wish to have a contract with God. Perhaps they are worried about the surety. Why? Is not one person bound to another by an obligatory note on a tiny piece of paper? God supplies the guarantee for so many and so large volumes, and you are going to refuse him a loan? But you say: "For the sake of argument, grant him the loan, but who will enforce the repayment?" He himself, because he is not able to lie; he himself is at the same time both executor and debtor. He will not be difficult in making restitution, since he is lavish in generosity. O man, entrust to God what God has given to you; when the Benefactor wishes to be in debt, it is because he wants to make a larger repayment.

SERMON 26

A Fifth on the Same <or On What Follows: And Peter Asked: "Lord, are you speaking this parable to us?">[1]

HE PARABLE THAT THE LORD told in response to Peter's question in today's reading, many in the audience surely thought was spoken only to the apostles themselves, to the teachers, and to those who preside over churches. *Peter asks: "Lord, are you speaking this parable to us or to everyone?" The Lord answers him: "Who do you think is the faithful and prudent servant whom the master sets over his household to give it a measure of wheat at the right time? Blessed is that servant whom the master finds doing this when he returns. I tell you, he will set him over everything he possesses. But if that servant should say: 'My master is delayed in returning,' and begins to beat the male and female slaves, to eat and drink and get drunk, the master of that servant will return on a day he is not expecting and at an hour he does not know, he will divide up his portion and rank him with the unfaithful"* (Lk 12.41–46).

2. Certainly this analogy encompasses first of all the leaders of the Church, but this parable exempts absolutely no human being, no mortal; while the Lord speaks it to the steward, he responds to everyone even though only one person asks the question. If there is anyone who receives nothing from God, he will not be fearful about an examination of stewardship, about the office of steward. But if you, O man, have received the very thing that you give, how will you deny that you have received what you have? From heavenly storehouses, from Divine silos the Distributor will settle accounts and will ensure justice for

---

1. Lk 12.41–48. This sermon may have been preached after *Sermon* 22 or *Sermon* 24. See F. Sottocornola, *L'anno liturgico*, 71–72, and A. Olivar, *Los sermones*, 261.

the Church; and the greater the credit one receives, the greater the debt that he is certain to repay, as the Lord says: *To whom more has been entrusted, from him more will be exacted* (v.48). And in another place: "The powerful will suffer torments powerfully."[2]

The higher a person ascends, the deeper will he slip and fall. What is higher than heaven? The one who transgresses in heaven falls from heaven. He is more hopeless in his sin when he commits the offense before the very eyes of the Lord, and he has no excuse when he commits his deed with the Judge himself as witness. Or for what defense can he hope whom the testimony of a witness accuses? Thus the devil, although he was an angel, although he was always so radiant and brilliant while he dwelt in heaven and in the presence of God, the moment he tried God's ears, the moment he grew haughty in God's sight, he fell to earth, he was cast down to hell, he was changed from an angel into the devil; he who was the minister of favors became the one in charge of punishments. This is why the Apostle urges the person of our order not to fall into haughtiness and the snare of the devil.[3]

3. Therefore, the steward of the divine word and the distributor of heavenly teaching, who stands continually before God, is always engaged at the altar, and never departs from the eyes of God, receives, bears, and offers the sins, the trials, and the sorrows of the people; he who in every regard is the substitute for an angel pours out prayers, he takes up, brings back, and restores all that has been petitioned by humanity; he has no place to sin except before the very face of God amidst the holy of holies,[4] with the result that he contracts guilt onto himself from the very place where he had been accustomed to bring back forgiveness to others.

In just this fashion when Dathan and Abihu the priests, sons of Aaron the priest, presume to contaminate the altar with a foreign fire, they are consumed by the fire of that very altar, such that those who had made a sin out of propitiation received their punishment from the sacrifices.[5] Drunkenness had

2. Wis 6.6.   3. See 1 Tm 3.6–7 and 6.9.
4. See Ex 26.34 and Heb 9.3.   5. See Lv 10.1–3.

stirred up their sin, for the smell of wine had banished the smell of incense, and the fumes of that very drunkenness had ignited the flame on the altar. Consequently, from the place where those who had alienated themselves by wine had brought an alien fire,[6] the next moment they are killed by a divine fire. In another person drunkenness is a sin, but in the priest it is a sacrilege, because whereas the other person kills his own soul with wine, the priest extinguishes the spirit of sanctity, as the Apostle says: "Do not extinguish the spirit."[7]

4. Rightly among all the things of which today's discourse accuses the wicked steward, it specifically condemns the madness issuing from wine when it says: *But if that servant should say: "My master is delayed in coming," and begins to beat the male and female slaves, to eat, to drink, and to get drunk.* It noted in particular: *to eat, to drink, and to get drunk,* as well as *to beat.*

Drunkenness is the mother of bloodshed, the parent of quarrels, the in-law of madness, and is disgraceful since it teaches impudence. The one who has it does not have himself; the one who has it is not human; the one who has it does not commit sin but is himself sin. Drunkenness is a seductive demon, a sweet poison, voluntary madness, an invited enemy, and an alluring violator of integrity and modesty. May no Christian have any acquaintance with it, so that no priest become contaminated by hearing about it, lest one who is the paragon of the virtues become and be discovered to be an example of the vices.

5. Inasmuch as enough has been said regarding us and regarding churchmen, let us inquire how the response of the Savior comprises all people, and how there is no one who is found to be estranged from God's dispensation. The Apostle says: "There is no power except from God."[8] If every power is from God, the king also has acquired from God the dignity of his royal authority.

---

6. Chrysologus's wordplay is difficult to render adequately into English. Those who have been *alienati* by wine bring an *alienum* fire. As the priests' disposition becomes different, even foreign, after the consumption of wine, so they then light a fire that is different, and hence foreign or alien, from what is commanded.

7. 1 Thes 5.19.   8. Rom 13.1.

So too the general, the soldier, the rulers of provinces and of cities, all of them are going to render an account: as to whether in no case did they exceed the limits of the power entrusted to them, whether the king guarded justice, maintained fairness, restrained his use of power, did not omit mercy, and kept the weight of his authority in such balance that in no respect did he abuse his power by making any biased or hasty judgment; whether he bore the care of all, attended to the peace of his citizens, and regulated taxation in such a way that neither the soldier lacked what he needed nor was the taxpayer overwhelmed.

The general too will answer before God for his responsibilities: whether he has distinguished himself to his troops as a paragon of virtue, been vigilant on night watch, tireless in his official duties, and through his own efforts has diligently sought the peace of all. The soldier too will render an account, whether he has obeyed orders, struck no one, and has performed sufficient labor for the wages he has received. The judge also will defend his judgment before the heavenly Judge.

6. And you who are master of your household, I want you to believe that you have been given the position of steward rather than master, so that you manifest true charity to your wife, and you prudently impart to her the teaching that you have learnt in church, since the Apostle prescribed that she be silent in church, and learn at home with you as her teacher, when he said: "Women should be silent in church, but question their husbands at home."[9] May you extend sober affection to your sons, concerned care, and rear them faithfully in the instruction of the Lord; may you render the food and clothing that is owed to your slaves, forgive their faults, be moderate in your threats, see to it that they receive instruction, and have as brothers in the heavenly family those whom you possess as your subjects in worldly servitude.

You slaves also owe fidelity to God in your very condition as a slave because the one who does not render with a dutiful and pure heart the obedience that is owed to a carnal master will be held answerable to God, who sees hearts, even before he will be

9. 1 Cor 14.34–35.

answerable to a human being; God has made you equal through grace, you whom your condition in lowly slavery had made unequal.

7. What am I to say about the wealthy person? The more one has, the more he owes. In short, he returns it all at once and hands it over to another all at once, if he does not wish to pay out what has been entrusted to him a portion at a time. And you who are poor, do not think that the stewardship[10] of poverty entrusted to you is a small one: if you should bear it patiently, if you should not be ungrateful, if you should be sober and frugal even in privation itself; if you should give thanks to the donor and not blasphemously heap insults on the one who does not give; if you should seek only as much as mercy gives, and not as much as insolent greed urges. Certainly even you who are poor, who willingly seek, should also willingly give.

But perhaps you say: "I have nothing." May you have the spirit of giving, and the means for generosity will not be lacking to you. Offer your chair to the one who approaches, offer your table, your candlestick, your lantern. By all means gladly provide out of whatever you receive. God, who sees that a guest has come, will himself the next moment furnish for you by means of that guest the necessities to be bestowed. Thus Elijah, and thus Elisha, while they went down to the scanty and impoverished dwellings of widows supplied in abundance what those widows did not have.[11]

8. But the Lord added these remarks to reinforce this parable: *The servant who knows his master's will and does not do what is fitting will receive a severe beating; but the one who does not know his master's will and does not do what is fitting will receive fewer lashes* (vv.47–48). Certainly the one who sins knowingly deservedly suffers more severe punishments on account of that knowledge; but even the other one, whose ignorance is to blame, will not avoid a beating on account of that ignorance. Just as it is wrong for God to be defied, so it is wrong for him not to be known.

---

10. *Dispensatio.*
11. See 1 Kgs 17.7–16 and 2 Kgs 4.1–7.

SERMON 28

On Matthew Sitting at His Tax Booth[1]

HAT POVERTY IS RELATED to the virtues, earthly and heavenly teaching attests. The athlete goes to the contest naked, the sailor battles the waves naked, the soldier maintains his post on the battle line only if he is unencumbered. Whoever is inclined toward philosophy first scorns everything having to do with material goods. So poverty is related to the virtues. And if poverty is the parent of the virtues, and is thus considered the ally of the virtues, it will be fitting to understand why Christ thus chose the poor for the office of virtue.

Peter and Andrew, James and John, two sets of brothers, or rather two groups impoverished, are appointed as the leaders of the apostles; poor in property, humble in station, lowly regarding their trade, undistinguished in life, ordinary in their labor, relegated to vigils, consigned to the waves, denied honors, used to injuries, with the help of only a net they seek their food and clothing by catching fish. But in them as lowly as they were in the sight of the world, so precious were their souls then under the gaze of God.

They were poor in property, but rich in innocence; humble in station, but lofty in holiness; lowly regarding their trade, but precious regarding their simplicity; undistinguished in life, but shining brilliantly as their life deserved; ordinary in their labor, but extraordinary in their resolution; relegated to vigils, but now called to heavenly victories; consigned to the waves, but not submerged by the waves; denied honors: rather, enriched by honors, not denied them; used to injuries, but not abandoned to injuries; catchers of fish, but now selected as fishers of human beings. "Come," [Christ] says, "and I shall make you

1. Mt 9.9–13.

115

fishers of human beings":[2] so that by casting living bait, so that by the hook of the heavenly word they might lift souls out of the abyss of death to light eternal. Catchers of fish become fishers of human beings: they go from the one labor to the other labor, because a labor well practiced is unable to become tiresome.

Everything that is routinely done does not make one tired; virtue remains firm by being exercised. That is why Christ wanted his apostles to be trained in human labors, so that he could render them tireless in divine ones. God wanted them to remain strong, to be well practiced in virtue, because profit results from labor. He did not want them to lose their jobs, but to change them. It was indeed he himself who allowed them first to be used to hard work, who then afterwards granted that they endure in virtue. That is why they were so victorious over kingdoms, peoples, prisons, bonds, tortures, and the forms of death that raged all over the earth.

2. We have said that in the case of the apostles poverty was chosen as the friend of the virtues and dear to God. What then shall we say, seeing that Christ chose for the company of apostles Matthew, who was wealthy from his tax-collecting post, rich from moneylending, laden with worldly profits? Today Matthew begins as follows concerning himself: *And when Jesus was crossing from there, he saw a man sitting at his tax booth, Matthew by name, and he said to him: "Follow me"* (Mt 9.9). Matthew the tax collector causes us no small question with his monetary quests, and instigates a very busy deliberation for us with his business.[3]

But someone says: "What question? What busy deliberation? God receives the poor, but he does not cast off the rich; he accepts those who have, and he draws to himself those who have not. Abraham, Job, and David were all rich: and what is more blessed than Abraham? What is more steadfast than Job? What is holier than David? For Abraham encloses within the bosom of his consolation those devoted souls who suffered earthly sor-

---

2. Mt 4.19.

3. The juxtaposition of "question" with "monetary quests" and "busy deliberation" with "business" attempts to capture some of Chrysologus's Latin wordplay in *quaestibus quaestionem* and *negotium sua negotiatione*.

rows and now fly back to heaven;[4] and Job, put to the test regarding his wealth, himself conquered the devil, and left us an example of conquering him.[5] Abraham possessed wealth in such a way that he could often despise it when it was offered, and could trample it under foot when it was bestowed;[6] and in such a way that he resolved to possess wealth, and not be possessed by wealth; to have it as the means for generosity, not as the fuel for greed."

3. But to this the response comes: wealth was harmless to the holy ones, inasmuch as it was given by God, and not basely acquired; conceded for the needs of life, not for the deeds of death.[7] But his wealth so publicized Matthew the publican[8] as a master in greed, so baked him in the oven of avarice, so tied him in the bonds of pledges, so weighed him down under the burdens of purses, that he was unable to be raised to innocence, to rise to righteousness, to progress to virtue. Consequently, his *sitting* was now really "sinking," not "sitting." So unless the reason is examined more profoundly as to why Christ called such a one as this to his goods, why he chose him for divine goods, it creates the most profound question, and would that it were only a question, and not such a great stumbling block, which at that time the thoughts of those who were present brought to light.[9]

For how would the weak human condition not be troubled, when it saw money having such power over Christ that he gave faith to one who was fraudulent, grace to one who accepted bribes, the ministry of liberality to one who was a master in greed, the authority of sacred teaching to an expert in usury, and the secret of heaven to an earthly tax collector? It angered the onlookers that usury, which was devastating the earth, was being raised to heaven; and the thing that human beings detest, he was giving divine acclamation. Moreover, Matthew himself is the one who relates that the onlookers felt that way. He

4. See Lk 16.22.   5. See Jb 1.21–22.
6. See Gn 14.21–24.
7. *Ad usum vitae non ad mortis usuram.*
8. Chrysologus has a wordplay between *publicanum* and *publicabant.*
9. See Mt 9.11.

who was to speak the truth could not remain silent about himself in this matter, and so he says: *But when Jesus was dining at his home, behold, many tax collectors and sinners were coming in, and they began to eat with him and his disciples. The Pharisees, however, said to his disciples: "Why does your Teacher eat with tax collectors and sinners?"* (vv.10–11)

And the Pharisees said this inasmuch as it was a great evil, which was even able to displease those who were evil; and if it was something wicked that tax collectors were sharing merely in food with Christ, what was it then that a tax collector partook of divine goods? Brothers, on this question the talent of the interpreter would be strenuously tested, if the Lord himself to whom this question was directed did not dispel the question in its entirety. So let us go back over the sequence of the reading, so that we may hear why Christ came to Matthew.

4. *When Jesus*, it says, *was crossing from there* (v.9). It did not say: "When he was standing there." Jesus crossed, and crossed over from there, so that Matthew would not remain there. Jesus crossed from there, so that Matthew could cross from there. Jesus crossed from there, so that Matthew would not remain there such as he was. *He saw a man.* It did not say: "He saw Matthew," because in Matthew he had freed a man, that is to say human beings, whom money was possessing. Those who serve money cannot serve God. "You cannot," he says, "serve God and mammon."[10]

And he said to him: "Come, follow me." He did not say: "Bring to me," because he was seeking Matthew, not Matthew's purses. *Come, follow me.* That is, "Put down your burden, break your bonds, escape the snares, follow me; seek yourself, be done with usury, so that you can find yourself." But now let us hear what he responded to the Pharisees.

5. *The healthy*, he says, *do not need a doctor, but the ill do* (v.12). See why Christ had come to Matthew: to heal the wounds of avarice, to cure the infection of usury. *Go*, he says, *and learn what this means: "I desire mercy and not sacrifice"* (v.13). He desired mercy, in order that Matthew might extend in mercy what he

10. Mt 6.24.

had procured by misery; and pay retribution from the source from which he had acquired his guilt.

I have not come to call the righteous, but sinners (v.13). In saying this he has not rejected the righteous, but he has excluded the unrighteous who pretend to be righteous. And so, that Christ came to sinners meant that he wanted to destroy sins; he did not want them to remain in the sinners. Bestowing generosity on the avaricious is the equivalent of giving life to the dead. And so, the reason that Christ calls Matthew has nothing to do with money, but has everything to do with virtue. As a result, Matthew presently became poor on earth, so as to be considered rich in heaven.

SERMON 29

A Second on Matthew <or> On Avarice[1]

WHILE THE LORD CALLS FORTH and exalts Matthew the tax collector to the dignity of the apostolic ministry, he is giving a hand to those who have fallen, he is restoring hope to the hopeless, and he is bringing back to life those whom death was already holding subjected to it. *When Jesus was passing by*, it says, *he saw Levi sitting at his tax booth* (Mk 2.14). Indeed he was sitting, because he was unable to stand, weighed down by the burden of being in bondage and entirely stooped over by his acute awareness of fraud.

Gold, which is heavy by its own nature, is made very much heavier by avarice. That is why it weighs down the one possessing it more than the one carrying it, and puts a more severe strain on the heart than on the body. It has its origin deep in the earth,[2] it runs along the foundations of mountains, and it makes its way through the depths in dark winding channels; and while seeking always to return to its natural origin, it casts heavenly souls down to hell, it always darkens the senses, and it always plunges lofty thoughts back down to earth. To give gold away is good, to hoard it is bad, to despise it is beneficial, to flee from it is safest of all. Just as to conquer it is a virtue, so to have escaped it is happiness.

Passion for gold seethes more ardently in the human heart than furnaces burn with all their fire; and it dissolves the human being from within more fiercely than it melts in the heat

---

1. Mk 2.14–17. A. Olivar, in *Los sermones*, 261, is of the opinion that this sermon was preached on the next occasion after *Sermon* 28, inasmuch as Chrysologus customarily treated consecutively each Gospel's account of the same Scriptural story: on the call of Matthew (or Levi) first in the Gospel of Matthew (*Sermon* 28) and then in Mark's Gospel (this *Sermon* 29).

2. See *Sermon* 22.3 (FOTC 17.67).

of flames. The master of cruelty, a savage enemy, wounds by loving, makes naked by enriching;[3] even a mere glance at it holds
one captive, breaks faith, does violence to affection, wounds
charity, disturbs the peace, carries off innocence, teaches theft,
prompts trickery, and commands robbery.

And why should I say more? This is what the Apostle said:
"Avarice is the root of all evils."[4] There is really only one thing
to do with it, if the prudent person should send it along to
heaven,[5] rather than like a fool be sent by it down to hell. Let
him send it ahead through the hand of the poor person, because the entirety of whatever he gives to the poor person on
God's account, he transfers to God without delay.[6]

2. In his desire that Matthew be released from such chains
that held him shackled, fittingly the Lord rouses him when he
says, *Follow me* (v.14). That is, "Follow me as I make my course
higher and higher, rather than gold, which plunges one deeper
and deeper." "Where your treasure is, there your heart will be
also."[7] O gold! It so corrupted and eliminated all fraternal devotion from the stock of the Patriarchs, the holy progeny, the
singular crown of so illustrious a brotherhood that they handed
over Joseph to the Egyptians, their brother to barbarians, the
innocent one to the guilty, one of noble lineage to slavery.[8] So
much did it blind their minds, weigh down their hearts, and
transform what they had of human feeling into beastly madness, that it did not allow them to be mindful of the affront to
God, the grief of their holy father, or any sensitivity for their
own blood.

Consider if there is anything that is harsher than gold,
which, when it destroys the morals of human beings, also destroys their nature. Gold so captivated the Jewish people by its
appearance, it so bound them with its attraction, it so thoroughly deceived them with its luster, that they believed it to be
a god, and they denied the true God, the God who was known

3. Reading the textual variant *ditando* instead of *vitando* in Olivar's CCL text.
4. 1 Tm 6.10.
5. See also *Sermon* 22.3 (FOTC 17.67).
6. See *Sermons* 7.6, 8.4, and 25.2.   7. Mt 6.21.
8. See Gn 37.25–36.

by his many benefits to them. It so changed human beings into beasts[9] that they believed that the head of a calf was their own Head, and that they preferred a head of cattle to the Head of all things.[10]

Notice how this madness must be avoided, which, after it destroyed the morals, the honor, and the life of human beings, wanted and aspired also to rob humanity of God himself. This is why it made Judas a traitor, in order to force man first to deny God, and then to sell him;[11] first to estrange his blood brother[12] and then to estrange the very creator of his blood, and to charge a price for the very blood that the Lord, of his own accord, was going to give for our ransom. But so that many examples on this point do not become tiresome, let us move on to the rest.

3. *"Follow me"; and getting up, he followed him* (v.14). One reads that often even in an enemy there is a useful virtue, often in an adversary a virtue is evident. Matthew is not being taken away from his work, but is being changed; and he takes his tax booth with him rather than leaving it behind, so that he may search after what will abide for God, not what will pass away for the human being; not so that as a grim accountant he may collect coins numbering thirty-, forty-, and fifty-fold, but so that he may happily store up thirty-, sixty-, and one-hundred-fold joy,[13] happy profits, full of divine favors. *And getting up, he followed him.* It is a noble spirit that so easily despised as though nothing at all those things that he had thought to be great! It is apparent that earlier through ignorance he had sought after present gain, from which, as he realized and saw, he was thus snatched away to divine gain.

4. *It happened*, it says, *that when he was dining at his home, many tax collectors and sinners reclined at table with Jesus and his disciples*

9. See *Sermon* 22.6 (FOTC 17.69).
10. See Ex 32.1–8. The particular reference to the worship of the golden calf's *head* is found, e.g., in Lactantius, *Divine Institutes* 4.10 (FOTC 49.265) and Ambrose, *Letter* 64 (FOTC 26.433).
11. See Mk 14.10–11 and parallels.
12. Jesus was Judas's "blood brother" because of their common humanity and, perhaps, the tight bond between Jesus and the Twelve.
13. See Mt 13.23.

(v. 15). Jesus was reclining more in Matthew's mind than on his dining-couch; and he was feasting not on food, but on the return of a sinner, in order to call back by a party, by fellowship, by a kind disposition, by very pleasant dinner conversation those whom he knew could be undone by his power as Judge if it were recognized, who could be overwhelmed by terror before his majesty, and who could at that moment be knocked prostrate if God's presence were uncovered.

He who wanted to be at one with humanity is concealed in a human body; he who wanted to help the guilty keeps the Judge hidden; he who considered servants worthy of not betraying his trust concealed that he was Lord; he who was eager to embrace the weak with a parent's love covered up his majesty.

But the Jews were offended and said: *Why does he eat with tax collectors and sinners?* (v. 16) Do you wonder, Jew, why there mingles in a party of sinners the One who for the sake of sinners both wanted to be born and did not refuse to be killed? Do you rant and rave at why the wine of sinners is being drunk by him who poured his own blood out on behalf of sinners? And if you want to know more: he himself has taken sin on himself so as not to lose sinners.[14] The Judge flung back onto himself his own sentence, so that he might show that he loved sinners more by paying the debt than by pardoning it.

5. But let the Lord's own response to such remarks be sufficient: *The healthy have no need of a doctor, but the ill do. I have not come to call the righteous, but sinners* (v. 17). And who was not sick since the very nature of the human race was so sick? Therefore he came for all people in order to cure them, since he found all to be ill. But clearly he deserved to die, he who despised the doctor so as not to accuse himself nor admit that he was sick.

But next the Lord discloses the meaning of his metaphor when he says: *I have not come to call the righteous, but sinners.* Here the Lord is not rejecting the righteous, but the haughty; and he is referring to those who, although they are not righteous, boast that they are. And where were those righteous ones

14. *Ne perderet peccatores* could also be rendered, "so that sin not destroy sinners." The expression *suscepit peccatum* is found also in *Sermon* 45.6.

when, according to the prophet, there was not anyone who did good, there was not even one?[15] In order for them to recognize the illness, let them admit the doctor[16] so as to be cured; let them admit that they are sinners, so that Christ, their parent[17] and table-companion, may bestow pardon on them right now, and so that later as Judge he may not render against them in their obstinacy the unending sentence that is their due.

15. See Ps 13 (14).1 and 3.
16. For other references to Christ as *medicus* in Chrysologus's sermons, see R. Benericetti, *Il Cristo*, 235, n. 16.
17. For other references to Christ as *parens* in Chrysologus's sermons, see ibid., 236, n. 23.

SERMON 30

A Third on Matthew[1]

ODAY'S GOSPEL READING changed Matthew the tax collector into an apostle in such a way that he who was a defrauder of money became a distributor of grace, and from the school of impiety he attained to a teaching position of piety, and he who had been an instructor in avarice became a teacher of mercy. *While he was crossing from there, Jesus saw a man named Matthew sitting in his tax booth* (Mt 9.9). *When Jesus was crossing from there.* It was well that he was crossing from there: he was crossing Judea in order to come to the gentiles; he was passing the synagogue in order to remain in the Church; he was proceeding through his homeland according to the flesh in order to return to the residence of his divinity. In Christ, brothers, fleshly harm is transitory, in whom the honor of divinity is eternal.

While he was crossing he saw a man. He saw with divine eyes more than with human ones. He saw the man in order not to see the man's sins; he saw his own work in order to disregard the works of sin. God saw him so that he might see God; Christ saw him so that he might see no longer the places where money was hiding. Christ saw him sitting, because weighed down by the burden of greed he was unable to stand up.

Brothers, this tax collector was sitting at his tax booth in a worse condition than the paralytic, about whom we have spoken earlier,[2] who was lying in bed, because he was suffering

1. Mt 9.9–13. This sermon was preached in a different year from that of *Sermon* 28 (on the same Gospel account). See F. Sottocornola, *L'anno liturgico*, 72. A. Olivar, in *Los sermones*, 261, believes that this sermon was preached immediately after *Sermon* 50 *(On the Paralytic)*, to which it alludes (see n. 3, below). The Gospel text on which *Sermon* 50 is based is Mt 9.1–7, the passage immediately preceding the call of Matthew, which this *Sermon* 30 treats.

2. This likely refers to *Sermon* 50. See A. Olivar, *Los sermones*, 166–69.

from a paralysis of the flesh, but the tax collector from a paralysis of the mind; in the one the structure of his bodily members had been disturbed, in the other the whole order of his judgment had been confounded. The paralytic was lying overcome in the flesh, the tax collector was sitting, a captive in body and spirit. The paralytic was submitting to his sufferings unwillingly, the tax collector was a willing slave to his vices.

The one seemed in his own mind innocent of the guilt of avarice, the other recognized from his wounds that he was a sinner. He was piling up sins from his profits, while the other was wiping out sins by his groans in pain. Deservedly then is it said to the paralytic: "Have confidence, son; your sins are forgiven you,"[3] because he had made up for his sins by his sufferings. However, it is said to the tax collector: *Come, follow me* (v.9); that is, so that by following me you may repair what you have destroyed in your pursuit of money.

2. But someone says: "Why is the tax collector, who is seen to be greater in terms of sin, considered greater in terms of office? For soon as an apostle, endowed with a certain dignity, not only did he receive forgiveness himself, but he also bestows forgiveness of sins on others, and makes the whole world shine by the splendor of his preaching of the Gospel; and the paralytic is considered barely worthy of pardon alone." Do you want to know why the tax collector has obtained more? Because, according to the Apostle: "Where sin abounded, grace has also abounded all the more."[4]

Likewise, let the tax collector comprise a type of the gentile people, and let the paralytic be a figure of the Jewish people, who even today are confined in their bed of illness, such that, unless they are carried by the faith of the gentiles, brought to Christ by the compassion of the holy ones, and rescued by the belief of the Christian people, they are unable to reach the house of faith, the safe harbor of their homeland.[5]

3. *And while he was dining at his home*, it says, *tax collectors and*

3. Mt 9.2.
4. Rom 5.20.
5. Reading the variant *portum patriae* for the *domum patriae* of Olivar's CCL text.

*sinners came in and began to dine with him and his disciples. But
when the Pharisees saw this they said to his disciples: "Why does your
teacher eat with tax collectors and sinners?"* (vv.10–11) God is being
blamed for turning to humanity, reclining with a sinner, hun-
gering for a penitent, thirsting for sinners to return, receiving
dishes of mercy, and taking up the cup of devotion. Brothers,
Christ came to the meal; Life came to the feast, so that he
might make those destined for death live with him; the Resurrection lay down, so that those who were lying down might rise
from the tombs;[6] Forgiveness reclined, so that he might lift sinners up to pardon. Divinity came to humanity, so that humanity
might come to divinity; the Judge came to the meal of the
guilty, so that the guilty might receive a compassionate sentence; the Doctor came to the enfeebled in order to refresh the
weary by eating with them.

The Good Shepherd lowered his shoulders to carry back to
the fold of salvation the sheep who had been lost.[7] But the
Pharisee detests this and finds it blameworthy, since he thinks
that the Lord's meal does not have to do with virtue but with
the stomach; not with the spirit but with the flesh; not with Divine goodness but with human desire; with earthly self-indulgence not with heavenly grace. Thus indeed, the one who does
not look upon God sees [merely] himself.

Who blames a doctor for lowering himself next to those who
lie low in illness except one who is an enemy of human health?
Who reproaches a shepherd for stooping down to a weary
sheep except one who knows nothing about love for a plump
flock? Who judges a judge guilty of kindness except one who
will have been completely without hope himself? Who spurns
the communion of God except one who has no regard for what
is sacred? Who despises forgiveness except one who is cruel?

4. *Why does your teacher eat with tax collectors and sinners?* And

6. Chrysologus uses forms of the same verb *iacuit* and *iacebant* which denotes
"lying down" in sleep, temporally and eternally, "reclining" at table, and "lying
prostrate" under the burden of sin and death. All of these meanings are included, as Chrysologus intends to emphasize the gratuitous act of condescension by
Christ on behalf of humanity.

7. See Lk 15.3–7.

who is the sinner, except the one who denies that he is a sinner? In fact he himself is the greater sinner and, to put it more accurately, he himself is even the sin, who does not even understand that he is a sinner. And who is unrighteous except the one who judges himself righteous? You have read, Pharisee: "that not any living person will be righteous in your sight."[8] As long as we are in a mortal body, and frailty dominates us, even if we overcome sinful actions, we are unable to overcome and escape thoughts that are sinful and unrighteous. Even if we are able to avoid bodily evil, and if we can conquer any evil deliberations, how can we abolish faults of negligence and sins of ignorance?[9]

Pharisee, admit your sin, so that you might be able to come to the table of Christ; so that you might have Christ as your Bread, and he the Bread might be broken in forgiveness for your sins; so that Christ might become your Cup to be poured out in remission of your offenses.[10] Pharisee, eat with sinners so that you can eat with Christ. Acknowledge that you are a sinner, so that Christ might eat with you. Enter with sinners into the feast of your Lord, so that you can be a sinner no more. Enter the house of mercy with the forgiveness of Christ, so that with your kind of righteousness you may not be shut out in punishment from the house of mercy. Acknowledge Christ, listen to Christ, listen to your Lord, listen to the heavenly Physician silencing your slander once and for all: *The healthy do not need a doctor, but the ill do* (v.12). If you want a cure, acknowledge your illness. *I have not come to call the righteous, but sinners* (v.13). If you desire mercy, admit your sin.

5. *Go,* he says, *and learn what this means: "I desire mercy and not sacrifice."* (v.13; Hos 6.6) Christ desires mercy and not sacrifice. For what sacrifice will he seek who, in order to seek you out, became a sacrifice himself? *I have not come to call the righteous, but sinners.* It is not that he has rejected the righteous, but

8. Ps 142 (143).2.

9. Sins of ignorance are referred to in Lv 4.2 and 27, and 5.17.

10. See Mt 26.28. F. Sottocornola, in *L'anno liturgico,* 142, n. 19, finds in this sentence a reference to the reception of the Eucharist under both species and perhaps an allusion to the liturgical action of breaking the Eucharistic bread.

rather that no one on earth is considered innocent without Christ.

I have not come to call the righteous, but sinners. By saying this Christ has not rejected the righteous, but rather he has revealed that all are sinners. Listen to the psalmist: "The Lord has looked down from heaven to earth upon the sons of human beings, in order to see if there is anyone intelligent or seeking God. All have turned away, all together have become good for nothing; there is no one who does good, not even one."[11] Brothers, let us be sinners by our own admission, so that with Christ's forgiveness we may be sinners no more.

11. Ps 13 (14).2–3.

SERMON 31

A Fourth on Matthew <or> On What John's Disciples Said to Jesus:
"Why do we fast but your disciples do not?"[1]

OODNESS IS THE MOTHER of the virtues; malice is the origin of the vices. Glory accompanies the virtues; confusion clings to the vices as their relative.[2] Thus, vices are deceitfully concealed, and virtues are freely brought to light. That is why Christ, the light of the virtues, acted openly, spoke clearly, manifested himself as God, was longsuffering as a parent, and corrected as Lord.

But the Jews, the offspring of a viper, the death of their mother, the murder of their father, while slaying Christ burst asunder the womb of their mother the synagogue.[3] Truly, as Scripture has it, as a "brood of vipers"[4] they lowered their heads, they flattered with their tongue, they inflicted wounds by trickery, they poured out poison with their blasphemies; and as if their contempt was not sufficient for their hatred, and their scorn was not enough to inflict injury, they kept pursuing Christ with their plots, testing him with their trickery, battering him with questions, assaulting him with insults, and surrounding him with completely feigned enthusiasm; they did all this as well as objecting that people should be cured on the Sabbath to such an extent that had he not cured them, their contempt would arise from the impossibility of his doing so, but an accusation based on the Law would await him if he did cure them.

1. Mt 9.14–17. Although there are references to fasting in this sermon, it does not appear to have been preached during Lent. See F. Sottocornola, *L'anno liturgico,* 72.

2. Or, more colloquially, "confusion is a kissing cousin to the vices."

3. For similar language, see *Sermon* 137.6. For references in other writers, see J. H. Baxter, "St Maximus *Contra Iudaeos:* Parallels in Earlier Writers," *Journal of Theological Studies* 21 (1920): 176.

4. Mt 3.7.

They were asking "on what authority"[5] he was performing
powerful deeds at his own bidding, so that if he had said
"God's," they would stir up popular odium; if he had been
silent, they would charge him with the crime of practicing magic. For they were saying: "It is by Beelzebul, the prince of
demons, that he casts out demons."[6] And, just as was read today, in the presence of his disciples they charged the Teacher
for having been known to feast with tax collectors; in the presence of the Master they accused his disciples of being ignorant
about fasting and prone to gluttony. Moreover, in their spite
they were stirring up grounds for hatred and sowing seeds of
discord for the disciples concerning the Teacher, and for the
Teacher concerning the disciples.

2. *John's disciples*, it says, *came up to him and said: "Why do we
and the Pharisees fast, but your disciples do not?"* (Mt 9.14) And
what partnership was there between John's disciples and the
Pharisees, unless it was that envy had joined those whom doctrine had divided? Here jealousy broke its own laws; jealousy,
which usually divides, in this case joined them. The Jews could
not bear Moses being ranked second to the Lord, John's disciples did not want Christ to be given any preference whatever
over John; thus in both cases in their common spite they were
raging against Christ.[7]

Why do we and the Pharisees fast, but your disciples do not? Why?
Because with you fasting is a matter of the Law, not of the will.
What is at issue in fasting is not that one fasts, but that one does
it willingly.[8] And what benefit is fasting for you, since you un-

5. Mt 21.23.
6. Lk 11.15.
7. Other negative opinions about the disciples of John the Baptist in the
Christian writings in the patristic and medieval periods are indicated in F. G.
Cremer, "Zum Problem der verschiedenend Sprecher im Fastenstreitgespräch
(Mk 2,18 parr)," in *Kyriakon: Festschrift J. Quasten*, ed. P. Granfield and J. A. Jungmann, vol. 1 (Münster, Westf.: Verlag Aschendorff, 1970), 169–70.
8. There appears to be a typographical error in Olivar's CCL text, which has
iubentem and lists no variant readings, while PL 52.288 has *lubentem*. I am indebted to R. Benericetti for pointing this out in San Pietro Crisologo, *Sermoni e
Lettera a Eutiche*, trans. G. Banterle et al. (Rome: Città Nuova Editrice, 1996),
1:234, n. 3.

dertake the fast unwillingly? Fasting is the singular plow of holiness: it tills the heart, it eradicates sins, it uproots offenses, it stamps out vices, it sows charity, it nourishes the crop, and it furnishes a harvest of innocence.

Therefore, Christ's disciples, completely and firmly placed in the field of holiness and gathering handfuls of virtues, now providing a new kind of bread, are unable to engage in the old kind of fasts that are bragged about verbally, promoted with a pallid complexion, advertised by disfigurement, and pleasing to human eyes, but not to divine ones.[9]

3. *"Why do we and the Pharisees fast, but your disciples do not?" The Lord answered: "Can the children of the bridegroom fast, as long as the bridegroom is with them?"* (vv.14–15) What is this? When questioned, John testified as follows that the bridegroom is Christ: "The one who has the bride is the bridegroom. The friend of the groom, however, greatly rejoices, because he stands and hears the groom's voice."[10]

Appropriately, then, did he respond to John's disciples in the words of their master, so that they might at least believe him, and not force the sorrows of fasting upon the happy occasion of a wedding; because the one who is looking for his bride puts fasting aside, leaves austerities behind, gives himself entirely to rejoicing, indulges in feasting, conducts himself in an entirely charming, amiable, and agreeable fashion, and he does everything that the tender affection of his bride requires. So Christ, who was at that time espoused to the Church, used to eat heartily at meals and would not refuse those holding parties; in his kindness and charity he intentionally came across as humane, available, and charming so as to join the human to the Divine, and make a partnership[11] with heaven out of fellowship on earth.

4. The Lord said in addition: *No one sews a piece of unused cloth*

9. See Mt 6.16–18.
10. Jn 3.29.
11. *Consortium.* Other references to Chrysologus's use of this term to connote both the union of Christ's divinity with his humanity and the union of Christ with humanity in general and the Church in particular are found in R. Benericetti, *Il Cristo*, 94–95.

on an old cloak (v.16). He is saying that the outfit of the ancient Law is worn away by the factionalism of the Jews, corrupted by their ideas, rent by their sects, and made obsolete by their defilements; he is calling the unused cloth of the Gospel a garment. But you hear *cloth:* not a section torn off, but the original fabric. For then in the first place the material of the royal garment was being woven from the fleece of Christ, from the fleece that the Lamb gave, the "Lamb of God, who takes away the sins of the world."[12] A royal cloak, however, was being woven, which the blood of his passion would dye into a bright purple. Rightly then did Christ prohibit this unused cloth from being sown on age-old Judaism, lest the tear become worse if the newness of Christianity tore apart age-old Judaism.

5. And he gives a second example when he says: *New wine cannot be poured into old wineskins; otherwise the wineskins burst, and the wine spills out, and the wineskins will be destroyed. But they pour new wine into new wineskins, and both are preserved* (v.17). He calls the Jews old wineskins, he names the Christians new wineskins; because just as wineskins are cleansed of all dirtiness, and are treated with scented preservatives, so that they can keep the flavor of the wine intact, so too human bodies are cleansed by fasts from all the dirtiness of carnal offenses, and become skins ready for the divine winepresses, so that they can accommodate the new wine from the press of the cross and keep their newness incorrupt.[13]

But just as Christians accommodate this, so too the Jews, unless they are Christians, will not have this new wine, which is the word of the Gospel, since they are corrupted by vice and inveterate in evil; if they try to accommodate it, they will burst and spill it. It must be recognized, therefore, that by using these examples Christ was not unwilling for his disciples to fast, but he was unwilling to mix true fasting with false fasting.

12. Jn 1.29.
13. Other Fathers additionally interpret the "winepress" as, e.g., the Church and the martyrdom of Christians. See C. Leonardi, *Ampelos: Il simbolo della vite nell'arte pagana e paleocristiana* (Rome: Edizioni Liturgiche, 1947), 75–80.

SERMON 32

On the Withered Hand[1]

LL OF THE MIRACLES of Christ are marvelous works of his powers, and they must not be believed to have happened in a human fashion or by chance, but by Divine design, as today the words of the Gospel have shown us. *And Jesus entered*, it says, *into the synagogue; and there was a man there who had a withered hand* (Mk 3.1). Indeed Christ goes into the synagogue, but the Jew does not welcome him as he enters, nor does he recognize who is present, nor in his blindness does he understand who is at work. See how bodily presence means nothing where the mind is miserably far away; just as, on the other hand, bodily absence is no obstacle where hearts are joined through faith.

And there was a man there who had a withered hand. In this person the image of all people is being depicted, in this person is being accomplished the cure of all people, in this person is found the long awaited restoration of everyone's health. For the hand of the man had withered more by dullness of faith than by the dryness of nerves; and more by a guilty conscience than by physical weakness. For that infirmity was very ancient which had arisen at the very beginning of the world, and it could be cured by neither human skill nor human mediation, since it had been contracted according to the justified displeasure of God. For [man][2] had touched what was forbidden, he had taken what was prohibited, when he had reached out to the tree of the knowledge of good and evil.[3]

---

1. Mk 3.1–7.

2. Chrysologus does not specify the subject here. It could be either the man with the withered hand (who represents all humanity) or the hand itself.

3. See Gn 2.17 and 3.6. Similar exegesis relating Eden to the healing of the man with the withered hand can be found in Ambrose, *Expositio Evangelii*

For he needed the Creator, not to apply salve,[4] but to be able to suspend the sentence that had been rendered, and to release by forgiveness what he had bound by his displeasure. In this man only a shadow of our healing is being accomplished, while perfect health is being kept for us in Christ; that is, the pitiful withering of our hand disappears at the time when it is drenched in the blood of the Lord's passion, when it is stretched out on that life-giving wood of the cross,[5] when it plucks the potent fruit that comes from suffering, when it embraces the entire tree of salvation, where the Lord's body is fastened with nails, never to return with a withered will to the tree of concupiscence.

2. The Pharisees *were watching*, it says, *to see if he would heal on the Sabbath, so that they could accuse him* (v.2). To the disgrace of the judges and the shame of the witnesses, a charge is being sought from a cure, an accusation from an act of kindness, guilt from a miracle, punishment from health. But it is no wonder: good things always offend the bad, righteous things offend the unrighteous, holy things the unholy. Or when does the licentious not make accusations against discipline, the corrupt against virtue, the criminal against innocence? The priests were anxious to see, not if he would sin, but if he would heal on the Sabbath, so that they could accuse him. The lovers of sin were on the lookout, they were laying a plot in accusation of miracles, as though the Sabbath were provided against healing and not for healing.

If he would heal on the Sabbath. With this kind of interpreter of the Law, I do not say that the one who is infirm is excessively wearied, but that he completely expires! The Sabbath did not cruelly forbid a cure for the sick, but purely out of kindness furnished a certain period of quiet for mortals tired out from excessive labor.

---

secundum Lucam 5.39–40 (CCL 14.148–49), and Maximus of Turin, *Sermon* 43.4 (CCL 23.175–76).

4. See Is. 1.6.

5. For references to Greek patristic preaching on this theme, see M. Aubineau's comment in his edition of Hesychius of Jerusalem, Hom. 1.3 in *Homélies pascales*, SC 187 (1972), 84–86, and n. 20.

3. Then, *He said to the man who had the withered hand: "Stand up here in the middle"* (v.3). You who show your own infirmity, who require heavenly kindness, who attest to Divine power, who manifest the unbelief of the Jews, stand up here in the middle! Such powerful miracles do not prick their conscience, such works of healing do not humble them, but perhaps sympathy for such an infirmity might temper and soften them.

Then, *He says to them: "Is it permitted to do good or to do evil on the Sabbath? To make a soul well or to destroy it?"* (v.4) By saying this he commends the goodness of his own works, and he finds their conscience guilty of entertaining malice; because while he was striving to make a man well in body and spirit, they were taking great pains to destroy him out of their eagerness to bring an accusation against him. Even as they endured his healing on the Sabbath, they were plotting in their minds to attack him, so that when he had worked the cure, they would find him guilty out of their own malicious intent. Consequently, they were worse on account of such endurance than on account of their malice, and in more of a frenzy in their deceit than they were insane in their judgment.

4. *But they were silent. And viewing them from all sides with anger, he was very much saddened at their blindness of heart* (vv.4–5). It said *viewing from all sides*, and not "viewing"; that is, not only looking at the face as man does, but as God he gazes upon bodies, hearts, minds, intentions, the past, the present, and the future. *Viewing them from all sides with anger, he was very much saddened.* As Lord, he is angered, as parent he is greatly saddened, as man he is hurt, as God he is disturbed. Then, *He says to the man: "Stretch out your hand." And he stretched it out, and his hand was restored* (v.5). *Stretch out your hand.* What had been bound by a command was released by a command. *Stretch out your hand.* The punishment acknowledged the Judge, the work its God, and indulgence revealed the Creator.

Pray, brothers, that only the synagogue be darkened by such an infirmity, and that there be no one in the Church who has a hand that greed withers, avarice shrivels up, thievery makes infirm, and sick stinginess shackles. But if this very thing happens, let him listen to the Lord, and quickly stretch out his hand in an act of kindness, loosen it in mercy, and extend it in almsgiving. He knows no healing if he does not know how to lend to the poor.[6]

5. Then *the Pharisees went out with the Herodians and planned how they might destroy him* (v.6). The Jew is always joined with the Herodians in his grudge against Christians. *Jesus*, it says, *left with his disciples for the sea* (v.7). He did this so that by comparison with the waves he might prove and demonstrate that the error of the Jewish people was more intractable. But with a little boat at his service, that is, the Church, Jesus is separated from the confusion of the crowd, and the Captain of the Christian people is seated and not made weary by the various kinds of healing;[7] "and he gave orders to the winds and the sea,"[8] so that they would obey and finally be quiet and tranquil, according to the prophet: "Let us burst their bonds, and cast their yoke off us."[9] By remaining under the yoke of kindness may we deserve to be bearers of God's kindness.

---

6. In, e.g., *Sermon* 9.4 Chrysologus speaks about lending to God by means of the poor person.

7. See Mk 3.9–10.   8. Mt 8.26.

9. Ps 2.3.

SERMON 33

On the Ruler of a Synagogue Whose Daughter Was Ill[1]

OU ARE ABOUT TO HEAR TODAY,[2] my brothers, and, as Saint Mark the Evangelist relates it, you are going to learn together with me, how a leader of a synagogue falls forward and prostrates himself before Christ; and he confesses him as both God and Lord, when he offers homage as the Law commands when it says: "You shall adore the Lord your God";[3] and he points him out as the Restorer of life, when he begs him to heal his dying daughter. *A certain ruler of a synagogue by the name of Jairus,* it says, *came to him, and when he saw him, he fell down at his feet, and greatly beseeched him in these words: "My daughter is in mortal danger, but come, place your hand on her, so that she may be well and live"* (Mk 5.22–23).

2. Before my sermon should disclose the mystery of the Gospel's meaning, it is fitting at this point to speak a little bit about the sufferings that parents assume and endure out of their affection and love for their children. While the family is standing about surrounded by their tender, soothing, and supportive neighbors, the daughter is lying on a soft bed, and the father, prostrate on the dusty ground, tosses and turns in distress: she grows weak in body, he wastes away in mind and spirit; she endures unseen sufferings from her illness, he, wailing and

1. Mk 5.22–29.
2. This does not mean that the Gospel has not already been proclaimed, but that Chrysologus will proclaim it again in the course of his sermon. He makes similar references in *Sermons* 15.1 and 145.1 (FOTC 17.232). See A. Olivar, "Quelques remarques historiques sur la prédication comme action liturgique dans l'Église ancienne," in *Mélanges liturgiques offerts au R. P. Dom Bernard Botte, O.S.B.* (Louvain: Abbaye du Mont César, 1972), 430–32. See also F. Sottocornola, *L'anno liturgico,* 143, n. 21. On the date of the delivery of this sermon, see *Sermons* 34, n. 1, and 35, n. 12.
3. Dt 6.13 and 10.20.

all disheveled, is in full view for all to see; she is dying unto peace, he lives unto punishment.

And certainly we have left unmentioned the anxious vows of parents when they beget children; the succession of dangers, when they bear and rear their offspring; when the children are sick they bring gloomy labors and constant hardships for their parents, but the day of their death is worse, when their posterity precedes the parents in death. Woe is me! Why are children ignorant of such things? Why do they not understand them? Why do they not break a sweat so as to make some recompense to their parents? And nevertheless, the devotion of parents remains constant because whatever parents expend on their children, God the Parent of all[4] will pay back to the parents. But let us return to the passage at hand.

3. *A certain ruler of a synagogue by the name of Jairus,* it says, *came to him, and when he saw him, he fell down at his feet, and greatly beseeched him in these words: "My daughter is in mortal danger, but come, place your hand on her, so that she may be well and live."* The extent to which he laments his daughter's mortal condition with tearful supplication, and the extent to which he goes in asking for a cure for her illness, clearly show and attest to his desperation and his love. And so it is that he wants the cure to be properly carried out: *Come, place your hand on her.*

A sick person does not order how he should be cured, but asks only that he be cured. But since he was a synagogue ruler, he thus had knowledge of the Law, and, among everything else that was written there, he had read that the human being had been fashioned by the hand of God. Therefore, he had faith in God, that by the same hand by which he had learned that his daughter had been created, he asks that she be created anew and restored to life. We know what he means by: *Come and place your hand on her:* that he who of his own accord placed his hand on her for the purpose of creating, might a second time when requested place[5] it for the purpose of repairing.

4. God is called *parens omnium* by Minucius Felix in his *Octavius* 18.7, 19.15, and 35.4. For an English translation (but where *parens* is rendered "Author" and "Father"), see FOTC 10.353, 358, and 395, trans. R. Arbesmann (1950).

5. Reading *imponat* (see PL 52.294) rather than *implorat* (a typographical error in Olivar's CCL text).

This is what the prophet says, when he chants in the Psalms: "You have formed me, and placed your hand upon me."[6] Namely, he who placed it when he formed the human being from nothing, imposed it again in order to reform it from ruin. And so the same psalmist, since he knew the healing that came from this hand and obtained a generous portion of it, broke forth in a repeated cry: "The right hand of the Lord has done a powerful deed, the right hand of the Lord has exalted me."[7] And after he had been worthy of demonstrating what the synagogue ruler had requested, he added: "I shall not die but live."[8]

The synagogue ruler had said in petition: *Come, place your hand on her, so that she may be well and live;* the psalmist now after having obtained his request exults: "I shall not die but live." The right hand of the Lord is Christ, just as we are shown by these prophetic words. And truly he has done a powerful deed, by waging war on the devil, by shackling that strong one, and, as he himself said, by stealing the property of that strong one;[9] by destroying hell, and by putting death itself to death.[10] And he has truly exalted us, whom he has lifted from the depths and raised to heaven.

But now let our sermon make its way to the woman who sought a cure for a wound that was hidden and for an infirmity of which she was ashamed; she sought a cure in such a way that she protected her own modesty and showed fitting reverence to the One who would cure her.

4. *And the crowds followed, and were pressing in on him. And behold, there was a woman there who had a flow of blood for twelve years, and had endured a great deal from many doctors, and had spent all her resources, and she had received no benefit, but became worse; when she had heard about Jesus, she came behind him, and touched his cloak and said: "If I touch his cloak, I shall be healed." And immediately her flow of blood dried up, and she felt in her body that she had been cured of her affliction* (vv.24–29).

Two seas do not become so convulsed with their waves as the

---

6. Ps 138 (139).5.   7. Ps 117 (118).16.
8. Ps 117 (118).17.   9. See Mt 12.29.
10. See Heb 2.14. In *Sermon* 146.8 Chrysologus refers to Christ as *mortificatorem mortis.* See FOTC 17.242.

spirit of this woman was agitated by a double deluge of thoughts. After the doctors' hopeless attempts, after costly drugs, after a futile and interminable treatment, when the skill and knowledge of the ones who attempted the cure had now failed, when the sick woman's entire substance had been exhausted, the fearsome sore encountered the Creator himself, and not by coincidence but by divine providence, such that what could not be cured by human skill after so many years, would be cured solely by faith and humility.

The woman was standing at a distance, whom her condition filled with shame, whom on account of this the Jewish Law had designated as unclean where it says: "She shall be unclean, and shall not touch anything holy";[11] she was afraid to touch him lest she might undergo the fury of the Jews and the sentence of the Law; she did not dare to speak lest she disturb and bother those who were present listening [to Christ]; lest she become the talk of the people, she whose battles with her afflictions had been for so many years in public view.[12] But on the other hand, inasmuch as her longstanding and constant pain did not allow her to bear and endure any more, and inasmuch as the haste in which Christ was passing by cut short any time for deliberation, she knew that healing for her disease would not be given to her if she were silent and hidden.

Amid these conflicting thoughts the woman found the sole way of healing: that she steal a cure, that she silently capture what she was unable to ask for both out of her own sense of shame and out of respect for the One who would perform it; and she who was bodily unworthy would reach the Physician with her heart, touch his cloak with only the hand of faith; she knew that this trickery, which was produced not by her will but by the shame and the urgency of her condition, would confer not only pardon but also a remedy, especially since she was seeking the benefit that would come from her theft, and would cause no detriment to the one from whom it was being taken.

It is a pious theft that is committed with the assistance of

11. See Lv 15.25 and 12.4.
12. Literally, "she who had been for so many years a stadium and arena of sufferings."

faith and at the instigation of faith. See where virtue has been sought by its opposite; where deceit, with faith conniving, obtained that for which it was striving. The woman approached while people were pressing around him, so that she not be known, and she presumed that she would be able to steal the cure by her faith alone, so that she might remain unnoticed in her bodily condition. She went behind him, and she considered herself unworthy to look at him. Faith cured in an instant what human skill was unable to cure throughout twelve years.

5. After this example it is one's own fault if he spends a lengthy period of time in ill health, and it is through his own negligence if he is afflicted for a long time, since he has not learned how to be cured by faith alone, but is burdened by expensive ointments. The woman touched his cloak and was cured, and she was liberated from her longstanding illness; we are wretched who daily handle and consume the Body of the Lord,[13] and are not cured of our wounds. It is not Christ who is absent from those who are afflicted, but faith. And so he, who in this fashion cured the woman who stayed hidden as he passed by, abides in us in a much greater way and will be able to cure us with our wounds.

6. It is sufficient for today, my brothers, that we have spoken about faith's theft and the power of the Lord as he passed by. But because of the length now of this sermon,[14] we shall relate

13. A. Olivar and A. Argemi, in "La Eucaristía en la predicación de San Pedro Crisólogo," *La Ciencia Tomista* 86 (1959): 616–18, argue from other sermons of Chrysologus on the Lord's Prayer, especially 70.2 (FOTC 17.122) and 72.7, that *cotidie* does not mean that there was in Ravenna a celebration of the Eucharist "every day," but that at every Mass the "daily bread" of the Eucharist was offered and distributed to the congregation. On this point, see also F. Sottocornola, *L'anno liturgico*, 144–47. Chrysologus, it is true, refers at times to the Eucharist being celebrated *cotidie*, but relying upon Chrysologus's own interpretation of this word in several of his sermons on the Lord's Prayer, Sottocornola emphasizes that it means "frequently," "continually," or "always," but not "daily" or "every day." For the contrary opinion, see B. de Margerie, *Introduction à l'histoire de l'exégèse: IV*, 97–106.

14. For other similar references to homiletic length, see A. Olivar's "La duración de la predicación antigua," *Liturgica* 3 (Montserrat, 1966): 147–48, n. 18; and his more recent work, *La predicacíon cristiana antigua* (Barcelona: Herder, 1991), especially 675–76, n. 32; 687–88, n. 74; 692, n. 87; 696–97, nn. 105 and 106; and 713–14, n. 131.

in the following sermon[15] why the Lord, in apparent ignorance, makes an inquiry about the woman who he knows has been cured by the working of his power.

15. The sequel is actually *Sermon* 36 (FOTC 17.75–80). See A. Olivar, *Los sermones*, 261–62, and F. Sottocornola, *L'anno liturgico*, 73.

SERMON 34

On the Woman Healed of Her Flow of Blood[1]

LL THE GOSPEL READINGS bestow upon us great benefits for both the present and the future life; but today's reading has, in addition, conferred everything conducive to hope, and excluded anything connected with despair. Our condition is a hard and lamentable one: our innate frailty compels us to sin, and the confusion related to sin prevents us from admitting it. To do what is evil is not a cause for shame, and to acknowledge it is a cause for shame. We are afraid of saying what we are not afraid to commit.

But today a woman, when she was seeking secret medicine for a shameful wound, found the silence through which a sinner can obtain pardon. Happiness of the first order is not to have fallen into sins' foulness; but a second class of happiness is to have found pardon for sins while the sins remain hidden. The prophet had recognized this when he said: "Blessed are those whose iniquities have been forgiven, and whose sins have been covered over."[2]

2. *Behold, there was a woman*, says the Evangelist, *who suffered a flow of blood for twelve years; she went behind him, and touched the fringe of his cloak* (Mt 9.20). The woman suddenly took refuge in faith, for whom a long treatment had failed; she who was ashamed to look for medicine wanted to steal a cure; she did not wish to be recognized by the One who she believed could heal her. As the air is disturbed in a whirlwind, so the woman was disturbed by the tempestuous confusion of her thoughts. Her condition was in conflict with faith, hope with fear, need

---

1. Mt 9.18–24. According to F. Sottocornola, *L'anno liturgico*, 73 and 158, n. 70, this sermon, *Sermon* 33, and *Sermon* 35 were each preached in different years and probably at the end of each year. See also *Sermon* 35, n. 12.

2. Ps 31 (32).1.

with shame. The chill of fear was extinguishing the heat of believing; the force of shame was darkening the light of faith; her humiliating need was breaking the confidence of her hope.

Thus the woman, like a great sea, was being tossed about by the raging and vacillating tide. She was searching for how to do something hidden from the public eye, how to do something secretly and away from the crowd. She wanted to ensure, both that health might return to her, and that shame would not come near. She was concerned that her cure not backfire and harm the One working the cure. She was exercising foresight so that health would be restored to her without tarnishing the reputation of the healer.[3] Therefore, with this being her intention, the woman fittingly reached from the top of the fringe up to the very height of divinity.

3. *She went behind him,* it says. But why behind? *And she touched the fringe of his cloak.* She went behind him, because her sense of shame did not allow her to face him openly. She went behind him; but where there was nothing behind him,[4] there she found the face that she was avoiding. There was in Christ a complex body, but a simple deity.[5] He was all eye, who thus saw the suppliant behind him.

She went behind him and touched the fringe of his cloak. Oh, what this woman saw dwelling in the interior of Christ, when she saw dwelling on the fringe of Christ the whole power of divinity! Oh, how this woman has taught how great Christ's Body is by demonstrating that there was something so great on Christ's fringe! Let Christians give heed, who daily[6] touch the Body of Christ, how great is the medicine that they can receive from this very Body, when a woman snatched complete healing from

3. The rhetorical brilliance of Chrysologus is evident in the Latin text of these two sentences: *Curabat, ne cura sua ad curantis redundaret iniuriam. Providebat ut redderetur sibi salus salva reverentia salvatoris.*

4. I.e., there was nothing escaping Christ's view, as Chrysologus makes clear in the next few sentences.

5. Chrysologus is contrasting Christ's human body, which he calls *multiplex*, with his divinity, which is *simplex.* Thus, the Incarnation is envisioned in terms of a kind of Neoplatonic descent from divine simplicity into the multiplicity of our world.

6. See *Sermon* 33, n. 13.

only the fringe of Christ. But what we should lament is that while the woman took the medicine that healed her wound, in our case the medicine itself works against the wound.[7]

This is why the Apostle is so insistent in warning and bewailing in the following words those who touch the Body of Christ unworthily: "For the one who touches the Body of Christ unworthily, brings judgment upon himself."[8] And that as a result rashness contracts an infirmity from which faith should receive healing, he related in opposition to them: "Therefore, many in your midst are infirm and sick, and many are asleep."[9] Moreover, those who are "asleep" he means are dead, since he mourns for them as already buried in a living body.[10]

Peter and Paul, the leaders of the Christian faith, spread knowledge of the name of Christ throughout the whole world; a woman was the first to hand on the teaching about how to approach Christ. A woman was the first to provide a pattern for how the sinner wipes out sin with a silent confession and without shame; how the wrongdoer, whose guilt is known to God alone, is not forced to reveal before human beings the shame on his conscience; and how a human being can prevent judgment by means of pardon.[11]

4. *But Jesus*, it says, *turned, saw her, and said: "Have confidence, daughter, your faith has made you well"* (v.22). *But Jesus turned:*[12] not by the motion of his body, but by the gaze of his divinity. Christ turned to the woman, so that the woman might be converted to Christ, so that she might receive healing from the very one from whom she had received life, and so that she might

7. For other references in Chrysologus's sermons to the importance of receiving the Eucharist worthily, see A. Olivar and A. Argemi, "La Eucaristía," 620–21.

8. 1 Cor 11.29.

9. 1 Cor 11.30.

10. In Chrysologus's interpretation, Paul is speaking about those who are dead spiritually but not physically.

11. Presumably, Chrysologus means that by being pardoned by God one avoids facing final condemnation. Elsewhere he uses similar expressions to indicate that by the offering of pardon to others one avoids condemnation himself.

12. The Latin verb is *convertor*, which can also mean "be converted," the meaning Chrysologus will intend when using it in reference to the woman's "conversion" to Christ.

know that the reason for her present wound was a matter of her eternal well-being.[13]

He turned and saw her: he saw her with divine eyes, not with human ones, in order to restore her to health, not in order to meet for the first time someone he already knew. He saw her: whomever God has seen is endowed with good things and lacks evil. Everyone recognizes this by employing the following customary expression about those who are happy: "God saw him." Therefore, God saw her whom he thus rendered happy by healing her. And why need I say more? Christ taught by the example of the woman how faith alone contributes to complete well-being.

5. But now let us speak about the synagogue leader who, while bringing Christ to his daughter, provided the way by which the woman could reach Christ. The introduction to today's reading began as follows: *Behold, one of the leaders came up, did him homage, and said to him: "My daughter has just died; but come and place your hand on her, and she will live"* (v.18). It was not hidden from Christ, who could foresee the future, that he would meet the woman previously mentioned.

Through her[14] the leader of the Jews would learn that God must not be thought of as changing location, or led on a journey, or brought along physically, but that it is to be taken on faith how God is present everywhere, is everywhere whole and entire, and is always everywhere; and how he can do everything by an order, and not by labor; to release power and not to lose any; to cast out death, not with his hand, but with a command; to restore life, not with some technique, but with an order. *My daughter has just died, but come.* That is to say: "The warmth of life still remains, traces of her breathing are still evident, her spirit is still on the way, our home still has a daughter, Tartarus[15] does

13. The noun *salus* denotes both physical "healing" and eternal "salvation," and so is translated in this sermon as "well-being."

14. Namely, through her faith in Christ, especially in being content with touching merely the fringe of Christ's garment.

15. The personification of Tartarus, the realm of the dead, is given a dramatic rendering in *Sermon* 65.6–9. See Jakob Speigl, "Petrus Chrysologus über die Auferstehung der Toten," *Jahrbuch für Antike und Christentum* 9 (1982): 145–46.

not yet know that she has died. So, hurry that you might be able to keep her breathing going."

The fool thought that Christ was not able to raise her when dead, but only keep her alive. That is why when Christ reached the house and saw that the girl was being lamented as though dead, in order to move their unbelieving minds to faith, he said that the leader's daughter was asleep, and not deceased, so that they might believe that she could rise from the dead as easily as[16] from sleep. *Your daughter*, it says, *is not dead, but is asleep* (v.24). And truly, before God death is sleep; for God raises the dead to life more quickly than someone who is sleeping may be aroused from sleep by someone else, and God restores life-giving warmth to bodily members cold in death sooner than a human being can invigorate bodies buried in sleep.

Listen to the Apostle: "In an instant, in the batting of an eye the dead rise."[17] Since the blessed Apostle could not relate with words the swiftness of the resurrection, he conveyed it by examples. Or how could he verbally harness such speed in this instance when God's power outstrips speed itself? Or how is time at issue in this instance when an eternal matter is being bestowed apart from time? Just as time has brought what is temporary, so has eternity excluded time.[18]

16. Literally, "no more easily than."

17. 1 Cor 15.52.

18. For an earlier and more in-depth discussion of the difference between time and eternity, see, for example, Augustine, *Confessions*, Book 11, especially 13.15–14.17 (FOTC 21.341–44).

SERMON 35

A Second on the Same, When the Most Blessed Bishop Peter of Ravenna Lost His Voice[1]

 HAT IT IS TO TOUCH CHRIST, today the woman who had long endured a hemorrhage has taught, who, when she touches Christ's fringe, strikes at the entire sanctuary of his divine heart and by faith's theft seizes the highest power from the end of the fringe. What happy trickery, which both conferred the asset of healing and the same moment removed the liability of shame. Hearing the Gospel reading attests to this. *Behold, there was a woman,* it says, *who was suffering from a flow of blood for twelve years; she went behind him, touched the fringe of his cloak, and said to herself: "If I touch his cloak, I shall be healed"* (Mt 9.20–21).

In the midst of difficult afflictions the force of the pain often gives advice. In hopeless situations necessity is often a teacher. The very suffering finds medicine for itself. That is why the woman discovered how to find relief from her shameful wound by making known by her silent faith what she was unable to make known by shouting publicly; and by the secret way of the spirit to reach the heavenly Physician, whom she was unable to reach by a bodily journey for all to see.

The compassion of the healer was giving her much courage, but the constraint of her shameful affliction was taking away her confidence. The magnitude of her pain was compelling her to approach Christ, but the hideousness of her sore did not allow her to come up to him. So the woman in her quandary, while even the advice of faith was confusing, preferred to be convicted of faith than to be perishing as she was from her foul wound.

---

1. Mt 9.20–21. On the date of the delivery of this sermon, see n. 12, below, and *Sermon* 34, n. 1.

2. *She went behind him and touched the fringe of his cloak*, knowing that one's touch does not pollute God, nor does one's appearance offend him, nor does one's odor nauseate him, nor does the sound of one's voice injure him, nor does human thought defile him. For if the sun touches dung, nevertheless it is not defiled by the dung;[2] all the more then does the Creator of the sun touch everything, and yet cannot be defiled by any of the things he touches. And if a doctor when he treats bloody wounds, when he cures the private parts of a body, does not consider it harmful but honorable, all the more does God not judge it to be harmful when he looks to cure our wounds, when he touches them to heal them, when he visits to make them well.

The wounds of sins, not of physical pain, are what are offensive in God's sight; the malady of iniquities, not bodily sufferings; the gore of vices, not the flow from organs; because the human being is held willingly in his sins, but he is kept unwillingly when physically infirm.[3] That is why the sinner receives punishment, and the sick obtains a cure. Therefore, the woman who was self-conscious not from a bad will, but from bad pain, who was in turmoil not by iniquity but by physical infirmity, went behind, to avoid the eyes of the crowd, not to evade the gaze of Christ; she wanted to be unrecognized by the people, but not by Christ; she was eager to escape the notice, not of God, but of humanity; since only by God alone could she keep out of sight but be seen, could she be silent but be heard, could she lie hidden but be cured.

3. *She went and touched the fringe* of Christ, because she believed that in Christ there was nothing to his back, and she judged that there was nothing remote; since God is not diminished in man,[4] nor is his power weaker on the fringe, nor does

2. See *Sermon* 94.2 for a similar reference. For a collection and a study of texts from one classical and many early Christian authors who employed this image, see A. Olivar, "L'image du soleil non souillé dans la littérature patristique," *Didaskalia* 5 (1975): 3–20.

3. In *Sermon* 30.1, on a prior section of Matthew 9, Chrysologus makes this same contrast between the paralytic who unwillingly submits to his physical affliction and the tax collector Matthew, who willingly is a slave to his vices.

4. See *Sermon* 58.5 regarding the incarnation as elevating humanity but not diminishing Christ's divinity.

the heavenly nature vary with the functioning of bodily members. That is why the woman behind his back reached his face, why through the cloak she penetrated his interior, and through the fringe she touched the top of his head.

This happens not without mystery. Listen to the prophet as he says: "Just like oil that runs down on the collar of his cloak."[5] You see, brothers, that onto the fringe of this cloak has penetrated the entire fullness of divine chrism,[6] the entire power of the divine head. Wisely then was the woman eager to touch the holy fringe of Christ, so that concerning the secret mystery of her wound she could take medicine.

4. Brothers, this woman is great and very marvelous who in her knowledge conquered the doctors of the Law, who in sign surpassed all the Jews, who in faith excelled an apostle. For Judea with her scribes and doctors despised God in his whole body. Thomas the apostle, in order to believe that Christ was God, thrust forth his hand, inserted his fingers, and exposed the wounds;[7] and, in order to believe Christ, he compelled Christ to suffer again.[8] But with a spiritual understanding[9] let us inquire into what role this woman has. Of what is she a type? Of whom is she an image?

5. Who is it that her own blood, natural weakness, and original fault led to such sources of death, to so lethal a wound, to so distressing and horrible an affliction? And whom did they make so filthy with vices, make so foul with iniquity, and so injure with secret wounds that skill could not cure, not even enough for eyes to see, nor for decency to be evident? Who is it that even the Law itself was unable to cleanse, but on the contrary had ordered her to be excluded from the Temple, to be prohibited from sacred things, to be kept away from all that was holy? And whom had it called unclean such that whatever it had touched was also considered unclean?[10] This is, my broth-

5. Ps 132 (133).2.
6. See *Sermon* 57.5 (FOTC 17.106–7).
7. See Jn 20.27–28.
8. See *Sermons* 81.5 and 84.8 for the same criticism against Thomas.
9. See *Sermon* 50.2, which also describes allegorical exegesis as *intelligentia spiritalis*.
10. See Lv 15.25–32.

ers, this is, this is the Church,[11] which was wounded by the first
sin of man, was overflowing in blood, from her origin was hastening with full speed unto death . . . [And blessed Bishop Peter lost his voice.][12]

11. See *Sermon* 36.3 (FOTC 17.79).

12. Both at the beginning and at the end of *Sermon* 86, on Zechariah and his
loss of speech, appropriately enough, Chrysologus alludes to this sermon, when
he lost his voice. This has led A. Olivar, *Los sermones,* 261–62, and F. Sottocornola, *L'anno liturgico,* 73, to believe that *Sermon* 86 was likely the next sermon
Chrysologus preached after this one. Since *Sermon* 86 was preached shortly before Christmas, Sottocornola maintains that this *Sermon* 35, as with *Sermons* 33
and 34, which treated the same story but in different years, was preached some
time in December. For an extended treatment on occasions when Chrysologus
became silent or refrained from preaching, see V. Zangara, "I silenzi nella predicazione di Pietro Crisologo," *Rivista di Storia e Letteratura Religiosa* 32 (1996):
226–68.

SERMON 37

On the Gospel Where It Says: A Wicked and Adulterous
Generation Seeks a Sign[1]

ROTHERS, THE DEEDS of the holy ones must not be considered as chance events, but as signs; and what are thought to be vices on their part, must be attributed to mysteries, not failings, as today the Lord's instruction pointed out and revealed when it said: *But as the crowds were increasing, Jesus began to address them: "A wicked generation seeks a sign, and no sign will be given to it except the sign of Jonah the prophet. For just as Jonah gave a sign to the Ninevites, so will he be also for this generation"* (Lk 11.29–30). See how the flight of the prophet is turned into a figure of the Lord himself; and what was believed to be a fatal shipwreck becomes a sign of the Lord's resurrection. For how Jonah held and fulfilled his role as a type of the Savior through all these events, the text of the account that has been written about him makes clear.

Jonah, it says, fled from the face of God.[2] Did not the Lord, in order to bear the face and the form of man, flee the face and form of his own divinity? This is what the Apostle says: "Who, although he was in the form of God";[3] and afterwards: "took on the form of a slave."[4] The Lord fled from himself into a man, in order to escape the notice of the world, in order to overcome the devil. And the type of Christ himself is well preserved in the words of Jonah; he did not say: "I am fleeing God"; but: "I am fleeing from the face of God."[5] There is no place where God, who is everywhere, can flee from himself. But Christ fled from the face of divinity not by place but by appearance, and he took refuge in all the features of our servitude.

---

1. Lk 11.29–30.
3. Phil 2.6.
5. See Jon 1.3, 10.

2. See Jon 1.3, 10.
4. Phil 2.7.

2. Jonah, it says, went down to Joppa in order to flee to Tarshish.[6] You hear the descent: "No one," it says, "has gone up to heaven except the one who came down from heaven."[7] The Lord came down from heaven to earth, divinity descended to humanity, heavenly dominion came down to our condition of servitude. And nevertheless, the one who had descended to the ship, boarded the ship as he was about to set sail. So Christ, who descended to this world, with acts of power and miracles boarded the ship of his Church.[8]

But what does the storm stirred up by the winds mean if not the devil, who in penetrating the heart of Judas lifted up and blew onto the waves kings, nations, peoples, the army, judges, and sailors, such that the rising and falling waves of the world might beg their Creator for calm?[9] Listen to the waves of the world, listen to the prophet speaking: "Why have the nations raged, and the peoples planned futility? The kings of the earth have taken their posts, and the leaders have come together as one against the Lord and against his Christ."[10] And because the lot that was going to reveal Jonah did not fail,[11] it fulfills David's prophecy about Christ: "And for my garment they cast lots."[12]

3. But the fact that Jonah is the instigator of his own submersion when he says: "Pick me up and cast me into the sea,"[13] points to the freely accepted passion of the Lord. For why did they wait for this command to be given to them when they were able to help themselves of their own accord in such a danger? For when the safety[14] of the many seeks the death of one, death is arranged such that it is freely chosen by the one suffering it, because the will of the person about to die can on the one

---

6. See Jon 1.3.

7. Jn 3.13.

8. See Lk 8.22–25. For other references to a ship or boat as an image of the Church in Chrysologus's preaching, see Mario Spinelli, "La simbologia ecclesiologica di Pier Crisologo," in *Sangue e antropologia biblica nella patristica*, ed. F. Vattioni (Rome: Pia Unione Preziosissimo Sangue, 1982), 1:550–54.

9. See Jn 13.2, 27. Apparently what Chrysologus means is that Judas's betrayal of Jesus led to his being handed over to earthly powers, which paved the way for the subsequent persecution of Christians.

10. Ps 2.1–2.   11. See Jon 1.7.

12. Ps 21.19 LXX; Ps 22.18.   13. Jon 1.12.

14. *Salus* denotes both "safety" and "salvation."

hand occasion a stay of execution, or on the other hand fore-
stall the danger of contriving delays.

But here, where the whole mystery of the Lord is being carried out in figure, the authority of the one dying is awaited, so
that death may not be forced upon him but be under his power.[15] Listen to the Lord as he says: "I have the power to lay down
my life, and I also have the power to take it up: no one takes it
from me."[16] How so? Because Christ, although "he emitted his
spirit,"[17] did not dismiss it,[18] because it is incomprehensible
how he who keeps and holds in his hands the lives of all could
lose his own life. Listen to the prophet as he says: "My life is always in your hands."[19] And in another place: "Into your hands I
entrust my spirit."[20]

4. But why need I say more? There races, there meets him,
there is present the beast from the deep who is going to fulfill
and reveal everything concerning the Lord's resurrection, and
indeed conceive and give birth to the mystery; the monster is
present, the horrible and cruel image of the underworld is
present, who, while he rushes toward the prophet with eager
jaws, sensed and tasted the vigor of his Creator.

For indeed hankering to devour him, but also trembling he
prepares and adapts the dwelling of his heart for his guest from
above to take residence, with the result that what had been the
whole cause for alarm would itself become an unusual vehicle
for a necessary voyage, saving its passenger and after three days
returning him to the land above; and with the result that the
Lord would give this sign to the gentiles which he had taken
away from the Jews.

When the Jews were seeking a sign, the Lord decreed that
only this sign would be given them by which they would know
that the glory to which they looked forward in the Messiah

15. See also *Sermon* 60.9 regarding Christ's death as a manifestation of his
power.
16. Jn 10.17–18.
17. Mt 27.50.
18. "Emitted" and "dismiss" attempt to capture the wordplay of *emisit* and
dimisit.
19. Ps 118 (119).109.
20. Ps 30.6 LXX; Ps 31.5.

would be conferred wholly upon the gentiles. *A wicked genera-tion*, he says, *seeks a sign, and no sign will be given to it except for the sign of Jonah. For just as Jonah was a sign for Nineveh, so will he be for this generation.* Because Christ was submerged into the depths of the underworld by the fluctuating faithlessness of the Jews, and he traversed all the hidden regions of hell during his three-day journey, he gave proof of the cruelty of the Jews, of his own majesty, and of death's demise, when he would rise.

5. Deservedly then will the Ninevites rise in judgment, and will condemn that generation,[21] because they were reformed by the cry of that one shipwrecked prophet, an unknown foreign-er. These, on the other hand, after such acts of power, after such miracles, with the full gleam of the resurrection, do not come to faith, are not moved to repentance. For indeed they do not believe the very sign of the resurrection, but are eager to dishonor it, while by bribery they shut the eyes of the sol-diers and they corrupt their hearts, so that the soldiers keep silent concerning what they had known and had seen; they paid for a lie in order to remove truth; they framed Christ's dis-ciples for their own crime when they said: "His disciples came and stole him."[22]

You are wrong, O Jew: a disciple had not taken him away, but the Master did; and he who had been slain in full view[23] is the one who stole himself. But I am amazed that the Jew is looking for Christ, whom he had placed to die between two robbers.[24] He commits an evil deed, hires guards in his wickedness, and looks for even more iniquity. O Jew, Christ is not able to be de-stroyed, but you have destroyed him for any benefit for yourself by your heinous act. She will come, the Queen of the South will come, and with you as your own judge she will condemn you on the charge that it was thought that he was stolen. She came from the end of the earth to listen to the wisdom of Solomon,[25] and you, most miserable wretch, killed the Wisdom of God,[26] who came to you.

The Ninevites then prefigured the gentiles who would be-

---

21. See Lk 11.32.   22. Mt 28.13.
23. *Videbatur occisus.*   24. See Mt 27.38.
25. See Lk 11.31.   26. See 1 Cor 1.24–30.

lieve, and the Queen of the South prefigured the Church. We are blessed, my brothers, since what preceded typologically, what was promised figuratively, we venerate, discern, and possess, not[27] in mere appearance, but in reality.

27. Reading the *non* contained in some manuscripts in preference to the *nos* in Olivar's CCL text.

SERMON 39

A Sermon on the Gospel Where It Says: Who among You Has a Friend and Will Go to Him at Midnight[1]

 IVINE THINGS ARE ALWAYS SUFFICIENT on their own for themselves, but frequently they are conveyed to human beings by means of human examples because heavenly providence pays heed, not to what it can say, but to what the hearer can grasp. So, a fountain begins its route by spurting out in shallow channels, and tentatively winds its way within narrow streams, until in due course it bursts forth into rivers of full width and flows vigorously. And that I might speak to you about ourselves, after a little child is born, nature simultaneously provides liquid appropriate for a newborn, changes food into drink, and by providing a lengthy period for consuming milk it builds up the throat still stiff and the intestines still numb.

In like fashion the Lord raises and forms us to grasp divine matters by commonplace examples when he says: *Who among you will have a friend, and will go to him at midnight, and say to him: "Friend, lend me three loaves of bread, because a friend of mine has come to me from a journey, and I have nothing to set before him"? And he from inside will answer: "Don't bother me; my door is closed now, and my children and I are in bed; I cannot get up and give them to you." I tell you: if he will not get up and give them to him because he is his friend, nevertheless, on account of his persistence he will get up, and he will give him however much he has that is needed* (Lk 11.5–8).

2. O how he wants to give, he who endures being disturbed and awakened in this fashion! O how he wants what is in his own power to seem to be a matter of compulsion for him! O how eager he is to meet the one knocking, who has thus placed

1. Lk 11.5–10.

right next to the door the bed where he is secluded! O how he does not want to say no, who shows in what way what is requested can be wrested from him even as he is saying no. O how the Lord was not only at the door, but actually was the door itself— "I am the door,"[2] he says—who while his servants were asleep was the first and the only one to listen to the need of the one who was knocking! O how compassionate and merciful is he who demonstrates and depicts by examples what he teaches by commands! "When you give alms," he says, "do not blow a trumpet." And again: "Do not let your left hand know what your right hand is doing."[3]

3. *If someone will have a friend, and will go to him at midnight.* It is not enough that the night was concealing the one doing mercy, and that the persistence of the petitioner was keeping the generosity of the giver secret, unless sleep also refers to the concealing of all acts of compassion. He declares in this act of kindness a double kind of need: of the one making the appeal and of the one sleeping, such that the guest forces the one to seek, and sleep forces the other to give; for he says to him that he will give at that moment, not because it seems right to come to the aid of a friend, but because it seems right to return to sleep; and because it seems more important to him to sleep than pleasing to him to give to the one making the appeal.

Why need I say more? See where sleep is a greater help to the one who knocks than is his voice. I do not think that it is of no purpose that he reveals the time of that petition; he points it out by saying, *Who among you will have a friend, and will go to him at midnight.* As if at the first or second or third hour of the night the persistence of the one who disrupts the quiet would not be troublesome and irritating, when slumber first spreads so soothingly into the bodies of those asleep, and sweetly and fully penetrates their inmost recesses tired out by the day's toil.

But this[4] is the time that provides evidence of someone spending the night in perpetual devotion. This is the time that the mind that is ardent—ardent for divine matters, that is—be-

2. Jn 10.7.
3. Mt 6.2–3.
4. Namely, midnight, in contrast to the first several hours of the night.

tween its past and future labors refuses to allot to the body or to quiet; but before it finishes the tasks of the day that is passed, it already begins and anticipates future ones. This is the most efficacious hour for making a request, this is a very easy hour for obtaining something. Aware of this, the prophet asserts that this was the time when he used to make supplication, as he chants: "I shall rise at midnight to confess to you."[5] At this hour that heavenly Bridegroom meets those who are always awake, as he says: "At midnight there came forth a cry, and the bridegroom arrived."[6]

4. It was impossible for him not to gain what he wanted, since he denied an uninterrupted rest in order to welcome his guest, and to give refreshment to his guest. Or how would he not respond to the one who sought and knocked in this way, since he professes that he is welcomed in the guest, when he says: "I was a guest,[7] and you welcomed me?"[8]

I think the one knocking would have spoken these words or perhaps something similar: "I did what you ordered, so render what you promised; I believed you when you said: 'Do not worry about tomorrow.'[9] And so I have nothing left to place before my guest of yesterday. Therefore, if I am a nuisance to you who have something, how much more of a nuisance is he to me, who have nothing? And yet I was not able to make any excuses to him, because I have been striving to obey you." The honor of the one who gives the order, more than that of the one who has nothing to give, is at issue now. "A guest is at my house, and you are sleeping; in fact, you who do not sleep[10] are sleeping. I have welcomed a guest: unless you give the bread, it is you who have refused bread to the guest."

5. Deservedly has he bestowed on the one knocking and petitioning him in this way however much bread he has needed. That lender in the Gospel has bestowed bread. What do they do who do not put themselves in bed, but in the very tomb;

5. Ps 118 (119).62.
6. Mt 25.6.
7. *Hospes* means both "guest" and "stranger."
8. Mt 25.35.   9. Mt 6.34.
10. See Ps 120 (121).4.

who give themselves over, not to sleep, but to death; whom the rooster does not awaken; whom the morning star does not rouse; whom even the sun itself does not call forth and lead to the light of day? They have lost the time of supplication, the reward for being a host, and the very works of day.

We are saddened, brothers, when we stand before the Lord at dawn, and do not see our sons with us.[11] That man [in the Gospel] in whose house a guest had come thus knocked at midnight; I ask you: Why are you not vigilant even at dawn, when you have[12] a guest at home? The attention that man gives to a favor, go ahead and give to laziness; what he gives to kindness, go ahead and give to your own need; be an even more devoted lover of sleep than of yourself! But so that you might be vigilant unto life, you who sleep unto death, at least listen to the following: *And I say, "Ask, and you will receive; seek, and you will find; knock, and it will be opened to you. For everyone who asks, receives; everyone who seeks, finds; and to everyone knocking it will be opened"* (vv.9–10).

6. But you say: "Granted that I can ask; how shall I be able to knock at heaven in its hidden mystery?" How? By repeating your prayers, and by waiting to see what judgment the Benefactor makes; by very patiently putting up with the delays of the Giver; because the one who, as soon as he knocks, becomes angry if he is not given an immediate hearing, is not a humble suppliant but an overbearing bully. Listen to the prophet as he says: "Wait for the Lord, act courageously, and let your heart be strengthened."[13] Even if he continues to delay into the future, patiently wait for your Lord. But you want to know where and what you ought to seek: if riches, then in the lap of the poor person, if the kingdom of God, then within yourself—the kingdom of God is within us, says the Lord.[14]

11. This is clearly a reference to some sort of gathering for worship in the early morning in Ravenna. See also *Sermon* 43.4 (FOTC 17.92). In *Sermon* 45.7 Chrysologus also laments people's refusal to give an hour to prayerful supplication.

12. Reading the variant *cui est hospes* of other manuscripts instead of *cui es hospes* of Olivar's CCL text.

13. Ps 26 (27).14.

14. Lk 17.21.

7. But who is the friend who sleeps, and who is the friend who comes on a journey, and who are the children who sleep, and who is the one who knocks, and why does he ask only for precisely three loaves of bread? When I ask, seek, and knock, and am counted worthy of receiving a reply in my restless vigilance, I shall not refuse to tell you, who are the friends of my Lord. But you say to me: "Look, here is a friend of your Lord coming to you; he has been accustomed to give and not receive." Now at last this eager shepherd has packed his traveling bag chock-full, so as to taste only a very paltry appetizer from our poor fare. He the richest of guests did not allow me in the dead of night to ask for anything for him from anywhere else beyond what he already had himself.

It is no wonder, brothers; the rich person always wants to give when he stoops down to the poor. This one[15] always stays at the door of that friend[16] in the Gospel; in this one's bed the benefactor in the Gospel continues to stay with his children, he in whose heart the Father, Son, and Holy Spirit always make and establish a dwelling. Why need I say more? I have trusted asking from him, seeking in him, and knocking through him; and so I have not made a rash promise when I asserted that I would give it to you.[17]

15. Presumably Chrysologus himself.
16. Presumably the friend who is visiting.
17. The meaning of the bulk of this final paragraph is certainly cryptic. What seems to be intended, however, is that Chrysologus has a friend visiting who is a bishop of some eloquence and wisdom. From the abundance of his knowledge and from his intimacy with the Triune God this visiting bishop will now address Chrysologus's congregation and provide answers to the questions Chrysologus posed at the beginning of this section on the deeper, allegorical meaning of the Gospel account.

SERMON 41

On Fasting[1]

E HAVE READ OF VERY MANY who have won wars of nations but, nevertheless, have not been victorious in battles of the flesh; and we have heard that those who did not give their backs to their enemies gave their hearts to sins. Oh, the pain of it all! How is it that conquerors of nations are captive to the vices, that masters of peoples have become slaves to offenses in base servitude, that those who stood firm amid the clanging of swords have fallen amid enervating seductions, that the one who brought terror to kingdoms was a laughingstock for his sins, that by fasting they crushed the enemy's battle line, but by gluttony they broke up the camp of their virtues, and that they were knocked down full of wine, after they were unable to be knocked down when blood was flowing?

How is it? It is not from reason but from infirmity; not from life, but from a fever; from madness, not from nature. For as often as overindulgence in food robs one of vitality, sickens the stomach, poisons the blood, infects the body's fluids, stirs up bile, and creates the high temperature of a fever, so often does the sick person ruin his mind, lose his senses, he is carried away by his desires, he is afflicted by conflicting needs, he spits out what is medicinal, he seeks what is harmful, and he flees from treatment. Then the doctors diligently prepare to help him by a remedy of abstinence, so that abstinence may heal what gluttony had made flare up.

And if for a temporal cure the ill follow their doctors' orders by exercising a restraint that is difficult, why for eternal salva-

---

1. This sermon was delivered during Lent, to which the beginning of section 4 refers. See F. Sottocornola, *L'anno liturgico*, 74–75.

tion should it be hard to obey Christ with moderate fasting, to exercise self-control over the body, to regulate the mind by restraint, and to make the intellect clear with sobriety? Just as dark clouds obscure the sky, so immoderate feasts darken souls. Just as whirlwinds disturb the elements, so do heaps of food cause agitation. As a tidal wave submerges a boat, so does drunkenness submerge the body,[2] hand the human being over to the deep, remove whatever one has gained in life, and force him to suffer the shipwreck of death.

2. It is therefore a fever, it is a fever that the blessed Apostle laments is seething within human wounds, when he says: "I know that nothing good dwells in me, that is, in my flesh."[3] If nothing good, then certainly evil. What evil? Truly a certain frailty creeps within the flesh, seethes in the veins, enters the bones, is hidden in the marrow, boils within the blood, and thus bursts forth into a frenzy of vice. Frailty is the fever of nature, the mother of weaknesses, the source of the passions. Frailty is that which places us under the law of compulsion; and where there is compulsion there is no free will, there is a condition of captivity, and one's judgment is irresolute and impotent.

It is on account of frailty that the human being goes not where his will beckons, but where compulsion leads. Listen to the Apostle as he says: "I do not do what I will."[4] Frailty, while it deals with the things necessary for the human being, causes him to reach for what is unnecessary; while it provides food, it leads to gluttony; it encourages drunkenness while it serves a drink; it offers sleep in order to hand over laziness; it increases one's concerns for the belly, in order to remove any concern for health;[5] it gives everything to the flesh, in order to leave nothing for the soul; it makes the body the showplace of the passions; it causes the human being to be the death of himself and the life of the vices.

2. A boat or ship is usually a symbol of the Church for Chrysologus, but here, as in *Sermons* 7a.1 and 8.1, it symbolizes the human body.

3. Rom 7.18.

4. Rom 7.15.

5. *Salus* denotes both physical "health" and eternal "salvation."

Therefore, if a person feels that he is sick in this fashion, let him submit himself to the heavenly Physician, let him feel safe in acceding to his directives, let him be temperate when it comes to food, let him keep some for later, so that in this way he may be able to overcome the weakness of frailty, flee from frailty, and transform the fever of the passions and the frenzy of vice.

3. Abstinence is the first medicine the human being must take, but for a complete cure the expenditure of mercy is required. Abstinence puts out the fever; but the bodily members dried up by the fire of a long-lasting fever cannot return to full health unless they are bathed in a lavish amount of ointment, unless they are moistened with the most soothing of lotions, unless they are aided by taking other medicines. Thus, although fasting repels the diseases of vice, excises the passions of the flesh, drives out what causes offenses; nevertheless, without the ointment of mercy, without the flow of kindness, without the practice of almsgiving, it does not restore complete health[6] to the mind.

Fasting heals the wounds of sins, but without mercy it does not cleanse the scars made by the wounds. Listen to the Lord as he says: "Give alms, and then everything will be clean for you."[7] Engaging only in fasting tears out the vices, eradicates offenses, prepares the field of both mind and body for a good harvest, but unless mercy sows the seed of kindness, of the one fasting. . . .[8] Fasting is a holy oblation, a sacrifice that is pure, but without the fire of mercy it cannot ascend as a fragrant offering to God.

What the soul is to the body is analogous to what mercy is to fasting.[9] When fasting lives off mercy, then it gives life to the one who is fasting. Fasting, the ship of the virtues, carries what one has gained in life and transports the profit of salvation; but the one who enters the seas of the flesh, who cuts across the

6. *Salus.*
7. Lk 11.41.
8. There is a lacuna at this point. The apodosis would probably have gone something like this: "the abundant crop of the one fasting is never gathered."
9. This same analogy is used in *Sermon* 8.2.

waves of the vices, who passes between the rocks of offenses, and traverses the shores of the passions, unless he quickly enters the harbor of kindness, he cannot exercise the virtues, and he cannot have the profit that comes from the virtues.

May the one who knows that he stands unsteadily in this life, who understands that he slips as he passes through the way of the flesh, and who realizes that he is subject to attacks from ignorance and to accidents from negligence, may he keep his fast in such a way that he does not omit mercy. Fasting opens heaven for us, and fasting admits us to God; but unless mercy then attends us as the patroness of our cause, since we are unable to remain steadfast in innocence, we shall not be secure about forgiveness, as the Lord says: "Without mercy will judgment be rendered on the one who has shown no mercy."[10]

4. The day is pleasant, but a clear day will be even more pleasant. Therefore, our fasting is all the more brilliant if the splendor of mercy gives us clear Lenten days. God cries: "I desire mercy."[11] Man, give God what he wants if you want God to give you what you want. "I desire mercy" is the voice of God; God asks for mercy from us; and if we give it, what will he say? What was read today: "I was hungry, and you gave me to eat; I was thirsty, and you gave me to drink."[12] And what else? "Come, blessed of my Father, and receive the kingdom that has been prepared for you from the beginning of the world."[13]

Whoever gives bread to the hungry will give the kingdom to himself; he will deny himself the fountain of life if he denies the one who is thirsty a cup of water. Out of love for the poor, God sells his kingdom, and so that every human being can buy it, he puts its price at a piece of bread, because he, whose asking price is only as much as he knows people possess, wants all to possess it. God sells his kingdom for a piece of bread: who will find an excuse for not buying it, when such a low cost incriminates him?

Brothers, may our lunch be the meal of the poor, so that the table of Christ may be set for our lunch, as he promises when

10. Jas 2.13.   11. Hos 6.6; Mt 9.13, 12.7.
12. Mt 25.35.   13. Mt 25.34.

he says: "You will eat at my table and in my kingdom."[14] Brothers, may the poor find delight in our fasts, so that our fasting at this time may be transformed into eternal delight for us. Man, by giving to the poor give to yourself, because what you do not give to the poor, another will have; you will possess only what you give to the poor.

14. See Lk 22.30.

SERMON 42

A Second on Fasting[1]

 N THE LAST SERMON, brothers, we touched upon the benefits of fasting as far as we could; and that prayer should be connected to fasting, we have made clear in the conclusion of that sermon. But since fasting without mercy is deficient, fasting without kindness goes hungry,[2] prayer without compassion is enfeebled, prayer without generosity grows weary, let us invigorate our fasting with an exhortation to mercy, let us arouse our prayer by hearing about kindness, let us invoke mercy as the patroness for our fasting, since it is the hunger of avarice to fast without mercy; it is the punishment of greed to fast without kindness; it is an act of spite, not of devotion; it is not fasting for God but for one's purse; it is wearing one's self out by abstinence and being puffed up all swollen with greed, relieving the stomach of food and weighing down the mind with the burden of money.

The one who does not know how to give money away, but only to lock it up, buries himself in the purse. He is the custodian of someone else's goods, he is not the lord of his own goods, because he provides for another and denies himself, since a merciful person will eventually distribute what the avaricious has hoarded away.

---

1. This Lenten sermon was very likely delivered by Chrysologus immediately after *Sermon* 12 and followed next by *Sermon* 43 (see F. Sottocornola, *L'anno liturgico*, 67–68, 75, 212–13). Contrary to A. Olivar's opinion in *Los sermones*, 262, that *Sermon* 43 preceded 42, Sottocornola's chronology is more convincing, in my opinion. *Sermon* 12 is almost entirely concerned with fasting, and only at the end refers to joining prayer with fasting, but with no mention of the third Lenten practice, almsgiving. *Sermon* 42 begins by referring to the prior sermon, which concludes with a mention of prayer connected with fasting (*Sermon* 12). *Sermon* 43 (FOTC 17.90–94), by contrast, deals with all three Lenten practices, and so would logically follow, rather than precede, this *Sermon* 42.

2. *Ieiunium . . . ieiunat.*

2. A field tilled without seeds is the one who fasts without compassion. A tilled field has no briars, is cleared of weeds, and is free of everything that has to do with negligence or neglect; but without seeds it becomes sterile, despite all the tilling it bears no fruit, it bears pain, it is unable to yield a good crop. In a similar fashion fasting cultivates the soul, it purges the senses, it cleanses the heart, it prunes away the vices, it eradicates offenses, it tills the mind, it tones the body; but without mercy it does not yield the fruit of life, it does not attain to the reward of salvation.

What the king's palace is without the king, this is what fasting is without generosity. The king's palace gleams with gold, it shines with marble, it looks magnificent with all its paintings, it has a lavish amount of room, it rises to the heights, it has charming lawns, it is awesome in its privacy; but without the king it has no[3] honor, it lacks glory, it is an empty place of solitude, it is an enclosed desert, it is a dreadful place of solitude.

3. So too fasting shines with innocence, it radiates with purity, it gleams as it is practiced, it is beautiful in its conduct, it sparkles as it progresses, it is magnificently decked out in sanctity; but without mercy it has no glory, it goes without any recompense, it does not hold the palm of victory, it loses its confidence in making supplication,[4] it does not acquire any reward from its prayers, as Scripture attests when it says: "The one who shuts his ear from hearing the poor will himself also cry unto the Lord, and there will not be anyone to answer him."[5] How can one who has refused mercy ask for it?

"Without mercy," it says, "will the judgment be rendered to him who has not shown mercy."[6] The one who does not have mercy on another takes it away from himself. He will receive mercy who disperses it on the poor. "He distributed," it says,

---

3. The *non* is inadvertently omitted from Olivar's CCL text. See PL 52.318.

4. *Fiduciam supplicandi.* For a discussion on the use of the juridical term *fiducia* in the context of Christian prayer, see L. J. Engels, "Fiducia: Influence de l'emploi juridique sur l'usage commun et paléo-chrétien," in *Graecitas et Latinitas Christianorum Primaeva: Supplementa*, vol. 3 (Nijmegen: Dekker and Van de Vegt, 1970), especially 89–94.

5. Prv 21.13.

6. Jas 2.13.

"he gave to the poor; his righteousness remains forever."[7] The one who sows mercy on the person in need will reap mercy for himself.

"The one who sows in tears," it says, "will reap in joy."[8] Rain does not moisten the ground as much as the tears of the poor moisten fasting. Man, cast the seeds of your fasting onto the tears of the poor, since the virtues[9] of fasting are dried up, the harvests of fasting wither if they are not watered by the tears of the poor. Rain from heaven pours upon the earth, the tear of the poor wets heaven. Therefore, heaven is thirsty, and awaits from the wailing of the poor a replacement of its water, since mercy tills the fields of heaven, and kindness plows furrows through the celestial sphere; it is there that he casts the seeds of mercy that the hand of the poor has received; there he gathers his crop who saw to it here that his mercy was sown on the poor.

Blessed is this kind of sower for whom eternal silos are being prepared for everlasting life! It is this sower whom the blessed Apostle was describing when he said: "But I say that the one who sows sparingly will also reap sparingly; and the one who sows bountifully will also reap bountifully. Everyone [should give], just as he has determined in his heart: not out of sadness or compulsion; for God loves a cheerful giver."[10]

4. "Great are the works of the Lord":[11] the magnitude of his mercy goes beyond magnitude. For when the prophet had said: "Great are the works of God," he added in another place: "His mercy is over all his works."[12] Mercy, brothers, fills heaven and fills up the earth. "Lord," he says, "your mercy is in heaven."[13] And likewise he says: "The earth is full of the mercy of the Lord."[14] And truly, brothers, everything that God had made

---

7. Ps 111 (112).9.

8. Ps 125 (126).5.

9. Or, alternatively, "power" since *virtus* bears both meanings.

10. 2 Cor 9.6–7. The variant reading, *in benedictione de benedictione,* found in one of the manuscripts and in conformity with the Pauline text, has been chosen instead of the *in corruptione, de corruptione* preferred by Olivar in his CCL text.

11. Ps 110 (111).2.

12. Ps 144 (145).9.

13. Ps 35.6 LXX; Ps 36.5.

14. Ps 32 (33).5.

would have perished if mercy had not come to its aid. Guilt and vengeance were sweeping away whatever had come into this world, both because frailty was always inclined to fall, and because the Judge was always being compelled to issue a sentence of punishment.

Thus an angel is cast out of heaven,[15] thus the human being is exiled from paradise,[16] thus the world is destroyed by the flood,[17] thus peoples are confused in their languages,[18] and are consigned to the sword;[19] thus cities are consumed by divine fire,[20] thus the people led out of Egypt have to eat in the desert,[21] thus the earth opens to devour people;[22] and in conclusion, thus the Roman army, avenger of Christ's blood, destroyed Judea.[23]

5. That is why only the great and bountiful mercy of Christ, which has reserved all judgment to only one day, has deemed the whole of a human being's life as an extended time for penitence, so that what infancy takes up from the vices, what adolescence carries off, what youth seizes, old age at any rate may correct; and then, at least, he may repent of sin, since he feels that he is now not able to sin; so that then at any rate he may give up his wrongdoing, since now wrongdoing has left him alone; so that he may make a virtue out of a necessity,[24] and die in innocence after he had lived entirely guilty.

That is why the prophet runs totally to mercy, because he did not have any confidence in his own righteousness: "Have mercy on me, God," he says, "according to your great mercy."[25] And why is it great? "Because your mercy," he says, "is great towards me, and you have plucked my soul from the depths of the underworld."[26] And if God restores through mercy what had utter-

---

15. See Is 14.12.
16. See Gn 3.23–24.
17. See Gn 7.11–24.
18. See Gn 11.9.
19. See Gn 14.1–16.
20. See Gn 19.24–25.
21. See Ex 16.1–15.
22. See Nm 16.31–35.
23. See Tacitus, *Histories* 5.1, 11–13.
24. *Faciat de necessitate virtutem:* see Jerome, *Apology against the Books of Rufinus* 3.2 (FOTC 53.164) for the same expression.
25. Ps 50.3 LXX; Ps 51.1.
26. Ps 85 (86).13.

ly perished through judgment, what, oh man, were you imagining would stand, would stand firm for you without mercy?

6. It has therefore been demonstrated to you that not only fasting, but also all the other virtues as well totter without mercy. The ardent generosity that he had extended to God made Abraham the leader of the heavenly banquet.[27] For because he welcomed the two men together with God to his earthly table, he welcomes the people from the east and the west to the heavenly table. "They will come," it says, "from the east and the west and will recline with Abraham, Isaac, and Jacob in the kingdom of heaven."[28] Because Lot welcomed the angels with hospitality, he prevented judgment; in this fashion he conquered Gehenna in the flesh.[29]

The divine fire is unable to consume the merciful. Let the one who wants to have no fear about the flames of Gehenna show mercy. At last when Christ comes he will conduct an investigation about mercy before he will pronounce judgment on guilt. When he sits, as he says, on the throne of his glory he will say: "I was hungry, and you gave me to eat."[30] He did not say: "You killed, you stole"; but: "I was hungry, and you gave me to eat." One will not face charges of sin, when the evidence of his mercy is undeniable. Why? Because "give alms, and notice how all will be clean for you."[31]

He will not be judged for his faults, when praise from the Judge is on record concerning his beneficence. He does not exact punishment when he acknowledges an indebtedness to the defendant's generosity. "I was hungry," he says, "and you gave me to eat."[32] In heaven God eats the bread that the poor person has received on earth. "As often as you did it to one of these least ones, you did it to me."[33] So, give bread, give a drink, give clothing, give shelter, if you want to have God as your debtor and not as your Judge. Nothing will harm us on earth, if we have mercy as a patroness in heaven.

---

27. See Gn 18.1–10.
29. See Gn 19.1–22.
31. Lk 11.41.
33. Mt 25.40.

28. Mt 8.11.
30. Mt 25.35.
32. Mt 25.35.

SERMON 45

On the Sixth Psalm[1]

OUR DISPOSITION SHOWS AND ACKNOWLEDGES with me that the response that we have sung today with the prophet as he makes supplication is opportune for this time and appropriate for the present evils. *Lord,* he says, *do not rebuke me in your anger, nor reprove me in your rage* (Ps 6.2[1]). And is God swollen with anger, and seething with rage? Far from it, brothers! God is not subjected to passion, nor is he enkindled by anger, nor is he agitated by rage. But God's anger is the punishment of evildoers, and God's rage is the chastisement of sinners.

Brothers, formed out of dust, molded from clay, we are trampled by the vices, we are under the sway of sin, we are worn out by anxiety, we wither in our members, we disintegrate in death, we shudder at the stinking tombs; and we are found so incapable of virtue, and so capable of vice. So the prophet, mindful of human frailty, and aware of his carnal nature, and because he put no trust in his own merits, fled hastily to be helped by mercy, so that God's judgment in his regard might consist of kindness rather than severity.

2. *Lord, do not rebuke me in your anger.* That is to say: rebuke me, but not in anger; reprove me, but not in rage. Rebuke me as a Father, but not as a Judge; reprove me not as Lord, but as a Parent. Rebuke me, not to destroy me, but to reprove me. Reprove me, not to do me in, but to correct me. And why should

1. It is likely that this sermon was preached during Lent, according to F. Sottocornola, *L'anno liturgico,* 76, because it contains a call to conversion, because sermons on the psalms were preached during Lent, and because *Sermons* 44–46, all on different psalms, immediately follow *Sermons* 41–43, indisputably Lenten, in the Felician collection of Chrysologus's sermons.

you do this? *Because I am sick* (v.3[2]a). *Have mercy on me, Lord*, he says, *because I am sick.*

What is sicker than a person whose understanding fails him, whose ignorance deceives him, whose judgment escapes him, who is deluded by vanity, for whom time is fleeting, who changes with the years—foolish in childhood, reckless in youth, and decrepit in old age? Therefore, that the Lord seethes in anger against him, that he flares up in rage is not, not at all the characteristic of a benevolent Creator, but of a very severe Prosecutor. *Have mercy on me, Lord, since I am sick.*

3. And what do you want? *Heal me, O Lord* (v.3[2]b). This one feels the wounds of his condition, he feels the bite of the ancient serpent, he feels the sin of his first parent. He recognizes that he has fallen into these afflictions by being born, and he recognizes that he has arrived at death from his natural condition. And because human skill was unable to do away with death, he is forced to appeal for divine medicine. And so as the more easily to obtain the cure for his illness, he reveals the causes of that illness, he describes its symptoms, he makes known its magnitude, he expresses how violent is his pain. *Heal me, O Lord.* Why? *Because my bones are trembling* (v.3[2]b).

The bones sustain the whole structure of the body; and so if the bones are trembling, how firm are the members, how strong are the nerves, in what deplorable condition is the substance of the flesh?[2] The bones tremble, brothers, under the weight of sins, out of fear of death, out of the terror of facing judgment. Hear this same prophet say elsewhere: "There is no health in my flesh because of your anger."[3] And my bones are trembling. "There is no peace in my bones," he says, "because of my sins."[4] And later: "My soul is filled with delusions, and there is no health in my flesh."[5] Rightly so did he add:

4. *And my soul is deeply disturbed* (v.4[3]a). Between the precepts of God and the passions of the body, between virtues and

---

2. Somewhat similar language is used by Augustine in his *Enarrationes in Psalmos* 6.4 (CCL 38.29), where Augustine mentions that the "bones" mentioned in the Psalm refer to the firmness and strength of the soul.

3. Ps 37.4 LXX; Ps 38.3.   4. Ibid.

5. Ps 37.8 LXX; Ps 38.7.

vices, between adversity and prosperity, between punishments and rewards, between life and death, standing on the battle line, enduring warfare, receiving wounds, rarely holding its ground, faltering in judgment, the soul is disturbed, deeply disturbed, because, being weighed down by the burdens of the flesh, it becomes a slave of the vices before it reaches the virtues.

The Apostle describes this warfare when he says: "The flesh lusts against the spirit, and the spirit against the flesh, so that you do not do what you want."[6] And elsewhere: "I see another law in my members fighting against the law of my mind, and taking me captive under the law of sin."[7] Therefore, in recounting these afflictions, this warfare, and these disturbances of mind, the blessed prophet addresses God in the following words:

5. *And you, O Lord, how long?* (v.4[3]b) That is: How long will you allow this, how long will you fail to notice, how long will you refuse to help? How long will you permit your work to be defaced, your image to be blotted out, your creature to perish? Where is your Christ, so often announced by the Law, by us—by the prophets—promised again and again in various ways? May he come, may he come before the world perishes and he can find nothing salvageable in the world. May he come, may he come so as to repair the flesh, to renew the spirit, and to transform nature itself into a heavenly reality. May he come to take away sin, to blot out death, to destroy hell, to restore life, and to confer heaven, so that earthly corruption may no longer find in us anything it can destroy. The following words, moreover, make clear that this is what the prophet is seeking:

6. *And you, O Lord, how long? Be converted,*[8] *O Lord!* (vv.4–5[3–4]) This is the way the human being speaks to God, the guilty to the Judge, the condemned to the Prosecutor? *Be con-*

6. Gal 5.17.

7. Rom 7.23.

8. The more customary rendering, "Turn!" is not as demonstrative and even radical as Chrysologus intends. He is fond of such "conversion" language, even for God the Father (see *Sermon* 68.1). For a discussion of the use of such language used Christologically, see R. Benericetti, *Il Cristo,* 104–5 and especially n. 127.

verted, O Lord! The human being sins, and God is the one to be converted? Yes indeed, my brothers, because according to the prophet, "He himself bears our sins, and suffers for us."[9] And blessed John says, "Behold the Lamb of God, who takes away the sin of the world."[10] He accepted sin, in order to take away sin, not to possess it. *Be converted, O Lord!* From what? From God into man, from the Lord into a slave, from a Judge into a Father, so that the conversion may show that you are kind, you whose power makes you threatening and frightening.

7. *Be converted, O Lord, and free my soul* from the depths of hell; *save me on account of your mercy* (v.5[4]). Not on account of my merit,[11] since distress impairs me, groaning consumes me, tears overwhelm me, anger disturbs me, and the enemy assaults me. But to clarify this, let the very prayer of the prophet be chanted: *Save me on account of your mercy.* Why? *Because there is no one among the dead who remembers you. I have been worn out by my groaning; each night I shall drench my bed, I shall flood my couch with my tears* (vv.6–7[5–6]). This, holy David used to say while firmly established on the summit of kingship, since he was holding the highest position of human power in such a way that he guarded in himself the sanctity of spirit[12] and the grace of prophecy. And we who stand before the full anger of God do not know enough to say: *Lord, do not rebuke me in your rage* (v.2[1]). The earth refuses its fruit, the sky calm weather, the air healthiness; as a result, a plague has spread throughout every city; throughout the fields it destroys every kind of living creature by a variety of diseases; and nevertheless we do not say: *Lord, do not rebuke us in your anger, nor reprove us in your rage.*[13] David, after his triumphs, used to fill his nights with groaning and his days with tears; but we who lie under the sword of the

9. Is 53.4.
10. Jn 1.29.
11. The same language *(non propter meritum meum)* is found in Augustine, *Enarrationes in Psalmos* 6.5 (CCL 38.30, ed. E. Dekkers and I. Fraipont [1956]), where Augustine is commenting on the same verse of this Psalm.
12. *Sanctitatem spiritus* could alternatively designate the Holy Spirit.
13. A. Olivar, *Los sermones,* 235, mentions that there were several plagues and epidemics from 442–47, so this sermon can be situated somewhere in this period. See also Introduction, p. 13.

enemy[14] give no periods of time to God, not even for an hour do we pour forth our tears to God,[15] but continually we give and commit ourselves to robbery, fraud, perjury, deceit, and slander, with the result that we enkindle the anger of God against us more and more with the fuel of our crimes. Come, brothers, come with the prophet: "Come, let us adore him and fall prostrate before him and cry aloud before the Lord who made us."[16] Come, let us say: *Lord, do not rebuke us in your anger, nor reprove us in your rage;* so that mindful of his mercy he may change his anger into mercy, he may restore what has been lost, he may free those taken into captivity, and may permit us at last to serve him with gladness.[17]

14. This likely refers to the threatening incursions of tribes from the north.
15. A similar lament is voiced in *Sermons* 39.5 and 43.4 (FOTC 17.92).
16. Ps 94 (95).6.
17. See Ps 99 (100).2.

SERMON 46

On the Ninety-fourth Psalm[1]

UST AS, WHEN A PERSON with a burning thirst is very dry and has been parched for a long time, to happen upon a fountain of cold water is a very happy and most welcome occurrence, so too, since we are overwhelmed by sadness and weighed down by the burden of numerous tribulations, the refrain of the prophet's song today rouses us to joy: *Come*, it says, *let us rejoice in the Lord* (Ps 94[95].1a). Come where? Or from where? From yourself, man, into yourself, where not a change of location, but a conversion of your attitudes casts out adversity, puts sadness to flight, dispels despair, drives away distress, and within the residence of a sincere heart prepares an eternal dwelling of divine gladness.

Then, what has become of: "Blessed are those who mourn,"[2] and "Woe to you who laugh"?[3] Clearly, blessed are those who mourn in the world, and woe to those who laugh in the world, but blessed are those who rejoice in the Lord,[4] and who gain no happiness from robbery, from deceit, or from the tears of their neighbors. *Come, let us rejoice in the Lord.* The one who by word, action, or deed rejoices not in himself but in his Creator rejoices in the Lord. *Come, let us rejoice in the Lord.* The one for whom God is always his only and complete happiness rejoices in the Lord.

2. *Let us sing joyfully*, it says, *to God our Savior* (v.1b). These are

1. LXX numbering. In Hebrew, this is Ps 95. It is likely that this sermon was preached during Lent. See F. Sottocornola, *L'anno liturgico*, 76, and *Sermon 45*, n. 1.

2. Mt 5.4.

3. Lk 6.25.

4. Augustine speaks similarly in his *Enarrationes in Psalmos* 94.2 (CCL 39.1331).

not the words of the sheep, but of the shepherd; but with a
sweet, joyful melody and a variety of songs he leads his flock to
pasture, or under a shady grove he gathers the weary sheep to
rest, or he encourages them to climb high hills in their desire
for better grass, or to make their way downward into the valleys
gradually and very carefully. But blessed are those sheep who
listen to the voice of their shepherd,[5] who attract it, who foster
it, who assemble in its presence, and who really do sing joyfully
to their shepherd; who strive to increase for the Lord the number of offspring in the flock.

3. *Let us stay ahead of his face by confession* (v.2a).[6] And who
stays ahead of the One who knows his intentions, scrutinizes
hearts, is aware of his thoughts, has foreknowledge of the future, and is present always and everywhere? But we are to stay
ahead of the Lord not by the proximity of our senses, but by a
keen, innate attentiveness and by a confession duly circum-
spect and humble. In fact it did not say: "Let us stay ahead of
him," but: *Let us stay ahead of his face by confession.*

That is, when there is hope of mercy, when it is the time of
pardon, when there is the opportunity for repentance, let us
confess to him as Father, so that we do not experience him as
Judge;[7] let us disclose to his kindness what we have done so that
we are not forced to explain to his severity what we hide in silence; let us tell our sins in the time of indulgence, lest if we
keep silent we weep when we receive a sentence. And why
should I say more, brothers? This most compassionate prophet
exhorts us to stay ahead, not of the Judge, but of judgment.

4. *And in psalms*, it says, *let us sing joyfully to him* (v.2b). So that

5. See Jn 10.27.
6. *Praeveniamus* is translated "let us stay ahead of" in an attempt to capture in
one English expression the two senses that Chrysologus intends simultaneously:
the proximity of "coming before" another's face, and the advantage gained by
"outstripping" or "arriving ahead of" another. Chrysologus is playing upon the
idea of the penitent avoiding condemnation in the next life by making a prior
confession of one's sins in this life. *Confessio* is translated "confession" because,
in what follows, this is clearly the sense in which Chrysologus takes it, although
in the Psalm text it more properly bears the meaning "praise."
7. Literally, "let us confess to the Father, so that we do not experience the
Judge."

our jubilation may not be relegated to an irrational feeling, let us sing joyfully in psalms, so as to delineate the mysteries, and so that there may resound in the psalms what is divinely signified and what may move the minds of the listeners forward to advance to salvation. *Since God*, it says, *is a great Lord* (v.3a). Here is revealed the mystery of the Lord's Body, since God even in our body is the *great Lord and great King over all gods* (v.3b), and as it says elsewhere: "Who will be like God among the children of God?"[8] Since, while all the heavenly powers rule over all the rest, they themselves, nevertheless, are ruled by Christ.

5. *Since in his hand are the boundaries of the earth* (v.4a). Since those things that are in the hand of God are unable to be obtained without God: if we desire to broaden the boundaries, to extend the limits, and to recover what was lost, then let us implore God for the strength of faith.[9] By offending him these things were lost to us, but by appeasing him they return to us increased; he who gives as he wills, also takes things away when he wills. He who is unable to restore them is not considered omnipotent. He does many things as a proof of his majesty, as an example for our improvement and correction. Assistance from others is useless if help from our King is not forthcoming.

6. *His is the sea, and he made it* (v.5a). Do not think of it as obtained and invented, but not created by God: *His is the sea, and he has made it.* Where are those who imagine that God shaped the world out of matter, and especially out of water?[10] Our God brought forth all things in heaven and on earth[11] out of nothing, not as an inventor but as the Creator of matter.[12]

7. *Come*, it says, *let us adore* (v.6a). For those who are unfamiliar with it, brothers, the prophet shows that what follows was, as it were, the sadness of his jubilation: while he invites us to re-

8. Ps 88.7 LXX; Ps 89.6.

9. Chrysologus is alluding either to the incursion of the Vandals into Africa and Sicily from 439–42 or to the attack of the Huns in 447–48. See A. Olivar, *Los sermones*, 235–36.

10. An allusion, perhaps, to the ancient philosopher Thales; see Cicero, *De natura deorum* I.10.25.

11. See Ps 134 (135).6.

12. Chrysologus vigorously affirms *creatio ex nihilo.* See also *Sermons* 25.1, 48.3, and 49.4.

joice, the next moment he summons us to weep. *Come,* he says, *let us adore him and fall prostrate before him, and weep in the presence of God who made us* (v.6). He had said: *Come, let us rejoice;* but here the prophet wants us with him to shed his tears of joy, because just as tears are always produced by great grief, so also they are produced by joy; tears, in any event, expose and attest to the internal disposition of the heart.

So he wants us who used to bow down[13] before stones and wood, now that the true God is finally known, to adore, fall prostrate before him, and repay with tears and with continual, dutiful worship what we neglected for such a very long time. So he weeps, while he repents of the past, rejoices in the present, and is agitated and fearful about the future. I said that he was fearful, because I recognize while still in my body a disposition to have sung such things, just as he himself attests elsewhere, when in his gladness he sheds tears of joy: "The one who sows in tears will reap in joy."[14]

But that this was the weeping out of perfect gladness he thus demonstrates in the following: *Come, let us adore him, and fall prostrate before him, and weep in the presence of the Lord who made us.* And as if he were being asked why, he gives reasons, and he reveals his logic: *Because he himself is our God, and we are the people of his pasture, and the sheep of his hand* (v.7a–c). Certainly from this it is clear that as devoted as the person is who rejoices, truly just as ungrateful is the one who is sad. But let us listen now still more attentively to what he advises.

8. *Today if you hear his voice, do not harden your hearts to provoke me, like the day of testing in the desert, where your fathers tempted me: they put me to the proof although they saw my works. Forty years I was next to this generation, and I said: "They always go astray in their heart"; I swore to them in my anger: "See if they will enter into my rest"* (vv.7d–11). When he says *today,* he is addressing you, he is speaking to you, whatsoever person you are who hear him, so that once you have heard his voice you do not incur the guilt of contempt and the sin of insolence, refusing to be corrected by

---

13. Reading *prosternebamur* for *prosternebatur* in Olivar's CCL text.
14. Ps 125 (126).5.

either his commands or his example. For it was on account of this that he described the hardness of the Jews in a long discourse,[15] so that he might make you, O Christian, more cautious, with whom God lives and dwells not only for forty years, but during your entire lifetime he is at your side and fights for your salvation.

15. This is an allusion to another Psalm, perhaps 105 (106).

SERMON 48

When Jesus Came to His Homeland[1]

S THE EVANGELIST TODAY was about to relate the envy of the Jews towards Christ, he began as follows: *Jesus came*, he says, *to his homeland and his home, and was teaching them in their synagogues, such that they were amazed and said: "Where did he get this wisdom and these powers? Isn't he the son of a carpenter? Isn't his mother called Mary? Aren't his brothers and sisters all here among us? So where did he get all this?"* (Mt 13.54–56)

Clouds do not cover and darken the sky, night the day, and gloom the sun as much as envy covers and darkens the mind. The jealousy of the Jews[2] attests to this; they marveled at Christ's wisdom, they were amazed at his powers, they extolled his works, they received what he had to say; nevertheless, so that divinity would not be seen in him, so that his deity would not be recognized, they recall and publicize the names of his parents according to the flesh.

Jesus came, it says, *to his homeland and to his home.* Let no one marvel if the Creator of the universe, the Lord of the heavens, the God of all, obtains a homeland in a particular place, when he encloses himself in a womb, is measured for a cradle, clings to the breasts, envelops himself in a lap, allows himself to be embraced, and, in order to remove humanity's exigencies, he submitted and adapted himself to humanity's exigencies.[3] O man, God puts himself through these things for you, he follows you through these things, he seeks you through these exigen-

---

1. Mt 13.54–58.
2. See Olivar, *Los sermones*, 164–65, for several other instances of this expression as applied to the Jews in Chrysologus's sermons.
3. See *Sermon* 50.3.

cies, so that the one whom he formed by his handiwork he might reform by his example; so that the one whom he cast off by his judgment he might lead back by his affection; and that he might preserve in himself the one whom he sees was lost without him.

2. *Jesus came*, it says, *to his homeland, and was teaching in their synagogues.* Not in his Temple, but in their synagogues. The synagogues could not be his, since in them the crowd of faithlessness, not of faith, was congregating; in them there came together the people of envy, not of love; in them was seated "the company of evildoers,"[4] not the council of good instruction. *He was teaching in their synagogues, such that they were amazed.* They were amazed out of indignation, not favor; they were astonished with jealousy, not with praise; they were furious because what haughty judgment-seats were not able to grasp, humility taught perfectly while standing up.

Such that they were amazed and said: "Where did he get this wisdom?" Thus says the one who is ignorant of God, the Source of wisdom and the Source of power. Thus says the one who does not know that Christ is the Wisdom of God and the Power of God.[5] Solomon shows where wisdom comes from, when as a child he accepted the crown of kingship, and in order to rule the people entrusted to him with virtue, not arrogance, with wisdom, not pride, and with his heart, and not all high and mighty, he wanted, asked for, and received wisdom from God.[6]

Where did he get this wisdom and these powers? It is a power that gives eyesight to those deprived of it from birth; that restores hearing to those afflicted with being deaf; that in the mute unbinds what had been shackling their speech; that puts those who had been lame back on their course; that compels souls now bound in Hades to return to their own bodies; only one who is envious of salvation[7] could deny that this power is from God.

3. But the Jews admitted that the works of Christ were of di-

4. Ps 21.17 LXX; Ps 22.16.
5. See 1 Cor 1.24.
6. See 1 Kgs 3.4–15 and Wis 8.19–21.
7. Or, alternatively, "health" or "well-being."

vine power, that they were not humanly possible; but by the cloud of jealousy and the smoke of malice, the vision of the onlookers was darkened[8] such that they did not see the light of Christ nor that it was the time of the Gospel, and they said: *Isn't he the son of a carpenter?* They were saying: "He is the son of a carpenter," but the son of which carpenter they did not say. They were saying *son of a carpenter* so that by a meanspirited kind of craftiness the Creator's craft might be concealed, and so that the carpenter's name might keep the name of the deity hidden.

Christ was the Son of a Craftsman,[9] but of the One who formed the structure of the universe, not with a hammer, but with his command; who joined together diverse elements, not with clever inventiveness, but with an order; who forged together the mass of the world with his might, not with coal; who set the sun ablaze, not with an earthly fire, but with heat from heaven, who adjusted the moon, the darkness, and the periods of night; who made the stars distinct with varying degrees of light; who made all from nothing; and he made it, O man, for you, so that by pondering the work you would think of the One who made it.[10] But you, O Jew, you observe that he is the Son of this Craftsman, to whom for such great benefits you ought to pay compensation to the Son. The reason why you do not receive any future benefits is because you are ungrateful for the present ones.

4. *Isn't he the son of a carpenter? Isn't his mother called Mary?* Again, O Jew, you call out the name of his mother, but you conceal that of his Father. You say, "Father,"[11] but you don't say his name; you say, "Craftsman," but you don't say what his work is. These things elude you, but they do not elude those who will believe. *Isn't his mother called Mary, and aren't his brothers and sisters all here among us?* If his mother, his brothers, and his sisters

8. For similar language, see Ambrose, *De Abraham* 2.4.16 (CSEL 32.575).

9. Chrysologus uses the same word *faber* throughout to indicate "carpenter" and "Craftsman."

10. This typology between the earthly "carpenter" Joseph and the Divine Craftsman is developed in Hilary of Poitiers, *Commentary on the Gospel of Matthew* 14.2 (SC 258.10–12); and in Ambrose, *Expositio Evangelii secundum Lucam* 3.2 (CCL 14.76).

11. In this text from Matthew's Gospel the actual term "father" is not used.

are there among you, what about his Father? He is not with you, because God hates pretenders, he abandons the envious, he turns away from the ungrateful, and he does not permit the unbelievers and the irreverent to stay with him.

Aren't his brothers and sisters all here among us? With cunning you bring up his brothers, you mention sisters, so that by numerous offspring the virginity of his sacred mother be kept hidden, so that her purity remain obscured, and so that everything that is human about the Son be noted, but nothing that is divine.[12] O Jew, those whom you call the brothers and sisters of Christ, are the children of Cleopha, Mary's sister, and not of Mary; both divine law and human custom call the children of brothers and sisters[13] "brothers."[14] Therefore, it was not his mother's virginity that made them Christ's brothers, since she remained a virgin after his birth,[15] but the declaration of being related through his mother's sister. Blessed Mary, if she had had other children, in the very time of his crucifixion and at the very moment of his death would not have been entrusted by Christ as mother to a disciple and commended to a stranger's care.[16]

5. Envy cast an angel out of heaven,[17] drove man out of paradise,[18] was the first to contaminate the earth with a brother's

12. For other references in Chrysologus's sermons to the antithesis between the human and the divine, see A. Olivar, *Los sermones,* 331.

13. Cousins, in other words.

14. See *Sermon* 49.4 on the same theme.

15. For other references to Mary's perpetual virginity in Chrysologus's preaching, see A. Olivar, *Los sermones,* 325, and B. Kochaniewicz, *La Vergine Maria nei sermoni di San Pietro Crisologo* (Rome: Pontifical Theological Faculty "Marianum," 1998), 111–14. Although Chrysologus frames his remarks in an anti-Jewish context, he is also directing his argument against Helvidius, a Christian of the fourth century who denied Mary's perpetual virginity. See R. Benericetti's n. 3 in San Pietro Crisologo, *Sermoni e Lettera a Eutiche,* trans. G. Banterle (Rome: Città Nuova Editrice, 1996), 1:337.

16. See Jn 19.26–27. Chrysologus makes the same point in *Sermon* 49.4. This text from John's Gospel is also used as a proof text for Mary's virginity in Hilary of Poitiers, *Commentary on the Gospel of Matthew* 1.4 (SC 254.96–98); and Ambrose, *Expositio Evangelii secundum Lucam* 2.4 (CCL 14.32). In contrast to Chrysologus, however, Hilary believes that Jesus' "brothers and sisters" are Joseph's children by an earlier marriage.

17. See Is 14.12.

18. See Gn 3.24.

blood,[19] compelled brothers to sell their brother,[20] put Moses to flight,[21] aroused Aaron to insult his brother,[22] defiled Miriam with jealousy toward her brother;[23] and in short, what causes the mind to shudder, the sight to become blurred, and the hearing to fail to grasp: it aimed for and attained the very blood of Christ.

Envy is worse than all other evils: those whom it captures cannot be freed; those whom it wounds can never be cured nor return to health. Envy is the venom for offenses, the poison for iniquity, the mother of sins, the origin of the vices. The one who does not see it sees good things; the one who is unfamiliar with it is unfamiliar with evil; the one who flees from it lives. One can avoid envy by flight, but once engaged in conflict with it one cannot win. But now let us hear what response the Lord makes.

6. *A prophet is not without honor except in his homeland* (v.57). Indeed Christ came to his homeland, because it is written: "To his own he came, and his own did not receive him."[24] But by saying: *A prophet is not without honor except in his homeland,* he teaches that if a person shows potential among his own, they will bite him; if one stands out among his fellow citizens, he will get burnt; one neighbor's glory inflames the rest of the neighborhood; if relatives should be obliged to give some honor to another relative, they consider it enslavement. *And he did not do many miracles,* it says, *because of their lack of faith* (v.58). A miracle is not done in a place where the lack of faith does not deserve it. Even if Christ does not demand pay when he heals, he is, nevertheless, offended when insult is offered to him instead of honor.

19. See Gn 4.8.   20. See Gn 37.28.
21. See Ex 2.15.   22. See Nm 12.1–8.
23. See Nm 12.10. Miriam became "defiled" with leprosy.
24. Jn 1.11.

SERMON 49

A Second on When Jesus Came to His Homeland[1]

S OFTEN AS THE HOLY EVANGELIST mentions that the Lord endured or did human things, so often does a fleshly understanding[2] throw everything into confusion like a tidal wave. For weak minds are not able to hear, to discern, and to interpret the mysteries of the Lord's Body, as is evident in today's reading, which says, *And Jesus left there and went off to his homeland* (Mk 6.1). From where does he leave, to what place does he go, inasmuch as he is contained and confined in no place? To what homeland does he travel, who made and possesses the whole world? As the prophet says: "Yours are the heavens and yours is the earth; you have founded the world and its fullness."[3]

Truly it is not for himself and for his own sake,[4] but for your sake, for you that Christ leaves and enters, until he admit you after you were expelled, recall you from exile, and lead and carry you back after you were cast out. Therefore, Jesus went off to his homeland, not for him to return to his homeland, but for you to return to your homeland, which Adam had lost.

2. *He went off to his homeland.* If he has been born, how is he not a man? If a man, how is he not a citizen? If a citizen,[5] who should be amazed that he has a homeland? But he is speaking here on a human plane, not on the level of divinity; because he who is and was before the ages our God wanted to be our Parent throughout these last ages so that he might save with kind-

1. Mk 6.1–4.
2. That is, a literal interpretation of the Biblical text.
3. Ps 88.12 LXX; Ps 89.11.
4. There is a transposition error in Olivar's CCL text where *sibi non per se* should read *non sibi per se* (see PL 52.337).
5. For another reference to Christ's human citizenship, see *Sermon* 50.3.

ness those whom he had made with power; and by sharing their sufferings welcome those whom he had banished[6] by his accusation and decree. For whatever we read that Christ did or accomplished through the man assumed,[7] let us hear it not as insulting to divinity, but as conducive to the glory of the human being.

3. *And his disciples*, it says, *were following him* (v.1). It is appropriate that the disciples follow Christ on his return to his homeland, since they were already inscribed in the register of a higher order as citizens and inhabitants who claim heaven as their homeland, thanks to so great an election, the fullness of such great grace, as the Lord says: "Rejoice, because your names have been written in the book of life."[8] *And on the Sabbath*, it says, *he began to teach in the synagogue, and many of those who heard him were amazed at his teaching and said: "Where does he get all this, what wisdom has he been given, and how are such miracles accomplished through his hands?"* (v.2)

The unhappy and detestable wickedness of the Jewish mind, always more ready to argue than to believe, is anxiously aroused by the divine miracles, not to faith, but to slander, as if it even deserved to hear such great wisdom! But maliciously curious or complaining concerning where everything comes from, suspicious of good things, very easygoing about harmful ones, it despises the teaching about which it is amazed; it disregards the precepts that it approves, it is hesitant toward God but very well disposed towards idols, clever in divine matters, completely uninhibited when it comes to wood and stones, rebellious toward the prophets, opposed to the truth, ruinously attached to soothsaying and lies.

I ask: who is concerned because a blind person sees? Who is worried because a dead person rises? Who has hesitations because a mute person speaks? Really, who would not know that it is God, at whose mere command every infirmity is healed? Moses had performed many signs,[9] Elijah had given the great-

---

6. See *Sermon* 50.3.

7. For other references to *homo susceptus* in Chrysologus's preaching about Christ, see R. Benericetti, *Il Cristo*, 97–99.

8. Lk 10.20; see Phil 4.3.   9. Cf. Ex 7–8, for example.

est demonstrations of power,[10] and Elisha had accomplished deeds no less comparable:[11] why does no one probe into their person? Why does no one stir up a question about their status? Why was there no one with such curiosity and lack of gratitude to search out from where they came, or who they were, and from what means and through whom they did those things?

But he alone is judged who alone did not want to judge, lest he punish; with shameless severity he is probed, he who in order to bestow pardon asked no questions;[12] and when he who alone was innocent found everyone else guilty, at the tribunal of his immense kindness he preferred to undergo punishment than to inflict it, so that by having been put to death he might give back and restore to mortals the life that they had formerly lost. Truly, as the Apostle said, great is the mystery of his kindness, that he is manifested in our flesh.[13]

4. Nevertheless, this rival of the flesh[14] increased its curiosity further, for whom a blood-relationship is always something hostile, and cannot endure the belief that Christ is God by virtue of his miracles and wisdom, but by pointing to his neighbors, his parents, his brothers, and his other relatives, it claims, strives, and hopes for him to be known as merely a man, when it says: *Isn't he the son of a craftsman and of Mary, and the brother of James and Joseph, of Simon and Jude? Aren't his sisters here with us?* (v.3)

Caiaphas prophesies with an unholy mouth and, since he was a priest, he conquers his inclination to falsehood by his duty to truth; and he proves his pronouncement not on his own authority but by the authority of the one who was handed over.[15] Balaam blesses with a mouth bent on cursing, and although hired for wickedness he speaks all the mysteries of truth.[16] And just like a rose amid thorns,[17] that is, as on a prick-

---

10. See 1 Kgs 17–18.   11. See 2 Kgs 2.15–8.15.
12. See Is 53.4–9.   13. See 1 Tm 3.16.
14. The "rival of the flesh" refers to Jesus' opponents, who are of the same "flesh" as he. Additionally, however, as in the first sentence of this sermon, "flesh" has the pejorative connotation of those who are content to remain on the "fleshly" or "literal" level and are not interested in plumbing the deeper mysteries that Christ has come to reveal.
15. See Jn 11.49–52.   16. See Nm 23–24.
17. For other references to roses in patristic thought, see S. Poque, "Des

ly shrub little flowers with wondrous aroma are grown, so too sometimes the perceptions of the worst people are triggered against their will by the impulse of divinity for the good, such that what they say derives not from their merit but from the [particular] mystery.

This then is what we see has happened to the malice of the Jews, which, while it intended to insult the Lord's lineage, when by a sly reference to Joseph it enlarges Christ's family, confesses the truth and indicates a characteristic of his true Father when it says: "He is the son of a craftsman." It was wisely silent about the person, so as to reveal the Father by his skill, by saying the Son, not of Joseph, but of the Craftsman. And who is as great a Craftsman as the One who created such a great and impressive world out of nothing? And who is as great a Craftsman as the One who is the sole Creator, the sole Provider of every good skill? So call him, O Jew, the Son of the Craftsman, so that you may involuntarily acknowledge that he is Son of God;[18] call him Son of Mary, so that you are forced to confess that he is true man but also Son of power;[19] call them brothers, so that you may declare and reveal how very gracious your Creator is.

And although you yourself are attempting to hide in this way the virtues of his holy mother, nevertheless, the Evangelist attests and asserts as truth that those whom you call brothers were the children, not of Joseph and Mary, but of her sister Cleopha. For it is recognized even in contemporary parlance that the children of brothers and sisters[20] are called brothers. For the Lord would never have acted against the order of family devotion and entrusted his mother to an outsider, that is to John, from the cross, if she had had other children besides him;[21] but he gives a Virgin to a virgin, so that among such as

roses du printemps à la rose d'automne: La culture patristique d'Agrippa d'Aubigné," *Revue des études augustiniennes* 17 (1971): 155–69, especially 156–63.

18. See *Sermon* 48.3 for a similar treatment.

19. *Virtus* means both power and virtue; the latter meaning may also be intended as well, to indicate the "virtue" of Mary.

20. That is, cousins.

21. See Jn 19.25–27. Chrysologus presents the same kinds of arguments in *Sermon* 48.4. For other patristic references, see *Sermon* 48.4, nn. 15 and 16, and

these their only concern would be with the mystery, their only partnership would be a religious one; so that so great a disciple as he would not be taken up with worldly cares, but as he was going to preach about the Virgin's offspring,[22] he would have in his home the proof for those who might be in doubt. James for his part was unable to care for this one woman and mother, since all by himself he governed the Church of Jerusalem at its origin and while the Jews were then raging furiously.[23]

5. Fittingly then did the Lord add: *A prophet is not without honor except in his own homeland* (v.4). See how wise citizens according to the flesh are! See how earthly relatives think and give honor! Blessed is the one who has deserved to have God as his Father; he requires no other homeland except for the heavenly one!

G.-M. Bertrand, "Saint Joseph dans les écrits des Pères," *Cahiers de Joséphologie* 14 (1966): 10–83. For a collection of all the references in Chrysologus's sermons to St. Joseph, see G.-M. Bertrand and G. Ponton, "Textes patristiques sur Saint Joseph," *Cahiers de Joséphologie* 9, no. 2 (1961): 391–415.

22. R. Benericetti, in *Il Cristo*, 90, n. 49, finds a basis for Chrysologus's assertion that John's Gospel affirms Christ's birth from the Virgin in that his text of that Gospel had a singular subject and verb for Jn 1.13. That is, Jesus is the one who was "born not of the will of the flesh or of the will of man, but of God." That the singular forms in Jn 1.13 are the correct ones, see J. Galot, *Etre né de Dieu: Jean 1,13* (Rome: Institut Biblique Pontifical, 1969), especially 123–24.

23. See Acts 21.18; Gal 2.9; Eusebius Pamphili, *Ecclesiastical History* 2.1.2 and 2.23.1 (FOTC 19.84–85 and 124–25).

SERMON 50

On the Paralytic[1]

HAT CHRIST CARRIED OUT divine mysteries in human actions and that he performed invisible actions in visible things[2] today's reading has made clear. *He entered the boat,* it says, *and crossed the sea, and came to his own town* (Mt 9.1). Is he not the one who made bare the depths of the sea by pushing back its waves, so that the people of Israel could cross dry of foot between the waters that had become rigid[3] like mountain gorges?[4] Isn't he the one who made the eddies of the sea secure under Peter's feet, so that a liquid path would be submissive in offering solid footing to human steps?[5] And why is it that he denies himself the compliance of the sea such that he must cross such a small lake in a chartered boat?

He entered the boat, it says, *and crossed the sea.* And what is so remarkable, brothers? Christ came to take up our infirmities, and

---

1. Mt 9.1–7. Although this sermon's authenticity has been a subject of some dispute, A. Olivar in *Los sermones,* 150–69, argues extensively and convincingly that not only is it authentic but it actually contains a plethora of Chrysologus's most linguistically and theologically characteristic elements. Both F. Sotto-cornola (somewhat tentatively) in *L'anno liturgico,* 72, and A. Olivar in *Los sermones,* 167 and 261, believe that this sermon immediately preceded *Sermon* 30. See *Sermon* 30, n. 1, in this volume.

2. See Heb 11.3. The antithesis between invisible and visible is presented also in *Sermon* 140b.2; see also Ambrose, *Expositio Evangelii secundum Lucam* 4.46 (CCL 14.122); and Augustine, *Tractates on the Gospel of John* 24.1.3 (FOTC 79.232).

3. Literally, "the waves being stunned" *(stupentes undas);* the same expression with reference to the Exodus account is also found in Zeno of Verona, *Tractatus* 1.46B.2 and 2.26.1 (CCL 22.120 and 200).

4. See Ex 14.22.

5. See Mt 14.28–31. In commenting on Peter's walking on the sea, Maximinus the Arian, *De Lectionibus Sanctorum Evangeliorum* 1.2 (CCL 87.7), uses *obsequium* ("submissiveness"), the same term as Chrysologus, to describe the conduct of the waters.

to confer his own power upon us; to experience human things, to bestow divine ones; to accept insults, to return honors; to endure what is irksome, and to restore health, because a doctor who does not bear infirmities does not know how to cure; and the one who has not been a fellow patient[6] is unable to confer health.[7] So if Christ had remained in his own powers, he would have had nothing in common with human beings; and if he had not made the ways of the flesh his own,[8] his assumption of the flesh would have been for no purpose. Therefore, he endured these limitations so that he would be shown to be true man by these human limitations.[9]

2. *He entered the boat,* it says. Christ always enters the boat of his Church[10] to calm the waves of the world, so that he might lead those who believe in him tranquilly across to his heavenly homeland, and make citizens of his own city those whom he made sharers in his humanity. Therefore, Christ does not need the ship, but the ship needs Christ, because without a Pilot from heaven the ship of the Church is unable to pass through the sea of the world amid so many grave perils and reach heaven's harbor. We have said these things, my brothers, insofar as it pertains to a spiritual understanding; but now let us pursue the course of the narrative itself.[11]

3. *He entered the boat,* it says, *and crossed the sea, and came to his own town.* The Creator of the universe, the Lord of the world, after he confined himself in our flesh for our sake, began to have a human homeland, began to be a citizen of a Jewish town, and he himself the Parent of all parents began to have parents, in order that his love might invite, his charity attract, his affection bind,[12] and his kindness persuade those whom his

6. Literally, "infirm with the infirm."

7. See 2 Cor 11.29.

8. Literally, "fulfilled the order of the flesh."

9. For more on the Christological ideas contained in this section, see R. Benericetti, *Il Cristo,* 97–99, 128–30, and 255–56.

10. For other references in Chrysologus's sermons to a boat or ship as symbol for the Church, see *Sermon* 37, n. 8.

11. Chrysologus contrasts the *intelligentia spiritalis* with the *ordo historiae.* Unusual here is that he considers the allegorical meaning before the literal sense. See Introduction, pp. 26–27 and n. 137.

12. Similar language is found in *Sermon* 67.2 (FOTC 17.116).

sovereign might had put to flight, dread had scattered, and the force of his power had made exiles.

He came to his own town, and they brought him a paralytic lying on a bed. And when Jesus saw their faith, it says, he said to the paralytic: "Have confidence, son! Your sins are forgiven you" (vv. 1–2). The paralytic hears about forgiveness, and he is silent, and he makes no response to grace, because he was more interested in a cure for his body than for his soul, and he was lamenting the temporal afflictions enfeebling his body so much that he failed to lament the eternal punishments of his soul that was even more enfeebled, and so considered his present life dearer to him than the future one. Rightly then does Christ regard the faith of those who brought him and overlook the folly of the man lying there in such a state, that by virtue of the others' faith the soul of the paralytic would be cured before his body.

4. *Regarding their faith,* it says. Notice on this occasion, brothers, that God does not seek the will of the foolish, he does not wait for the faith of the ignorant, and he does not examine all the senseless desires of the infirm, but he comes to help thanks to someone else's faith, so that he may grant through grace alone, and not deny, whatever is of the divine will.

And really, my brothers, when does a doctor ever either seek or regard the will of his patients, inasmuch as one who is sick always desires and asks for the opposite treatment? This is why he administers and prescribes now iron, now fire, now bitter potions against their will, in order for them to be able to appreciate the cure when they are well, which they could not[13] appreciate when ill. And if a man pays no heed to insults[14] and disregards curses, in order to confer of his own accord life and health to those afflicted with diseases, how much more so does Christ the Physician[15] with divine goodness draw to salvation[16] those afflicted with diseases, that is, laboring under the mad-

13. *Non* was inadvertently omitted from Olivar's CCL text; see PL 52.341.

14. *Iniuria* could also refer to any physical harm that might come to the doctor if the patient fought off his attempts at treatment.

15. See R. Benericetti, *Il Cristo,* 235, n. 16, for the numerous references to Christ as *medicus* in Chrysologus's preaching.

16. *Salus* means both physical health and eternal salvation.

ness of sins and offenses, even when they are unwilling and do not want it?

O, if only we were willing, my brothers, if only we all were willing to give our full attention to the paralysis of our minds! We would then discern that our soul was deprived of virtue[17] and lying prostrate on a bed of vice; it would be clear to us how Christ each day both regards our damaged wills, and drags us and urges us on against our wills to remedies that can heal and save us.

5. *Son,* he says, *your sins are forgiven you.* In saying this he wanted to be understood as God although still hidden from human eyes through his humanity. For he was comparing himself by his miracles and signs with the prophets, who themselves had accomplished their miracles through him; however, granting pardon for sins, since it is not in the power of human beings but is proper to God alone, was introducing into human hearts the idea that he was God. The jealousy of the Pharisees attests to this; for when he had said: *Your sins are forgiven you,* the Pharisees responded: *He blasphemes: for who can forgive sins except God alone?* (v.3)

Pharisee, in your knowledge you are ignorant, in confessing you deny, when you give testimony you contradict it: if it is God who forgives sins, why do you not consider Christ to be God, who by his one work of forgiveness is shown to have taken away the sins of the whole world? "Behold," it says, "the Lamb of God who takes away the sins of the world."[18] But so that you can receive greater indications of his divinity, hear that he has penetrated the solitude of your heart; see that he has reached the sanctuary of your thoughts; realize that he lays bare the unspoken designs of your heart.

6. *And when Jesus had seen their thoughts,* it says, *he said to them: "Why do you think evil in your hearts? What is easier to say: your sins are forgiven you, or to say: stand up and walk? But so that you may know that the Son of Man has power to forgive sins"*—he then said to

17. Another meaning for *virtus* is "strength," which may also be intended here.

18. Jn 1.29.

the paralytic: "Stand up, pick up your bed, and go home." And he stood up and went home (vv.4–7). The Examiner of souls[19] anticipated the wicked designs of their minds and demonstrated his divine power with an action that would provide the testimony, by straightening out the members of a deteriorated body, tightening the muscles, joining the bones, perfecting the inner organs, strengthening the joints, and prompting the footsteps that had been buried for so long in a living corpse to set out on their course.

Pick up your bed, that is, "Carry what used to carry you, reverse the burden, so that what is a testimony to your infirmity may be a proof that you are healed; so that the bed of your pain[20] may be evidence that I cured you; so that the amount of its weight may attest to the amount of strength you have regained." *Go home,* so that you who have been healed by Christian faith may linger no more on the paths of Jewish faithlessness.

19. For other similar references to Christ in Chrysologus's preaching, see *Sermon* 163.7 and R. Benericetti, *Il Cristo,* 263, n. 165.

20. See Ps 40.4 LXX; Ps 41.3; Ambrose, *Expositio Evangelii secundum Lucam* 5.14 (CCL 14.139).

SERMON 51

On a Deaf and Dumb Spirit[1]

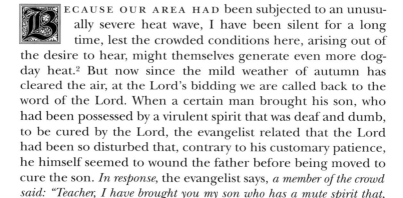ECAUSE OUR AREA HAD been subjected to an unusually severe heat wave, I have been silent for a long time, lest the crowded conditions here, arising out of the desire to hear, might themselves generate even more dogday heat.[2] But now since the mild weather of autumn has cleared the air, at the Lord's bidding we are called back to the word of the Lord. When a certain man brought his son, who had been possessed by a virulent spirit that was deaf and dumb, to be cured by the Lord, the evangelist related that the Lord had been so disturbed that, contrary to his customary patience, he himself seemed to wound the father before being moved to cure the son. *In response*, the evangelist says, *a member of the crowd said: "Teacher, I have brought you my son who has a mute spirit that, whenever it seizes him, throws him down; and I told your disciples to cast it out, and they could not." And the Lord replied: "What an unbelieving generation!"* (Mk 9.17–19)

2. *In response, a member of the crowd said.* Why is it that although only one asks the question, many are dealt a blow? Why is it that while only one has a complaint, all are accused of unbelief? Why is it that at the voice of just one the whole generation is called insolent in its lack of faith? Why is it? It is because he had come not to God, but to a teacher, demanding a cure not from power, but from skill; attributing the delay of the cure not to the real reason but to the one doing the curing; ascrib-

---

1. Mk 9.14–24. As the first two sentences of this sermon indicate, this was preached in early autumn. F. Sottocornola, *L'anno liturgico,* 289, suggests that it was during the second half of September.

2. For other instances when Chrysologus refrained from preaching, see V. Zangara, "I silenzi nella predicazione di Pietro Crisologo," *Rivista di Storia e Letteratura Religiosa* 32 (1996): 225–68.

ing what was impossible for the disciples to the lack of skill of their teacher, and with Jewish jealousy[3] he was reinforcing the envy of the scribes by complaining as follows: *And I told your disciples to cast it out, and they could not.*

That is to say, that there is a devil that would not yield to Christ; that there is a demon that is able to have little respect for the power of Christ's name. It was not by their own name but by Christ's that the disciples were casting demons out of the bodies of those possessed:[4] therefore, that a demon did not yield to the command of the disciples, this man was imputing to the weakness of the name of Christ, and not to the fault of the disciples. And so, as the Lord saw that the crowds of Jews present understood it in this way, he thus branded upon the children the faithlessness of their fathers, in their ancestors he knocked down the venomous offspring[5] as follows: *What an unbelieving generation!*

3. *When the Lord came to his disciples,* it says, *he saw around them a large crowd and scribes disputing with them, and as soon as they all saw him, they were amazed and awestruck* (vv.14–15), fearing certainly that they would lose at the Teacher's arrival the claims they had made against his disciples; and that as soon as so great a demon was expelled what had been an occasion of shame for the disciples would become a cause for glory. This is why the Lord responded to all while only one raised the query: *What an unbelieving generation! How long shall I be among you?* (v.19) Because of their lack of faith not even one demon was expelled from the body of the person taken captive.

How long shall I be among you, "and not undertake a mission to the gentiles, where at the voice of just one of my disciples temples fall, graven images flee, altars are consumed by fire, idols retreat, groves are chopped down, every demonic power groans, trembles, and wails as it is being driven out of its ancient and obsolete abodes; shrines are changed into churches, pagan altars are turned into Christian altars, victims consisting

3. See, e.g., *Sermon* 48.1; several other such references are noted in Olivar, *Los sermones,* 164–65.
4. See, e.g., Lk 10.17.
5. See Mt 23.30–33.

of dead beasts are exchanged for a living offering of the heart; auguries, divinations, and dreams are established solely according to God's command, only in accord with God's will?"

How long shall I be with you; how long am I to endure you? (v.19) He endures with patience, not with fear; not out of necessity, but out of mercy; he endures[6] this with hope, not with anxiety. He bears it and has hope since he wills for the unholy to return, and not to perish.

4. *Bring him to me* (v.19). As if he could not cure him if he were a distance away! But bring the reason for your lack of faith, the epitome of your incredulity, and the proof of your faithlessness. Bring him, so that you, who through the ages have been unwilling to believe when God was your teacher, may at least believe when a demon confesses and may realize that you are more wicked than the devil himself, when, in a moment, you see him confess and tremble in the presence of his Judge.

And they brought him forward, and the spirit threw him into convulsions, and he fell down and began to roll around on the ground (v.20). The man was rolling around, but it was the devil that was being tormented; the cure was causing the one who had been possessed to tremble, but the majesty of the Judge was exposing the intruder; the one who had been captured was standing trial, but it was the enemy that was being punished; the punishment of the devil was apparent in the torment of the human body. We need, brothers, we truly need God's light, so that our human eyes do not fail to discern God's work.

5. *He asked the boy's father: "How long ago did this happen to him?"* (v.21) The Author of time asks about the time of suffering, the Physician asks about the time of suffering; he does this not as one who does not know, but, as One who does know, he discloses it to those who do not know. And so, with such a question he reveals how long it has been, he makes known the extent of time, he goes back over his infancy, so that the cause of so great an evil not taint the offspring, but the parent, who con-

---

6. Reading *patitur* rather than *patior*, a typographical error in Olivar's CCL text. See PL 52.343.

signed the child entrusted to him by God to the service of the devil, and as payment to demons, as Scripture says: "And they offered their sons and their daughters to demons."[7]

What sort of crime, what sort of offense did infancy commit, so as to admit the devil into itself? But children are possessed by a demon when they are offered by their parents to the devil, when they are given over to the demons' keeping. In short, he who had been in bondage because of his father's infidelity is set free by his father's faith. The father says: *If you can do anything, have pity on us and help us* (v.22). That is, "Help us, have pity on us whose offense puts a burden on one who is innocent, and whose punishment is intensified by the peril to the child."

And rightly so does the Lord once again seek faith from the parent, when he says: *"If you can believe, all things are possible for the one who believes." And the father responds: "I do believe, but help my lack of faith"* (vv.23–24). The father believed, such that, just as we said, the one who had been condemned by his father's infidelity was now freed by his father's faith. For how could the father's faithlessness not have harmed the one who was helped by his father's faith? But how he was healed, or why the disciples, who had cast out many demons, were unable to put this one to flight, with the Lord's help we shall reveal in the next sermon.[8]

7. Ps 105 (106).37.
8. See *Sermon* 52, n. 1.

SERMON 52

A Second on a Deaf and Dumb Spirit[1]

HE OFFICE OF THE TEACHER is to explain what has been read, and to elucidate and point out with clear speech what mystical meanings lay hidden,[2] so that an inferior understanding may not wreak havoc on the listener out of the very place from which it should have and could have conferred saving knowledge. And so, today's reading is a case in point: *And in response a member of the crowd said: "Master, I have brought my son who has a deaf and mute spirit"* (Mk 9.17).

He did not say: "I have brought my deaf and mute son"; but: *I have brought my son who has a deaf and mute spirit*. Is it that spiritual wickedness is apportioned among the members of the human body, is confined within the human senses, in such a way that it endures our weaknesses and our sufferings? Is it that it is unable to see unless it has our eyes as windows,[3] to hear unless it uses the openings of the ears, to speak except by means of the tongue or the mouth? Is it for this reason that it cannot bear the wretched condition of one who is deaf and mute, inasmuch as its rarefied and airy nature has no knowledge of flesh,[4] does without bones, and, just like a breeze, as it blows it crosses

---

1. Mk 9.17–25. This sermon was delivered probably in late September, just after *Sermon* 51. See F. Sottocornola, *L'anno liturgico,* 77 and 289, and A. Olivar, *Los sermones,* 169.

2. See *Sermon* 112.1 (FOTC 17.180) for similar remarks.

3. See *Sermon* 139.2 regarding the eye as "the window of the soul." See also Jerome, *Letter* 64.1.4 (CSEL 54.587–88) and Augustine, *Sermon Guelferbytanus* 20.1 (=265C) in *Miscellanea Agostiniana,* ed. G. Morin (Rome: Tipografia Poliglotta Vaticana, 1930), 1:505.

4. For similar references to the rarefied nature of angels and demons, see also Tertullian, *Apology* 22.5 (FOTC 10.69); Lactantius, *Divine Institutes* 2.14 (FOTC 49.152–54); Augustine, *City of God* 15.23 (FOTC 14.471); and John Cassian, *Conlationes* 7.13 (SC 42.257–58).

the whole world in a moment of time, it assumes different appearances, changes into various forms, penetrates hearts, uses
souls as its plaything, and inspires thoughts that are unholy and
very filthy?

Nor can anyone figure out where it comes from or where it
is going, and so, like a javelin in flight, it pierces innocent
minds with a lethal blow with the greatest of ease. It would have
been insufficient, if only the father had spoken, when he made
his appeal: *I have brought my son who has a deaf and mute spirit*, if
the Lord himself had not cast out the unclean spirit with the
following words, with the following rebuke: *Deaf and mute spirit,
I order you: come out of him!* (v.25) But now let us pursue what
pertains to the solution to this question.

2. God, who is going to burn the demons to ashes in the
everlasting fire,[5] who already even now binds them with fetters,
distresses them with torments, and harasses them with punishments, is able, as soon as he gives the order, to maim them with
every weakness, and however they see, hear, and speak, to render them blind, and to make them deaf and mute, so that they
do not speak. But in this situation what is being shown is what
the devil did to the human being.

The ancient fugitive, when he discovered that the Lord had
come to earth, obstructed the ears of the man, bound his
tongue, and, having bolted the entryways to human percep-
tion, he made and prepared the human heart as his own cave
and hideout, thinking that the hearing of the word and the
power of the divine name would not come there. At the same
time, since he is sly and crafty,[6] he believed that he could mis-
lead the father and deceive the other relatives with such a
scheme, that they would despair that he who was unable either
to hear or to speak would ever be curable; and that they would
believe that what was actually of the devil's doing was merely a
matter of human infirmity; they would attribute to the child,
they would ascribe to nature what the enemy enclosed within
him had inflicted and injected.

5. See Mt 25.41.
6. See Gn 3.1.

3. In short, as Saint Matthew refers to the same event, also under yet another guise he had deceived the father of this poor boy, for there the father begs: "Lord, have pity on my son, because he is a lunatic[7] and is badly tormented."[8] The demon then wanted what had actually been of his own craft to seem to come from either human nature or a celestial body: making the torments of the man coincide with the course of the moon, he afflicted the body in proportion to the waxing of the moon, so that his family would believe that what was actually effected by the devil's wicked fury was caused by the moon.

But he deluded human beings, he deceived those who were unaware, before the sluggish he ruined the reputation of a creature that was made only to provide light and is unable to harm human beings whom, on the contrary, it has no choice but to help with continual servitude. But after the One who knows what is hidden came, that keenest of observers of what is secret, whom the hidden schemes of the devil were unable to hinder, the boy was brought forward to be healed by the divine command, so that whatever the devil had bound would be loosed. He did it, the enemy did it so that what was seen would seem to be a natural condition.

4. But why were the disciples unable to cast it out?[9] Because this man is brought forward as a type of the pagan people; because the pagans, according to the Apostle, had the spirit of the air: "The spirit of the air," he says, "which now is at work among the children of disobedience."[10] This one, therefore, was deaf and mute who was not able to hear the Law nor to confess God, but was being tossed about in the fire of Gehenna and through the waters of the ever bitter abyss,[11] and was unable to be healed by the disciples or by any other human being, since Christ was at that time called the Hearing of faith,[12] the Confession of salvation,[13] the Redemption and Life of the gentiles.

In short, when the devil was put to flight by Christ's com-

---

7. Or "epileptic": *lunaticus* derives from *luna*, "moon."
8. Mt 17.15.   9. See Mk 9.18.
10. Eph 2.2.   11. See Mk 9.22.
12. See Rom 10.17.   13. See Rom 10.10.

mand, what had been shut is opened, bonds are loosed, speech
is given back, hearing returns,[14] the man is restored, and only
the devil is in mourning that he has been forced out of the one
he had possessed for so long. This is why the one who comes
from paganism is first cleansed of the demon by the imposition
of hands in exorcism[15] and then receives the opening of his
ears,[16] so that he can acquire a hearing of the faith, so that he
can attain to salvation with the Lord accompanying him.

14. See Mk 7.35.
15. See *Sermon* 105.8 for another reference to the imposition of hands at
baptism.
16. A reference to the "Ephphetha" rite in the baptismal ceremony. The significance of Chrysologus's remarks here on the pre-baptismal ritual for studies
in the history of liturgy is indicated by A. Olivar, *Los sermones*, 169. See also Ambrose, *The Mysteries* 1.3, and idem, *The Sacraments* 1.1.2 (FOTC 44.6, 269).

SERMON 54

On Zacchaeus the Tax Collector[1]

UST RECENTLY WHEN THE BLESSED EVANGEL-
IST was describing the life and end of the inhuman
rich man, he moved our human emotions and sad-
dened us.[2] But today by mentioning the kindness and the faith
of the rich Zacchaeus he has exalted us and brought us to heavenly joy. *And after he had entered Jericho,* he says, Jesus *was walking
through the city* (Lk 19.1). Why was he walking through it, and
not merely walking? Because since Moses had walked, Christ
was walking through; and the people whom Moses led on a
journey, Jesus leads to the peace of the promised dwelling
place. *He was walking through Jericho.* Jericho is the very city that
Jesus son of Nave overthrew with the sevenfold din of trumpets.[3] But because Jesus came to save what had perished, he enters Jericho, so that what the Law had demolished with a terrifying cry, Jesus would raise up with the proclamation of holy
preaching.

2. After Jesus, he says, *had entered Jericho, he was walking
through the city. And behold there was a man named Zacchaeus, and
he was the chief tax collector, and he was rich* (vv.1–2). In Jericho
Zacchaeus was the chief tax collector: in a city that was ruined it
is written that Zacchaeus held the first place in a work of ruin.
From the place, the person, and the deed the enormity of guilt
is made manifest, so that from the magnitude of the sin the
magnitude of the Forgiver might shine brightly.

1. Lk 19.1–9.
2. Chrysologus preached on the rich man and Lazarus in *Sermons* 66 and
121–24, but it is unclear to which, if any, of these he is referring here. See A.
Olivar, *Los sermones,* 262–63.
3. See Jos 6.15–21. In Greek "Joshua" is spelled "Jesus" (Ἰησοῦς)—which
serves Chrysologus's exegetical purposes here well.

206

And behold there was a man named Zacchaeus, and he was the chief tax collector, and he was rich, and he wanted to see Jesus (vv.2–3). The one who wants to see Christ looks toward heaven, from where Christ comes, and not toward earth, from where gold comes. So the rich man who looks up does not carry his riches but tramples upon them; he is not burdened by his riches, but he is relieved; and he uses his riches in homage to the One who bestowed them, not as a slave to avarice for more riches. The slave of riches, not their lord, is the avaricious person; the merciful person shows that he has as many slaves as he has coins.

3. *He wanted to see Jesus, and he could not because of the crowd, since he was small in stature* (v.3). He was exceedingly large in spirit, although he seemed small in body; he who was not on a par with other men in his body was touching the heavens with his mind. Therefore, let no one be concerned about being short physically, which is impossible to augment,[4] but let him direct his energies to standing high in faith. *But he ran ahead to a tree. He wanted to see Jesus, and he could not because of the crowd, since he was small in stature. And he ran ahead and climbed a tree* (vv.3–4).

With what sort of steps do you suppose he reached the branches of a very high tree? He trampled on the earth, he went above the gold, he surmounted avarice, and he stepped over his whole pile of riches, so that by jumping up onto the tree of pardon he might hang[5] on the fruit of mercy, and from the watchtower of confession he might discern the Bestower of forgiveness. *He climbed a sycamore tree:* to signify a mystery, not a random event. *He climbed a sycamore tree:* in order that from the tree from which Adam had clothed his naked body,[6] from there Zacchaeus might cover the filth of avarice. *He climbed a sycamore tree, in order to see Jesus, since he was about to pass by there* (v.4). Correctly did he say *about to pass by*, because Christ had come through earthly journeys and human labors not to stay, but he had come to pass by.

4. *But when Jesus had come to the place, he looked up and saw him*

---

4. See Lk 12.25.   5. Or, alternatively, "depend."
6. See Gn 3.7.

(v.5): as though had he not turned his eyes, he would not see him, when he saw Nathaniel from afar under the same tree, although he was not present?[7] But *he saw him:* he saw for the sake of pardon, he looked up for the sake of grace, he noticed him for the sake of life, and he gazed upon him for his salvation. God desires to come to know the person he looks at, and not as a stranger, but as One who knows he wants to look at him for his glory.

He saw him and said: "Zacchaeus, hurry, come down, because today I need to stay at your home" (v.5). If it was right that he had climbed the tree, why is it said to him: *Come down?* It said above: *He ran ahead and climbed a tree* (v.4). The servant runs ahead of his Lord, and Zacchaeus climbs the tree before his Ruler would climb the cross. That is why it is said to him: *Hurry, come down* (v.5). Let *hurry, come down* suffice. Come down before the Lord from Adam's tree, so that after the cross of the Lord's passion you may climb up.[8]

"Unless one take up his cross and follow me."[9] It did not say: "go ahead of me." So come down, in order to put down the burdens of such fraud, the weight of greed, the pile of usury, the management of tax collecting, and the leadership of a very cruel position of authority; may you enter unencumbered into the school of poverty, the tutelage of mercy, the practice of kindness, the discipline of patience, the pursuit of the virtues, the knowledge of divinity, the endurance of sufferings, and the philosophy of death, and then, once perfected amidst the difficulties of the Tree of Life, climb up.

5. *Come down, because today I need to stay at your home.* When Peter had said to the Lord: "You will not wash my feet,"[10] the Lord responded: "Just allow me, for I need to do this."[11] And

7. See Jn 1.48.
8. The antithesis between the tree of the knowledge of good and evil and the tree of the cross is a frequent one in early Christian rhetoric. See, for example, Irenaeus, *Demonstratio praedicationis apostolicae* 34 (SC 406.130–31); Tertullian, *Adversus Iudaeos* 13.11 (CCL 2.1386–87); and Zeno of Verona, *Tractatus* 3.10.20 (CCL 22.28–29).
9. Mt 10.38.
10. Jn 13.8.
11. Mt 3.15: Chrysologus has confused his references. Jesus' response

now he says: *I need to stay at your home.* The one whose home Christ does not enter will not attain to the divine dwelling place; and the one at whose table Christ does not sit will not recline at the heavenly table. *And he came down and received him with joy* (v.6). He rejoices because he helps his helper,[12] because he gives nourishment to[13] his Shepherd, because the one who is guilty sways the Judge by means of his hospitality,[14] because by lending him food and drink he renders and acquires him as indebted to himself; and as a result this tax collector does not lose any profit, but he changes it.[15]

6. *And when they saw this*, it says, *they all began to murmur about why he had altered his course for a man who was a sinner* (v.7). And who is without sin?[16] And if there is no one, then he denies pardon to himself who finds fault with God for going to sinners. When God seeks the sinner, he seeks, not the sins, but the person, so as to despise the sin, which is the work of the human being, but so as not to lose his own work, which is the human being. Listen to the prophet as he says: "Turn your face away from my sins,"[17] that is, from my works. But concerning himself he says: "Do not despise the works of your hands."[18]

When the Judge wants to forgive, he regards the human being, not the offense. When the Father wants to show mercy to the son, he considers his affection, not the sin. So in the case of the human being God is mindful of his own work[19] so as to forget the human being's work. So you who criticize and murmur about why Christ altered his course for a sinner, come in and

---

comes, not to Simon Peter's complaint at the Last Supper, but to John the Baptist's protestation at Jesus' request for baptism.

12. It is impossible to capture the richness of the Latin *suscepit susceptorem suum* in a single English expression. Chrysologus is indicating both Zacchaeus's welcoming of Christ, who welcomed him, and, more theologically, his "taking into" his household Christ, who "took on" his human nature.

13. Literally, "he pastures his Shepherd."

14. Alternatively, *suffragio humanitatis* could be describing the Judge being influenced toward "a judgment of benevolence."

15. In *Sermon* 29.3 Chrysologus says something similar about Levi's change, rather than loss, of employment.

16. See 1 Jn 1.8–10.

17. Ps 50.11 LXX; Ps 51.9.

18. Ps 137 (138).8.

19. See Ps 8.5 (4).

grasp from this the way to salvation,[20] an example of pardon, and the hope for mercy; and be on your guard against your making a matter of blasphemy out of an opportunity for your salvation.

Where does a doctor go, if not to one who is sick? "Those who are well," Jesus says, "do not need a doctor, but those who are ill do."[21] Where does the shepherd go huffing and puffing if not after the lost sheep?[22] When does a king become involved with an enemy, except when he wants to free a captive? And one who drops a pearl of great price[23] does not disdain entering filthy places, and does not shrink from looking for it amid even dunghills.[24] Is there any peril into which a mother does not plunge after her child?

And they find fault with God, who created the human being to his own image and likeness,[25] because with his love as Creator he searches out the human being in the midst of his sins? Do you murmur, O man, about why God looks for the human being in the midst of his sins? What will you do when you see him penetrate the murky depths of hell for the sake of the human being? Nevertheless, listen to what Christ accomplished by going to a sinner's home.

7. *Zacchaeus*, it says, *stood there and said* (v.8). You see how the one who was lying prostrate is standing up straight. We lie prostrate in our vices, and we lie crushed; we stand when by our good works we are straightened up to go forward. *Zacchaeus*, it says, *stood there and said: "I give half of my goods to the poor"* (v.8). He believes that he will live after death who now sends half of his goods across to the future life. Granted that the perfect person is the one who always sends ahead all that he has from here to where he will be going. Nevertheless, that other person is his companion in the virtues, a partner in prudence, and a fellow believer, who gives away even half to God, because a human being loses what he leaves here.

And in truth, my brothers, just as a person expects to live

20. See Acts 16.17.
21. Mt 9.12.
22. See Lk 15.4–6.
23. See Mt 13.45–46.
24. See Tertullian, *Fragment* 4 (CCL 2.1335).
25. See Gn 1.26.

where he sends his goods across, so someone else does not expect that he will live there since he has provided nothing for himself there that he needs to have. For if we can bear temporal poverty only with difficulty, who will endure becoming a beggar for eternity? What soldier does not send back to his homeland whatever he procures by the sweat he expended in warfare, so that his being well-off in old age might compensate for the labors of his youth? And how does a Christian, whose term of military service is his life in this world,[26] not plan to make up for earthly trials with heavenly leisure? How a Christian is to do this, Zacchaeus himself both teaches by word and demonstrates by example.

8. *I give half of my goods to the poor, and if I have defrauded anyone of anything, I return it fourfold* (v.8). The one who gives away someone else's property, pillages more by the giving than by the stealing; from that act he does not quell the groaning of those aggrieved, but he prolongs it. I dare say the one who makes an offering to God out of what he obtained by fraud memorializes his crimes, he does not wash them away, because in such a gift what God looks at are the spoils taken from his people, not any acts of mercy towards the poor.[27]

In vain does a person cry out to God when another has justly cried out to God against him. These are God's words: "If you have taken a coat away from your brother, return it to him before sunset."[28] Just as a light reveals a thief, so the sun accuses those who commit fraud. If we want to offer our goods to God, if we want to possess in the presence of God those things that are ours, let us be counted worthy of hearing the kinds of things that Zacchaeus heard: *This one too*, Jesus says, *is a son of Abraham* (v.9).

9. *Today salvation will come to this house, because this one too is a son of Abraham* (v.9). The inhuman rich man, although he was a son of Abraham, became a son of Gehenna. But this man, al-

26. See 2 Cor 10.3–4 and 1 Tm 1.18.
27. See E. Bussi, "La donazione nel suo svolgimento storico," in *Cristianesimo e Diritto Romano*, ed. M. Roberti (Milan: Vita e Pensiero, 1935), 224, n. 4, for references to Augustine's sermons on a similar theme.
28. Ex 22.26.

though he was a son of robbery, by distributing his own goods and returning the goods of others is adopted as a son of Abraham. However, let no one think that by offering only half of his goods Zacchaeus did not reach the summit of perfection, because later he gave everything and even himself to the Lord when he was elevated to the office of bishop.[29] From the table where tax collectors make their profit he attained to the table of the Lord's Body, and having abandoned the fraudulent riches of the world, he found the true riches of the world in the poverty of Christ.

29. See Pseudo-Clement, *Homily* 3.63–72 (GCS 42.79–83), and idem, *Recognitions* 3.65–68 (GCS 51.139–42, 2d ed. [1994]), which relate that Zacchaeus was ordained bishop of Caesarea by the apostle Peter. See also *Constitutiones Apostolorum* 7.46, in *Didascalia et Constitutiones Apostolorum*, ed. F. X. Funk (Paderborn: F. Schoeningh, 1905), 1:452–53, where Zacchaeus is cited as the first bishop of Caesarea in Palestine. There is also a reference to a Zacchaeus as bishop of Caesarea some time in the second century who opposed the ideas of Valentinus and his followers, in an anonymous fifth-century work entitled *Praedestinatus* or *Praedestinatorum Haeresis* 1.11 and 13 (PL 53.590–91).

SERMON 55

On the Gospel in the Creed,[1] Where It Says: If One Asks His Father for Bread, Will He Give Him a Stone?[2]

FTER THE PRECEPTS OF THE LAW, filling up several al volumes and collected in books, were not sufficient to make us appreciate God's love, God's affection takes root and works its way into people's hard hearts through the use of comparisons and examples. *If one among you,* it says, *asks his father for bread, will he give him a stone? Or a fish, will he give him a serpent? Or if he asks for an egg, will he offer him a scorpion? Therefore, if you, although you are evil, know how to give good gifts to your children, how much more so will your heavenly Father give good things to those who ask him?* (Lk 11.11–13)

2. *If one among you asks for bread, will he give him a stone?* Charity is unable to play tricks, devotion is without deceit, affection rejects falsehood. If he is a father, he is unable not to love; if he loves, he is unable to give anything except what is good. He denies his father if he is suspicious about his father's generosity; he does not know that he is a son, if gifts from his father make him anxious. He is without any trace of devotion if he does not believe that whatever his father gives is beneficial. Or how will a father be able to give his children bad things instead of good ones,[3] when he has always been ready to endure bad things on his children's behalf, refusing to flee from death and never sidestepping dangers for the sake of his children?

For this reason God made you a father, for this reason he wanted a human being to be begotten from you. Now in view of

---

1. Olivar suggests that the reference to the confession of God as Father at the beginning of section 3 of this sermon could justify the reference to the Creed in this sermon's title (see CCL 24.308, n. 37).

2. Lk 11.11–13.

3. See Ps 34 (35).12.

the fact that he made you from the earth,[4] he certainly could
have made as many human beings as he wanted in that fashion;
but he ordained it that by begetting children you might know
how great is the affection of the begetter, and in yourself you
might show that the love of the Creator for you is as great as the
love that you, the creator of your child, try to lavish on your
child. To be sure, not only has God willed that you feel within
yourself what the affection of the begetter is, but also God
willed that you see this in the beasts, in animals and in birds.

When by his command he produced them solely from the
earth,[5] afterwards he compelled them to experience the labor
of begetting, to change their habitat, to procure places fit for
lairs, to keep their young safe within inaccessible locales, to
give birth with groans, to nourish them with the greatest of
labors, and not to refuse surrendering themselves to death if
they saw their offspring being captured. Therefore, if not by
comparison with a human being, at least with beasts, by the
similarity with animals, by the examples birds provide, learn
how great and genuine is a father's charity.

3. So if you believe and have acknowledged that God is Father, believe that whatever he gives, whatever he commands,
whatever he causes is enough to bring you salvation, and
enough to bring you life. It is not permitted to debate about a
mother's gifts; it is wrong to harbor doubts about a father's admonitions. Although a father's command may appear to be
rather harsh, nevertheless, it is the very thing that brings salvation[6] and life.

Thus Abraham, when he trusted God as Father, did not
dwell on the harsh and bitter aspects of his commands: he
looks upon circumcision as something shameful, but because
the heavenly Father orders it, he decides that it is a glorious
thing;[7] he considers the murdering of a relative to be something very wicked, but because God commands it, he under-
takes it with all devotion. So, although Isaac saw his father's

4. See Gn 2.7.
5. See Gn 1.24.
6. Or, more generally, "well-being."
7. See Gn 17.9–14.

sword above him, when he could have shuddered, when he could have lamented that he was the victim, he rejoiced.[8]

So Jephthah's daughter was full of joy as she fulfilled her father's obligation, fulfilled his vows by her own death.[9] Or why does one who already knows God argue about the Father's gifts, when a little, innocent child makes a request of his father and receives only good and profitable things? But let us examine why the Lord composed these parables.

4. *If one among you*, it says, *asks his father for bread, will he give him a stone?* He could have said: "Will he give weeds, will he give tares?" which from their closeness and similarity pose as bread, but cause distresses. But because Christ had come to his children, that is to the Jews, whom he complained about having begotten when he lamented: "I have begotten and raised up children, but they have spurned me,"[10] therefore he came to his children, he the Bread from heaven came, as he said: "I am the Bread that came down from heaven."[11]

However, for the Jews he turned into a stumbling stone and a rock of scandal, as the Lord says: "See, I place in Zion a stumbling stone and a rock of scandal."[12] Why a rock? Because they were striving to devour a rock, not to ask their Father for bread—"Many dogs," it says, "have surrounded me."[13] In short, after it is demonstrated that they have turned from human beings into dogs, the Bread of heaven has turned into a rock for them, through no fault of the Giver, but through the wickedness of the recipient, a rock, not to give them sustenance, but to kill them; and having been placed in the foundation, not to have those who were intent upon killing their Father to advance to the heights, but to plunge them into the abyss and roll them away to destruction.

5. He added another image: *Or will he give him a serpent instead of a fish?* Christ was also a fish lifted up out of the Jordan riverbed,[14] who, after he had been placed on the charcoals of his passion, he then after the resurrection provided living food

---

8. See Gn 22.
10. Is 1.2.
11. Jn 6.41 and 51.
13. Ps 21.17 LXX; Ps 22.16.

9. See Jgs 11.29–40.

12. Rom 9.33.
14. See Mt 3.13–17 and parallels.

for his own, that is, for his disciples.[15] But for the Jews this fish is changed into a serpent, as the Lord says: "Just as Moses lifted up the serpent in the desert, so must the Son of Man be lifted up."[16] The Jew perceived Christ in the serpent,[17] because the unholy eye cannot perceive God nor steadfast kindness.

6. He also gave a third example: *If he asks for an egg, will he offer him a scorpion?* It is a customary and usual practice that children always ask for an egg, and that parents never refuse an egg to the little ones who ask. But because Christ had come to gather his own, as a hen gathers her young,[18] he furnished his word as an egg, for the nourishment of the holy offspring of the Church. But because the Jew through envy was more desirous of breaking it than consuming it, he found a scorpion in its place, such that, according to the Apostle,[19] the command that was meant to bring them life, was now a source of death for them.

7. In commending steadfast devotion, the Lord has offered and shown us three examples, so that by three pieces of evidence, like three witnesses,[20] he might stir up the holy ones to trust in his love, and refute the unholy by showing that it was on account of their own vice, and not any vice on the Father's part, that they had not received the grace of charity.

---

15. See Jn 21.4–14; *esca vitalis*, as applied to the bait the first disciples supplied in fishing for human beings, is also found in *Sermon* 28.1. For references to Christ as fish, see, for example, Tertullian, *De Baptismo* 1.3 (CCL 1..277), and Augustine, *Tractates on the Gospel of John* 123.2 (FOTC 92.75, trans. J. W. Rettig [1995]): "The roasted fish is the suffering Christ." See also A. Olivar and A. Argemi, "La Eucaristía en la predicación de San Pedro Crisólogo," *La Ciencia Tomista* 86 (1959): 613, where references to Chrysologus's *Sermons* 67 and 71 are cited regarding Christ as the bread that is "baked" through his passion. See also C. R. Morey, "The Origin of the Fish-Symbol," *Princeton Theological Review* 8 (1910): 421–23. A recent and exhaustive treatment on fish symbolism in early Christianity and earlier sources is Laurence H. Kant's "The Interpretation of Religious Symbols in the Graeco-Roman World: A Case Study of Early Christian Fish Symbolism," Ph.D. dissertation, Yale University, 1993, especially p. 719.

16. Jn 3.14.   17. See Nm 21.6.
18. See Mt 23.37.   19. See Rom 7.10.
20. See, e.g., Dt 19.15; Mt 18.16; 2 Cor 13.1; and 1 Jn 5.7–8.

SERMON 56

On the Creed[1]

HE SUDDEN AND SURPRISING disruption occasioned by a premature delivery would be worrying me, the birth of children ahead of schedule would be causing me great distress, if those about to be born, by their persistence in bursting asunder any obstacles of time and by breaking through the confines of the womb with brute force, were not in such a hurry in their quest to grab hold of all the advantages of being alive. And so it is that a human being, perceiving the limit of the tenth month, often in the seventh month breaks out of the narrow confines of his first home and the constricted space of the womb and leaves it all behind, in order that this newborn warrior might rejoice that he has conquered time even before falling under the sway of time himself. And if this is possible for human nature, what will be able to prevent it from happening for the heavenly and divine nature? Or why can't the Holy Spirit do this, if the flesh can? Or how does grace from above not achieve what human frailty obtains and accomplishes?

2. Wasn't this the case with Paul as he afflicted the way and the womb of our Mother with sharp pain, so that with his heavenly whirlwind and violent tempest he might stay one step ahead of the Church as she labored to give birth, such that all of a sudden on the way he was born who would offer to the gentiles the way to faith?[2] Wasn't it right that he called himself one

---

1. On the term *symbolum* for the Creed, see J. N. D. Kelly, *Early Christian Creeds*, 3d ed. (Singapore: Longman, 1986), 52–61. *Sermons* 56–62a were all preached on the Creed and toward the end of Lent (see F. Sottocornola, *L'anno liturgico*, 77 and 158). *Sermons* 57 and 61 are already translated in FOTC 17.103–14.
2. See Acts 9.3.

217

who was prematurely born, and marveled that he had been born at all, since he knew that he had not spent any time in the womb?[3] Indeed he was still an enemy when he was striking the womb of our holy Mother from the outside, and was crushing her venerable children at the very moment of their birth. Suddenly he who had been the most ferocious persecutor of these very offspring is changed into a holy offspring himself.[4]

A eunuch was also brought to life on the road.[5] After human recklessness had castrated him so as to serve human beings, and a forced chastity had placed him in the court of the king, voluntary and vowed chastity would promote and transfer him to the glory of the heavenly court and to the service of the eternal King. Blessed is he to whom it was granted not to lose the privileges of the palace, but to change them.

3. My reason for saying this, my dear children, is so that after having received you now in sadness, at one and the same moment we may lead you forth in great gladness to your Mother's womb. Listen to the faith, learn the prayer.[6] But because of time constraints since we are unable to open up the mystery to you,[7] and you are unable to give a solemn recitation from memory to us of what is being handed over to you,[8] see to it now that you simply learn the words of the Creed, and that in the Easter season, when these things are explained more fully, you can understand the deeper meanings of this same mystery.[9]

Take the thing that you want, take possession of what you desire, since "the kingdom of heaven is enduring violence, and those who do violence, snatch it away."[10] Take the thing that

---

3. See 1 Cor 15.8.   4. See Acts 9.1–5.
5. See Acts 8.26–39.
6. Chrysologus is addressing those soon to be baptized. They are to listen to the "faith" enshrined in the Creed, and learn the "prayer," namely, the Lord's Prayer.
7. The period of catechesis for the *competentes* or elect was abbreviated because they were enrolled for the Easter sacraments very late. This is a recurring theme in Chrysologus's sermons on the Creed. See *Sermon* 10, n. 1.
8. Chrysologus is referring here to the customary *traditio* and *redditio symboli*. See J. N. D. Kelly, *Early Christian Creeds*, 32–37.
9. Unfortunately, Chrysologus's Easter mystagogical catecheses have not come down to us.
10. Mt 11.12.

you want; and may grace bestow what violence can take away. The entrance to life, the gateway of salvation, the beginning of faith is clearly shown to consist in a unique, innocent, and pure profession, as the prophet says: "Enter his gates with profession."[11] And so the same prophet, having been given such a reminder, soon afterwards asks for a means of access to God to have him speak to him, as he says: "Open to me the gates of righteousness, so that I might enter through them and profess to the Lord."[12] You see that one cannot profess if he has not entered this house of salvation and faith. And just as profession admits one to this house, so too there is no doubt that denial excludes one from it.

4. But let us hear what must be professed. "Believing with the heart," the Apostle says, "leads to justification, professing with your mouth leads to salvation."[13] And he shows what must be believed: he says that if you believe in your heart that Jesus is Lord, and you profess this with your mouth, you will be saved.[14] "Believing with the heart leads to justification, professing with your mouth leads to salvation." As a result, my dear children, we see that this summary of our faith is a great thing, since between the heart and the tongue the whole mystery of human salvation is up for consideration and is being accomplished.

You have, O man, the manner in which you ought to believe: "Believing with the heart leads to justification"; you have the manner in which you ought to make your profession: "Professing with your mouth leads to salvation." And what shall I say? The human being who has himself has everything within himself; however, he has himself if he has God: and he truly has God if he believes and professes that God is his Creator.

5. Make the sign of the cross![15] Faith, which is received by

11. Ps 99 (100).4.

12. Ps 117 (118).19.

13. Rom 10.10. That this verse was a favorite for those preaching on the Creed, see, for example, Niceta of Remesiana, *An Explanation of the Creed* 2 (FOTC 7.43); Augustine, *Faith and the Creed* 1 (FOTC 27.315); and Augustine, *Sermon* 214.1 (FOTC 38.130).

14. See Rom 10.9.

15. Regarding the sign of the cross as a customary part of Christian prayer, see, e.g., Tertullian, *The Chaplet* 3.4 (FOTC 40.237), and Prudentius, *Hymns for*

hearing,[16] is believed with the heart, and is uttered by the mouth for salvation, must be placed in the sanctuary of our mind, and must be committed to and kept alive in our very heart, lest it be written imprudently with paper and ink,[17] and not be reserved for the faithful for life, but be revealed to unbelievers for their destruction. You must keep secure within yourself, O man, what will likely go to ruin, with you to blame, if it is placed outside yourself.[18]

Every Day 6.129–32 (FOTC 43.44). For its place in one's entry into the catechumenate, see, e.g., Augustine, *Sermon* 215.5 (FOTC 38.147). For the same command *(signate vos)* at the time of the *traditio symboli*, see Ambrose, *Explanatio Symboli* 3 and 8, in SC 25bis, 48 and 56.

16. See Rom 10.17.

17. See 2 Cor 3.3, 2 Jn 12, 3 Jn 13.

18. This is a good example of the *disciplina arcani*, where the truths of the Christian faith were to be reserved for the initiated or soon-to-be initiated only. Although the "discipline of the secret" was more often associated with silence about the Church's liturgical and sacramental actions, that it was also observed regarding the Creed is attested in several other fourth- and fifth-century sources. See J. N. D. Kelly, *Early Christian Creeds*, 168–72.

SERMON 58

A Third on the Creed[1]

HE ONE WHO LOOKS for faith does not look for reason; the one who asks for divine things puts human ones aside. The one who is born of God as Father transcends nature; and the one who is deemed worthy of the Author of time owes nothing to time. Now look, devoted offspring of faith, we see that you want to be born before you are conceived; to carry off the kingdom of heaven before submitting to the narrow confines of the womb; to be so intent upon the joys of your Father that you bypass the anguish of your Mother; and you do not consider it a premature birth, which you believe is mature through Christ.[2] Thus Paul the apostle is born mature through faith, who proclaims that he is prematurely born through time.[3]

So, accept the faith by faith alone, and do not look for an explanation of that very faith to be revealed to you. So that you for your part do not have to provide an explanation, you have in your haste kept it securely enclosed within the faith. Today the faithfulness of your Creator invites you, my children, to faith; he fulfills the pledge he had promised before receiving your pledge of faithfulness; and this he has rendered to human affairs, as he had once promised verbally through the prophet: "Open your mouth wide," he says, "and I shall fill it."[4] That is: "Open wide in professing, and I shall fill it with the mystery of what you profess, I shall enrich it with mystical words, and fill it with all the eloquence of the secrets of heaven." And truly, children, whatever the one who listens and responds professes out

---

1. Regarding the term *symbolum* for the "Creed," see *Sermon* 56, n. 1.
2. See *Sermon* 56, n. 7.   3. See 1 Cor 15.8.
4. Ps 80.11 LXX; Ps 81.10.

of obedience, this is thanks to the grace of God, who gives and teaches.

2. Therefore, as you are about to receive the Creed, that is, the pact[5] of life, the pledge[6] of salvation, and the indissoluble bond of faith between you and God, prepare your hearts, not a piece of paper; sharpen your understanding, not your pen; and write out what you have heard, not with ink, but with your spirit at your service.[7]

Recognize that the eternal and heavenly secret cannot be entrusted to perishable, corruptible tools, but it must be placed in the safe of the soul itself, in the very library[8] of the spirit within you, so that no profane investigator, nor the power of the enemy may find anything to dissect and tear apart.[9] Otherwise what has been bestowed for the salvation of the person who professes and believes may become the ruin of the one who despises it and is ignorant of it. But when the prophet says to you: "Open your mouth wide, and I shall fill it,"[10] may you be able to respond: "In my heart I have hidden your eloquence, so that I may not sin against you."[11]

3. *I believe in God the Father Almighty.*[12] The one who has professed the Father also professes the Son, because without the Son, he cannot be called Father. And because there can be no increase or addition to God, the Son always was, because the Father also always was. The Son cannot have a beginning, be-

5. On the Creed as a pact, see also Augustine, *Sermon* 212.1 (FOTC 38.117), and Niceta of Remesiana, *An Explanation of the Creed* 13 (FOTC 7.53).

6. On the Creed as a pledge, see also Augustine, *Sermon* 214.12 (FOTC 38.142).

7. See *Sermon* 56.5, nn. 17 and 18.

8. The use of the term *bibliotheca* ("library") to refer to the human "memory" among early Christian authors is discussed in A. Mundó, "*Bibliotheca:* Bible et lecture du carême d'après saint Benoît," *Revue Bénédictine* 60 (1950): 77, n. 2.

9. On the topic of being foolishly inquisitive and with some of the same terminology, see Ps.-Augustine, *Sermon* 122.3 (PL 39.1990).

10. Ps 80.11 LXX; Ps 81.10.

11. Ps 118 (119).11.

12. For the entire text of the Creed of Ravenna, as well as of other creeds from Italy and Remesiana (in the Balkans) of the late fourth- and early fifth-centuries, see J. N. D. Kelly, *Early Christian Creeds*, 3d ed. (Singapore: Longman, 1986), 173–75. According to Kelly, all these creeds derive from an earlier old Roman creed, reconstructed on p. 102.

cause the Father cannot have an end;[13] the Begotten does not grow, where the Begetter does not grow old. The substance of the Father and the Son is eternal and coeternal, and that substance must not be judged according to human stages of growth, but according to divine powers.

4. *In Christ Jesus, his only Son, our Lord.*[14] Understand that Christ was anointed not with ordinary oil, but with the Holy Spirit, from whom he was born.

5. *Who was born of the Holy Spirit.* By such a birth humanity has been made holy in God, but divinity has not been diminished in God by this very gracious favor.[15] *Who was born of the Holy Spirit and the Virgin Mary.* Virginity believed in God, because only through God's initiative could the same person be both Virgin and Mother.

6. *Who was crucified under Pontius Pilate and was buried.* It refers to the judge in order to designate the time; it mentions that he was crucified, in order to convey the kind of suffering endured; and from this it gathers evidence of the divine power and of the truth of the resurrection, where godlessness had gleaned material for insult and opportunities for error. *He was crucified.* Lifted high on the cross, he suffered death before all his enemies, who both looked forward to it in all their cruelty and watched it in all their bitterness. He endures burial, lest the ungodly bandy it about that he did not undergo death in order to conquer it, but had merely pretended to die in order to delude. *He was crucified and was buried.*

7. *On the third day he rose.* And if in his passion he showed that he was the true substance of our flesh, by the symbol of the three days he rises unto the full glory of the Trinity.

8. *He ascended into heaven.* He ascended to bring us there, not to bring himself back, since he never left heaven.[16]

13. The Latin for "have an end" is *deficere*, which can also bear the meaning "be deficient," which the Father would be if he had ever been without the Son.

14. Olivar's text omits the *filium eius*, found in two of the manuscripts and included in all of Chrysologus's other sermons on the Creed.

15. On this topic and with some of the same terminology, see Ps.-Augustine, *Sermon* 193.1 (PL 39.2104).

16. See *Sermons* 62.11, 62a.7, and 72a.4.

9. *He is seated at the right hand of the Father.* There the arrangement is divine, not human. The Son sits at the right in such a way that the Father does not sit on the left. Unique and unparalleled is the divine seating plan, where heavenly power allows nothing on the left.[17]

10. *From there he will come to judge the living and the dead.* Let human beings stop, let heretics stop judging their Judge; let them hope for pardon, lest they pay the penalty for such presumption.

11. *I believe in the Holy Spirit.* Now your profession of faith in the Trinity is perfect, when you have professed with the words of faith the Holy Spirit, of one substance with the Father and the Son.

12. *And the holy Church,* as though united to Christ, in order to be conveyed to the full glory of divinity.

13. *In the forgiveness of sins.* Gain for yourself the pardon coming from faith, since he is his own worst enemy who does not believe that he is given what the very generous Bestower of mercy promises in all his kindness.

14. *The resurrection of the flesh.* The one who does not believe this has no faith in what was said above,[18] as the Apostle says: "If the dead will not rise, then neither did Christ rise."[19] Whom will God judge, and with whom will he reign, if the resurrection does not restore to life and to judgment those whom death has removed from the world?

15. *Eternal life.* It is clear that once death itself dies, eternal life takes its place.

17. *Sinister* connotes both a location on the "left" and "evil."
18. The same idea is expressed in Niceta of Remesiana, *An Explanation of the Creed* 10 (FOTC 7.50–51).
19. 1 Cor 15.16.

SERMON 59

A Fourth on the Creed

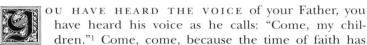OU HAVE HEARD THE VOICE of your Father, you have heard his voice as he calls: "Come, my children."[1] Come, come, because the time of faith has come, the day of believing, the hour of professing. Come, seekers of faith, bring a sincere mind, a clean heart, a pure voice so that what the word of salvation makes known through us, you may grasp by listening reverently. "Faith depends on hearing; hearing depends on the word."[2] Listen with complete simplicity of understanding to the pact[3] of faith, the pledge[4] of grace, the symbol of salvation,[5] until you can both listen to it and give it back[6] when it is time to profess it, because to give it back is to have it: the one who gives back the divine gift does not lose it.

2. When God was about to give the Law he ordered the people to wash their clothes, to wash their bodies, and to cleanse themselves entirely from every contagion of the flesh,[7] since the human being cannot draw near to God if he is polluted with bodily impurity or earthly filth. And if the Law, which contained a shadow and figure of grace, was right to require such purification and to demand such purity for those who are about to hear the entire mystery of divinity, how great must be their purity in both mind and body? So let us cleanse our hearts, let us purify our bodies, let us open our eyes, let us unlock our understanding, let us open wide all the doors of our soul, so that we can listen to, grasp, retain, and always preserve in the very depths of our heart the Creed, which is the pact of faith.

---

1. Ps 33.12 LXX; Ps 34.11.   2. Rom 10.17.
3. See *Sermon* 58, n. 5.   4. See *Sermon* 58, n. 6.
5. It is, of course, the Creed that is the "symbol" *(symbolum)* of salvation.
6. I.e., recite it from memory.   7. See Ex 19.10.

3. *I believe in God the Father Almighty*. We believe in God, if we deny the gods, if we renounce idols, if we reject the devil and his angels. "Hear, O Israel," it says, "the Lord your God is God alone."[8] And again: "You shall not have any other gods besides me."[9] Therefore, that one will have the true God, the only God, who will not have any other god.

4. We believe in God, and we profess that this same God is Father, and so let us believe that he always had a Son: but that he had a Son not begun at conception, not separated from him at birth, not increased in time, not diminished in rank,[10] not changed by age, but an Offspring abiding eternally within the eternal Begetter. "I am in the Father," he says, "and the Father is in me."[11] We have heard the Father, let us believe [that he has] a Son by divine power, not by human arrangement; by the mystery of God, not by earthly means; not by the law of the world, but by heavenly might. What it is right to know, it is not right to debate; what it is appropriate to believe, it is inappropriate to subject to an exhaustive analysis; for it is for this reason that we have called the Lord "Almighty," inasmuch as we consider nothing to be impossible for God.

5. *And in Christ Jesus, his only Son, our Lord*. From his anointing he is called Christ, from salvation he is called Jesus;[12] because, just like the anointing that had flowed symbolically as oil over kings, prophets, and priests, onto this King of kings, Priest of priests, and Prophet of prophets, divinity poured itself out in all its fullness through the Spirit, so that the kingdom and priesthood that divinity had sent in advance through others for a time, it might pour back onto the Creator himself and make them eternal. And Jesus, because he is called Savior—"Jesus" means "Savior"—is rightly called Salvation, since he both gave

8. Dt 6.4.
9. Ex 20.3.
10. See also *Sermon* 58.5 and n. 15.
11. Jn 14.10.
12. For the same kind of language about the etymology of "Jesus" and "Christ," see Niceta of Remesiana, *An Explanation of the Creed* 3 (FOTC 7.44), on "Jesus"; Augustine, *Tractates on the Gospel of John* 7.13 (FOTC 78.166–67), on "Christ"; and Rufinus of Aquileia, *Expositio Symboli* 6 (CCL 20.141), on both "Jesus" and "Christ."

existence to things, and he, one and the same, gives salvation to those that are perishing.

6. *And in Christ Jesus, his only Son, our Lord.* He is an only Son who is the only one to possess as his own and by nature what he grants that others have by his grace.[13] *Our Lord.* Just as we said above, the Lord God, the one God, abides in Christ, because whatever he is with both divinity and humanity, he is the one God. Any opposition of substances[14] has ceased in Christ, when the flesh began to be what the Spirit is; when what is human began to be divine, when what pertains to our body began to be the one majesty of divinity.

7. *Who was born of the Holy Spirit and the Virgin Mary.* Can it be any earthly being who is born when, thanks to the action of the Spirit, Mary is called a virgin in giving birth? Who would not believe that he is divine, when she who bore him experienced nothing human? The woman was carrying God in her virginal temple; this is why she both obtained the honor of Mother, and did not lose the glory of virginity.[15]

8. *Who was crucified under Pontius Pilate and was buried.* We say the name of the persecutor, so that the time of the passion, so that the truth of what occurred may be evident in this way. He was crucified, so that since death had come by means of wood, life would return by means of wood.[16] He was buried, so that he might undergo the entire process of death,[17] so that death be

13. Namely, filial adoption.

14. *Substantiarum diversitas. Diversitas* has a negative connotation of disagreement, lack of harmony, or contrariety, and so is translated "opposition." But because its secondary meaning is the more neutral term "diversity," some have taken Chrysologus to hold to a monophysite Christology by denying a diversity of substances or distinction of natures in the incarnate Christ, as though Christ's humanity was absorbed by his divinity. But he is in fact asserting the harmony between the divine and human in Christ, without denying the reality of the two distinct natures. For a more extended discussion, see R. Benericetti, *Il Cristo*, 108–13.

15. On the paradox of Mary being both virgin and mother, see also *Sermons* 58.5 and 59.7.

16. The tree of the knowledge of good and evil (Gn 2.15–17; 3.1–24) and of the cross. See *Sermon* 54, n. 8.

17. The Latin, *officia tota mortis impleret,* suggests that Christ is discharging official duties.

put to death by death,[18] so that by the seed of his body all the human bodies that had been planted would rise and be lifted up unto the harvest of life.[19]

9. *On the third day he rose.* So that in the three days the favor of the Trinity might be revealed; so that by means of a three-day period the human generations spanning the three periods might be saved, that is, before the Law, under the Law, and under grace.

10. *He ascended into heaven,* not seeking, but returning to heaven. "No one has ascended to heaven," he says, "except the one who descended from heaven."[20]

11. *He is seated at the right hand of the Father.* But he does not have the Father to his left: the divine seating plan has nothing on the left.[21] He is seated at the right, so that he not be less in status, inferior in rank; but that he reign together with the Father, one in divinity, equal in power. "I and the Father," he says, "are one."[22]

12. *From there he will come to judge the living and the dead.* If we believe that the Judge will come, let us prepare ourselves in innocence for the Judge. He denies that there is a Judge, he has no faith that he will come, he does not really believe that he must be judged, if he lives in wickedness. He judges the living, and he judges the dead whom he certainly raises in order to judge.[23]

13. *I believe in the Holy Spirit.* Seeing that we have made our profession of faith as far as the mystery of the birth of the Lord, of his passion, of his resurrection, of his ascension, and his future coming, we now come to profess faith in the Holy Spirit, so that just as we believe in the Father and the Son, we should likewise believe in the Holy Spirit, such that we proclaim one deity, power, and glory in the Trinity.

14. *And the Holy Church.* We also believe in the Church,

18. For a similar expression, see Rufinus of Aquileia, *Expositio Symboli* 14 (CCL 20.151).

19. See Jn 12.24.   20. Jn 3.13.
21. See *Sermon* 58.9 and n. 17.   22. Jn 10.30.
23. Olivar's CCL text has erroneously printed *iudicaturos* instead of *iudicaturus.* See PL 52.364.

which we believe and profess has been received and confirmed into Christ's glory.

1 5. *In the forgiveness of sins.* What will the one about to be born as a new human being have of the ancient guilt and the old sin? The one who does not believe that his past sins have been forgiven him has doubts about receiving future goods.

1 6. *In the resurrection of the dead.* Believe, O man, that you can rise in death, you who were nothing before you were living.[24] Or why do you doubt that you will rise, when everything there is in the universe thus rises daily for your benefit? The sun sets and rises; the day is buried and returns; when months, years, seasons, vegetation, seeds pass on, they die; when they return, they come to life from their own death. And so that you might be instructed with an ever-present and familiar example that you will rise again: as often as you sleep and awaken, so often do you die and rise.[25]

1 7. *Eternal life.* It is necessary that the one who rises live forever, because if he did not live forever, he would rise not to life, but to death.

1 8. Make the sign of the cross![26] May your mind retain and your memory preserve this pact of hope, this pledge of salvation, this symbol of life, this guarantee of faith, so that a common piece of paper may not cheapen the precious gift of divinity, so that black ink may not darken the mystery of light, and so that an unworthy and profane listener may not possess the secret of God.[27]

24. On this same theme, see Augustine, *De Catechizandis Rudibus* 25.46, in Patristic Studies 8, trans., intro., and commentary J. P. Christopher (Washington, D.C.: Catholic University of America, 1926), 104–5 and 294–95, for references in other early Christian authors.

25. For other references on this topic in Chrysologus's preaching, see Jakob Speigl, "Petrus Chrysologus über die Auferstehung der Toten," *Jahrbuch für Antike und Christentum* 9 (1982): 140–53, and Brian Daley, *The Hope of the Early Church* (Cambridge: Cambridge University Press, 1991), 164–66 and 254. For other authors' derivation of immortality or the resurrection from the cycle of nature, see Seneca, *Epistle* 36.10–11; Tertullian, *Apology* 48.7–9 (FOTC 10.119–20); Tertullian, *De Resurrectione Mortuorum* 12 (CCL 2.934–35); and Minucius Felix, *Octavius* 34.11 (FOTC 10.393).

26. See *Sermon* 56, n. 1 5.

27. See *Sermon* 56.5 and n. 18.

19. If your charity always showed me such silence, you would succeed in listening to all the points of my sermon.[28] But may our God see fit to give me confidence in speaking, and you the desire to listen.

28. Such an extemporaneous comment supports the contention that Chrysologus's sermons as we possess them are not abridgements but are what he actually preached, or at least what his stenographer heard. See Introduction, pp. 29–30. See also F. Sottocornola, *L'anno liturgico*, 138.

SERMON 60

A Fifth on the Creed

F THE CANAANITE WOMAN with an unexpected shout and with sudden faith both acquired what she wanted and extracted what was being denied her when Christ was going by;[1] if the Ethiopian eunuch while passing by found the mystery of the bath of life, seized it on the road, and received it during his travels;[2] if the centurion Cornelius, before being baptized, obtained the Spirit;[3] if the criminal at the very moment of death gained paradise and life:[4] who will refuse you what you seek in an instant?[5] Therefore, acquire faith from faith and, so that you might be capable of knowing the mystery of faith, work hard as the time approaches.

As Moses was about to convey the Law, he invoked heaven and earth; what kind of invocation will the priest make who is about to bestow grace? Moses said: "Listen, O heaven, and I shall speak, and let the earth hear the words of my mouth."[6] I say: listen, O God, so that I may speak, and let the human being hear the words of my mouth. Moses said: "May my discourse be awaited like rain, and may my words descend like dew."[7] I shall say: may your Spirit come like dew, may your grace overflow like a river, and may the water of the heavenly word come gushing out unto eternal life.[8] Moses said: "Since I shall call on the name of the Lord, give glory to our God."[9] I say: since I have called on faith, give your trust to your God.

2. And since the vessels of our bodies have now been re-

---

1. See Mt 15.22–28.   2. See Acts 8.26–38.
3. See Acts 10.44–47.   4. See Lk 23.40–43.
5. For other allusions to the brief time of catechesis before baptism, see *Sermon* 56.3, n. 7.
6. Dt 32.1.   7. Dt 32.2.
8. See Jn 4.14.   9. Dt 32.3.

stored by the Lenten fast,[10] it is now necessary for us to learn the pledge[11] of faith, the symbol of our interaction with heaven, so as to be steadfast in hope that, as we traverse all the seas of the world and the treacherous waves of this age, we are to acquire gain that will endure forever. So, receive the faith, await the reality: because for the one who does not first have faith as a seed, there never results the reality as its fruit. Make the sign of the cross![12] Speech gives rise to listening, listening produces faith,[13] faith produces belief, belief fosters professing, professing confers eternal salvation.[14] And so, in what follows, faith finds itself in my mouth and yours, belief is embraced, and salvation greets itself with the kiss of professing:

3. *I believe in God the Father Almighty*. This statement acknowledges and reveals the entire mystery of the Trinity. It says *God* and not "gods," because it believes that in the Trinity there is one God. Christian faith knows the Father, it knows the Son, it knows the Holy Spirit, it does not know gods. Divinity is threefold in persons, but there is one divinity in the Trinity. The Trinity is distinct in persons, but there is no division of substances. God is one, but in a Trinity;[15] God is alone, but not solitary. Divinity is not divided in the Trinity, nor is there any confusion in its unity.[16] Faith perceives this when it says: *I believe in God*.

4. The next word is *Father*. The one who believes in the Father, professes that there is a Son. The one who believes in the Father and the Son is not to think of ages, nor to consider ranks, nor to make hypotheses about periods of time, nor to inquire into conception, nor to understand a birth. The one who believes in God has professed divine not human matters. But the heretic says: "How is he a Father if he does not precede? How is he a Son if he is not subsequent? How does the Begetter

10. This suggests that Lent is almost over. Thus, this sermon and the others on the Creed were all likely delivered at the end of Lent, each in different years. See F. Sottocornola, *L'anno liturgico*, 78, and A. Olivar, *Los sermones*, 244.

11. See *Sermon* 58.2, n. 6.   12. See *Sermon* 56.5 and n. 15.

13. See Rom 10.17.   14. See Rom 10.9–10.

15. Reading the variant *trinitate* instead of the *unitate* of Olivar's CCL text.

16. For similar ideas with the same terminology to express the Triune nature of the one God, see *Sermons* 83.4 and 88.5 (FOTC 17.136, 142).

not provide a beginning? How does the Begotten not take his beginning from the Begetter? This is what reason teaches, this is what nature manifests."

You are wrong, O heretic![17] This is what human reason holds, but it is not what divine reason holds. This is what worldly nature proposes, this is not what the divine nature disposes.[18] Human frailty is conceived and conceives, it is produced and produces, it is begotten and begets, it has a beginning and transmits death, it receives and it gives back, and preserves in its offspring whatever pertains to its own condition and nature. God the Father, however, did not beget in time, because he does not know time; he who knows no beginning did not give a beginning; he did not transmit an end because he has no end; but he generated the Son from himself in such a way that everything that was in him was and remained in the Son. The honor of the Begotten is an honor for the Begetter; the perfection of the Begotten is the image of the Begetter; any diminution of the Begotten brings dishonor on the Begetter.[19]

But when you hear these things, O heretic, do not say: "How do these things happen?" You have said, *God*, you have believed in the Father, you have professed that he is Almighty. If you doubt, you have lied. If you say, *I believe*, how is it that you do not believe but you raise objections? If you think such things are impossible, then you have removed the omnipotence that you professed. But let us, who profess that the Father, Son, and Holy Spirit have one majesty and glory, now speak about our faith concerning the Lord's Body.

5. *And in Jesus Christ his only Son, our Lord.* After the Son of God "like rain on fleece"[20] with the entire ointment of his di-

17. The "heretic" in question is clearly an Arian.
18. "Proposes . . . disposes" is an attempt to render Chrysologus's wordplay *accipit . . . recipit.*
19. See *Sermon* 58.5 and n. 15.
20. Ps 71 (72).6. See also *Sermon* 143.5. This psalm text and Jgs 6.36–40 were frequently interpreted by early Christians to refer to the Incarnation. See, for example, Hippolytus, *Bénédictions d'Isaac et de Jacob* 7.19, in Patrologia Orientalis 27, 26–27; Theodoret of Cyrus, *Commentary on the Psalms* 72.4 (FOTC 101.415); Augustine, *Enarrationes in Psalmos* 71.9 (CCL 39.978) (here the "fleece" refers to the people of Israel in general and not just the Virgin Mary). For other patristic references, see *Homélie Anoméenne* 1.16, SC 146, ed. and

vinity poured himself into our flesh, from this "ointment" he was called "Christ"; and he was the sole bearer of this name who was so fully inundated and infused with God that man and God were one God. Therefore, with this anointing he has made his name flow upon us who from Christ are called Christians; and what is sung in the Song of Songs has been fulfilled: "Your name is ointment poured out."[21] *And in Christ Jesus his Son.* The former is the name of a mystery, the latter of a triumph; for just as the One anointed by God receives the name [Christ] from the anointing, so too when he restored to the world the salvation that had been lost, from the verb "to save" he took the name of Savior. Now we have often said that what "Jesus" means in the Hebrew language means "Savior" in Latin.[22]

6. *And in Christ Jesus his Son.* Whose? Certainly God the Father's. So when you say: in Jesus his Son, you profess that Jesus, who was born of Mary, is the Son of God. So be careful not to give more recognition to what was human in Christ, but always profess that he is God, as the Apostle says: "Even if we have come to know Christ according to the flesh, we now no longer know him in this way."[23] *Our only Lord. Only* is appropriate in two ways, since he is both the only [Son] of the Father, and he is our only Lord. Others have obtained by grace being sons and lords; Christ alone has and possesses by nature being Son and being Lord.

7. *Who was born of the Holy Spirit and the Virgin Mary.* If, according to the evangelist, "What is born of the Spirit is spirit,"[24] since "God is spirit,"[25] let the heretic[26] now profess that God is born of the Virgin's flesh, and no longer reduce a heavenly mystery, namely, the birth from virginity, to the world's man-

---

trans. J. Liébaert (1969), 78, n. 1; and *Homélies Pascales,* SC 187, ed. and trans. M. Aubineau (1972), 460–61, n. 48. See also R. Benericetti, *Il Cristo,* 181–82.

21. Song 1.2 (3).

22. See *Sermon* 59.5 and n. 12.

23. 2 Cor 5.16.

24. Jn 3.6.

25. Jn 4.24.

26. The heretic in question refuses to accept the virginal conception and birth of Christ. See Introduction, p. 19, n. 93.

ner of conceiving, to the impairment arising from earthly frailty.

8. *Who was crucified under Pontius Pilate and was buried.* You hear the name of the judge, so that you may recognize the time of the passion. Hear that he was crucified, so that you may observe the extent of his charity from the extent of his death; and that you may know that death, which came through wood, has been put to death through wood;[27] and that you may believe that greater goods have been returned to you through the tree of the cross than you were lamenting that you had lost through the tree of paradise. You say that he was buried, so that professing his burial may indicate that Christ had true flesh and that his death was not superficial.[28]

9. That he underwent and conquered death, that he entered the underworld and returned, that he came to the power of hell and destroyed the power of hell, this is not frailty but might. You profess that he rose on the third day; on the third day: so that you may understand that in the resurrection of Christ the victory belonged to the whole Trinity.

10. You say that he ascended the heavens, so that you believe that he is Lord of heaven; so that you acknowledge that he returned to the realm from which he had come; since after having overcome the devil, having trampled upon death, having freed the world, Christ enters in triumph above the heavens, when he was thought to have been conquered on earth.

11. You proclaim: *He is seated at the right hand of the Father,* such that, since the divinity of the Father and the Son is one and their power is equal, in the heavenly seating plan the insult of being seated on the left does not exist.

12. *From there he shall come to judge the living and the dead.* When Christ comes the dead will rise, and the living will stand for judgment, so that both at the same time will plead their cases by accounting for their deeds. And since we have now spoken about the mystery of the Lord's Body, we have reached the point of professing the divinity of the Holy Spirit.

27. See also *Sermon* 54.4 and n. 8.
28. See *Sermons* 58.6 and 144.4.

13. We believe *in the Holy Spirit*, whom the divine voice proclaims as God to us, when it says: "That God is Spirit."[29] We believe in the Holy Spirit, who is the fellow worker of the Father and the Son, as the prophet sings: "By the word of the Lord the heavens were established, and by the Spirit of his mouth all their powers."[30] Entirely God and the entire power of God is he who is shown to be the creator of the heavenly powers.

14. We believe in *the holy Church*, which Christ took to himself in such a way as to make her a sharer in his divinity.

15. We believe in *the forgiveness of sins:* since through Christ and the Church the one who is born as a new human being will have nothing of the old one.

16. We believe in *the resurrection of the flesh*, such that we believe that the reason for the passion, death, and resurrection of Christ was that we might rise from the dead. The flesh will rise; it will rise, such that we ourselves exist, and recognition of persons remains, so that both the martyr receive joy from the punishment of the persecutor, and the persecutor receive punishment from the honor of the martyr.[31]

17. We believe in eternal life, because after the resurrection there is no end of the good or the wicked.

18. Make the sign of the cross! Let us entrust the faith that we believe and are taught, not to ink, but to our spirit; let us commit it to our heart, not to paper; to memory, not to a book; so that human devices do no injury to the divine gift; so that no profane inquisitor may obtain the heavenly secret; so that what is conducive to life for believers, may not be the ruin of unbelievers. For the bleary-eyed the sun bestows not light, but darkness; wine does not restore the strength of those who have a fever, but it debilitates them even more. Without a doctor the cup of life becomes lethal: so too for unbelievers the mystery of

29. See Jn 4.24. Augustine makes a similar point in his *Sermon* 215.8 (FOTC 38.149).

30. Ps 32 (33).6.

31. Niceta of Remesiana, in his *Explanation of the Creed* 12 (FOTC 7.52–53, trans. G. Walsh [1949]), states somewhat similarly that after death the martyr enjoys the "eternal and blessed life," while pagans, among others, do not.

faith is very destructive without faith.[32] As the Apostle says, let "faith" be obtained "from hearing,"[33] but let hearing be obtained from the word. And let the pledge of life, the pact of faith, the law of salvation not be attached to those destined for death, but to the minds of the living.

32. Regarding the *disciplina arcani* ("discipline of the secret") in this context, see *Sermon* 56.5 and n. 18.

33. Rom 10.17.

SERMON 62

A Seventh on the Creed

NLESS THE ONE WHO IS DEVOTED to bringing up children regresses to childhood in every way, he never leads the child to mature adulthood. For this reason at such a moment, he softens his voice, he emphasizes his words, he nods and gestures, he suspends his judgment, he changes his diet, he reduces his strength, he neglects to exercise, he slows his pace, he strives not to walk but to crawl; he pretends to laugh, he feigns fear, he sheds false tears, because in his case to lie shows his dedication, to have acted foolishly indicates his prudence, and his weakness is his strength. I think that blessed Paul did this when he says: "I have become a little child in your midst, just like a nurse fondling her children."[1]

But perhaps someone may be amazed at seeing someone involved with child-rearing doing such things: he does not laugh if he is a parent; if he is a father he is not surprised; whoever knows how to love cannot call this foolishness. And so you who are already fathers, already strong, and already prudent, I beg you to put up with the duty I must discharge of rearing the little ones of my Lord, and with my uttering of words today that are more suitable for coaxing than for imparting knowledge; allow me not to be robust in my remarks, but to water them down,[2] and to have them flow like milk for their still-delicate throats, as the Apostle teaches: "I gave you milk to drink, not solid food":[3] to modify my way of speaking, to have a propensity for a variety of emotions, and—what more can I say?—to be con-

---

1. 1 Thes 2.7.
2. The Latin—*non quadrare, sed liquare sermones*—implies that Chrysologus's preaching on this occasion will not be the usual fare, a good "square meal."
3. 1 Cor 3.2.

sumed in mind, heart, and body with the weak minds of the little ones.[4]

2. But now I urge you, dear offspring of the Church, in the words of the prophet: "Come, my children, listen to me."[5] Rather, listen through me, and through my voice listen to the commands of your true Father, because God is calling you by means of my mouth. "Come, my children." To where do you come? For what purpose? "I shall teach you," he says, "the fear of the Lord."[6] And who would come to that fear? The one "who wants life"; the one who "desires to see good days";[7] the one who wants to do good and to flee evil; the one who desires to possess the quiet of divine peace after the struggle between flesh and spirit.

"Come, my children, listen to me: I shall teach you," he says, "the fear of the Lord. Who is the person who wants life and desires to see good days? Restrain your tongue from evil, and do not let your lips speak any deceit."[8] Just as a guilty conscience corrupts the flesh, so does deceit pollute the lips, curses defile the tongue; and consequently one who is impure[9] in lips and tongue is unable to make profession before God. And since "faith in the heart leads to justification, confession with the mouth to salvation,"[10] sanctify your hearts, cleanse your lips, make your tongue upright, so that your voice, which conveys your faith, may proceed from a pure heart in a complete manifestation of sanctity.

3. Make the sign of the cross![11] We are taught that even in a human contract a pledge[12] or a pact,[13] which contains hopes for immediate or future gain, is called a symbol;[14] nevertheless, duplicate documents always confirm that symbol between the two parties, and human wariness makes a person cautious in such

---

4. That is, his audience includes both longstanding Christians and candidates for baptism. See F. Sottocornola, *L'anno liturgico*, 140.

5. Ps 33.12 LXX; Ps 34.11.   6. Ibid.

7. Ps 33.13 LXX; Ps 34.12.   8. Ps 33.12–14 LXX; Ps 34.11–13.

9. Reading the variant *inquinatus* for *dilatatus* in Olivar's CCL text.

10. Rom 10.10.   11. See *Sermon* 56.5 and n. 15.

12. See *Sermon* 58.2 and n. 6.   13. See *Sermon* 58.2 and n. 5.

14. On *symbolum* as the word for the "Creed," see *Sermon* 56, n. 1.

agreements so that treachery, always the enemy of contracts, may not sneak up on him and cheat him. But this is the case between human beings, among whom fraud does damage, either by whom it is done or to whom it is done.

But between God and human beings the symbol of faith is confirmed by faith alone; it is entrusted not to the letter, but to the spirit; it is entrusted and committed to the heart, not to a sheet of paper,[15] since divine credit has no need of any human warranty. God does not know how to commit fraud and is incapable of suffering it, since he is not hindered by time, nor restrained by age, nor deceived by anything concealed; he sees what is hidden, he retains what is stolen, and he possesses what is refused him. For God his account is always solvent, since there is nowhere for what he has entrusted to another to be lost. And the following is the case for the human being, not for God: it is lost for the one who rejects it, but it is not lost for the one who lends it.

But you say: "Why is it that the One who is unable to be deceived demands a pledge? Why does he want a symbol?" He wants it for your sake, not for his; not because he has any hesitations, but so that you might believe. He wants a symbol, since the One who entered into your death does not disdain entering into a contract with you. He wants a symbol, because whoever is always lending everything wants to be in debt himself. He wants a symbol, because now he is calling you, not to the reality, but to faith; and through the present pledge he entices and invites you to future gain. The Apostle reminds us of this when he says: "From faith to faith."[16] And elsewhere: "The just one lives by faith."[17]

4. Therefore, let no one be unmindful of the symbol or forgetful of the agreement he has entered into with God and demand the reality when he has only now taken up faith; let no one when he has just begun to hope complain because he has not yet received what he has hoped for. Listen to the Apostle as

---

15. See *Sermon* 56.5 and n. 17.
16. Rom 1.17.
17. Ibid., Hab 2.4, Gal 3.11, and Heb 10.38.

he says: "By hope you were saved; hope that is seen is not hope. For why hope for what one can see? We hope, however, for what we do not see, and we await it with patience."[18] Hope aims for the future, faith is the means to what is promised: when the reality comes, and what is promised arrives, hope ends, and faith ceases.

A letter is sweet, but only until the one who sent it comes in person. A bond[19] is necessary, but only until the debt is paid off. Flowers are pleasant, but only until the fruit grows. But the writer's presence puts an end to the letter, payment wipes out the promissory note, flowers are destroyed by the fruit; and so by faith you will recognize that you have been marked out now as an offspring of your heavenly Father, an heir of God, a co-heir of Christ,[20] a sharer in the heavenly kingdom, one who professes the divine Judge, a resident of heaven, a possessor of paradise; you will recognize that you have been promoted now with hope, not with the reality.

And so receive faith, hold fast to hope, learn the Symbol, so that you may be able to attain to the reality and those good things that we mentioned earlier. Make the sign of the cross! Today, O man, your soul has been brought back to God.

5. *I believe in God.* Your soul, which for a long time earlier was addressing God, but did not know it; which was calling upon God, but was unaware of it—it certainly was unaware of him whom it was so eagerly seeking through stones and wood—therefore, let it now say, let it say: *I believe in God the Almighty Father.* For the long time when it used to look upon rocks, it did not see the One in whom to place its trust. And he is truly God who granted you to see by not seeing, while the pagan gods, by contrast, had made you not see by seeing. Listen to the Lord as he says: "I came into this world for judgment, so that those who do not see might see, and those who see might become blind."[21]

---

18. Rom 8.24–25.
19. See Col 2.14 and Rufinus of Aquileia, *Expositio Symboli* 13 (CCL 20.150).
20. See Rom 8.17.
21. Jn 9.39.

6. *I believe in God the Father.* There is devotion in God, there is always affection in God, Fatherhood abides permanently with him. So believe that there was always a Son, lest you blaspheme that there was not always a Father. But you say: "If he begot, how did he always have [the Son]? If he always had him, how did he beget him?" You who ask such questions deny the faith that you profess. *I believe,* is what you said: if you believe, where does that "how" come from? "How" is the word of one who doubts, not of one who believes.

I believe, you said, *in God the Father Almighty.* If there is something he cannot do, he is not almighty. But you suppose that he begot his Son from something else, since you profess that he made everything from nothing; it certainly would have been from something else, if it had been a temporal action. But if the Father is not subject to time, the Son knows no beginning. But what a travesty it is that you make him temporal who has seen fit to make you eternal. Therefore, the Father begets the Son for us, not by a conception within time, nor by fleshly passion, but insofar as he reveals it.

7. *And in Christ Jesus his Son, our only Lord.* Be aware with what reverence the faith is taught and handed on to you: you hear the Father in order to recognize, understand, and believe in, but not to dispute about, the Son; and so, profess that he is, but do not be so reckless and inquisitive as to investigate from where and when and how he is. This is why immediately after this heavenly discourse proclaims the Father to you, it refers you with good reason to Christ, to Jesus, to the Son, to our only Lord, so that when you see that you are unable to comprehend, evaluate, and grasp his human dimension you do not dare to intrude upon his divine dimension.

8. *I believe in God the Father Almighty. And in Christ Jesus his only Son, our Lord, who was born of the Holy Spirit and the Virgin Mary.* Come, O man, if you are a man after all; advance with your heart, ascend with your mind, expand your understanding, master the extent of your talents, arouse the vigor of your knowledge, activate all of your reasoning capacity, examine, dispute, scrutinize, and then to the world's amazement explain all by yourself how the Spirit begets, the Virgin conceives, bears,

and remains a Virgin after giving birth;[22] how the Word becomes flesh, how God becomes Man, how man is brought into union with God; how a cradle contains him whom heaven does not contain; how the One who sustains the whole world is carried on people's shoulders; why he, who made all things, established the universe, and keeps everything in order, willed to be born from you and to be ruled by you, and ordained that he be brought up, so that he would live with you as his parent, after he had earlier noted your servile condition.

And if out of the recesses of divinity you will have been able to attain to this and speak about the mystery of God, then go deeper, ascend higher, be more bold in your gaze. And then as a new explorer, as a unique discoverer, and as a revealer of divinity make plain the times of the Father, the origins of the Son. Be greater than Isaiah, who said: "Just as a sheep was led to slaughter, and as a lamb that was silent before its shearer, so too he did not open his mouth in his lowliness. He was taken away in condemnation; who will describe his generation?"[23] Whose generation? His, who like a sheep was led to the slaughter.

Whether it is Christ's human generation, or whether it is his divine one, both generations are indescribable, so what surge of water, O man, what tidal wave has brought you to such a shipwreck? What wind has propelled you to fly through the air to your ruin? The Father, Son, and Holy Spirit are one deity, one power, one eternity, one majesty. But whatever inferiority the Son has, whatever he receives, whatever he does not know, comes from my body, not from his substance. Or are you surprised, O man, that he invokes his Father in heaven while deeming it fitting to have a mother on earth?

22. For another reference to the three phases of Mary's virginity in a catechesis on the Creed, see Augustine, *The Creed* 3.6 (FOTC 27.294–95). On the sources and background for the doctrine of Mary's perpetual virginity, see David Hunter, "Helvidius, Jovinian, and the Virginity of Mary in Late Fourth-Century Rome," *Journal of Early Christian Studies* 1 (1993): 47–71. See also Chrysologus's *Sermon* 148a.3.

23. Is 53.7–8 LXX. Is 53.8 was a popular prooftext for theologians from all sides of the Trinitarian controversies in the fourth century. See R. P. C. Hanson, *The Search for the Christian Doctrine of God* (Edinburgh: T. and T. Clark, 1988), 833 and n. 55. See also Augustine, *Sermon* 215.3 (FOTC 38.144–45).

9. *Who was crucified under Pontius Pilate and was buried.* Why, O man, do you find fault with him, who in himself is equal to the Father, for the sole reason that he willed to be inferior in you?[24] You hear that he stands while Pontius Pilate is seated, that he is judged while Pilate interrogates him. Why then do you accept only that he is delivered over to slanderous accusers and condemned by a guilty judge? But it was also his will to be born from your flesh, his will to cling to your breasts, to lie on your chest, and his will to be carried on your shoulders, since it was always his will to be loved and not to be feared by you.[25]

Look at what was his first command in the Law, and then you will see what he has desired with respect to grace. As the evangelist has told us, after the Lord had been asked what was the first commandment in the Law, he said: "You shall love the Lord your God with all your heart, with all your soul, and with all your mind."[26] This is why he came to your heart, he came to your mind, and he took on your soul, because from the beginning he wanted to be loved by you with your intellect, your heart, and your body—he *who was crucified under Pontius Pilate and was buried.*

10. Up to this point the Jew follows, and the heretic[27] lies in wait: but let no one go along with their opinion on the last statement, since they are fed and fattened on the injuries inflicted on Christ. But you, my little children, listen, so that after the sadness of the passion, death, and burial, you may glow with the joy of the resurrection. *On the third day he rose:* so that the resurrection of our body might be the power, grace, and favor of the Trinity.

11. *He ascended into heaven:* in me, since in himself he was never absent from heaven.[28]

24. This "inferiority in you" is a reference to "your" human nature that Christ assumed in the Incarnation.

25. See Olivar, *Los sermones,* 361–62, for other references in Chrysologus's sermons to the notion that God wants to be loved rather than feared.

26. Mk 12.30.

27. The heretic in question is probably an Arian who, in Chrysologus's view, is intent upon diminishing the Son's divinity.

28. See *Sermon* 58.8, n. 16.

1 2. *He is seated at the right hand of the Father:* according to the order of divine power, not of human honor. We have said: the Son is seated at the right hand in such a way that the Father is never seated on the left.[29]

1 3. *To judge the living and the dead.* And how can death pay what is owed to the Judge? This is the reason why one rises, so that he must pay what is owed.

1 4. *I believe in the Holy Spirit.* The one who denies the Holy Spirit denies the One in whom he has believed.

1 5. *In the holy Church:* because the Church is in Christ, and Christ is in the Church. The one who confesses the Church[30] has professed that he has believed in the Church.

1 6. *In the forgiveness of sins.* Give yourself, O man, pardon by believing, since you fell into all the sins by despairing. *In the forgiveness of sins.*

1 7. *The resurrection of the flesh.* This is the complete manifestation of faith, if you should believe that the flesh, which has broken down, has become putrefied, and has decomposed, can rise, can be restored, and can return through the action of God, whom you swore could do all things just then when you professed that he is Almighty.

1 8. *Eternal life.* It was right to add *eternal life* so that one would believe that he would rise.

29. See *Sermon* 58.9 and n. 1 7.
30. Following the manuscripts that omit the preposition *in* before *ecclesiam.*

SERMON 62A

An Eighth on the Creed[1]

BELIEVE IN GOD THE FATHER ALMIGHTY. If you have believed, do not doubt; do not create faithlessness out of belief; do not join vice to virtue. You have said: *I believe in God the Father.* You have professed the whole Trinity in one God.

2. *And in Jesus Christ.* He is mystically named Jesus as Savior and Christ as the anointed one.[2] He is called Savior because he has become the Savior of his own creation. Moreover, just as kings have oil poured over them, so too does he have the fullness of divinity poured over him.

3. *His only Son our Lord.* Others have been granted through his grace to be sons and lords; but that he is Son, and that he is Lord, he possesses through his own nature.

4. *Who was born of the Holy Spirit and the Virgin Mary.* The Virgin and the Holy Spirit form a powerful partnership,[3] a heavenly union,[4] and a standard of majesty. Therefore, that a virgin

---

1. A. Olivar, *Los sermones*, 369–84, makes a convincing case for this sermon's authenticity by offering numerous linguistic and theological connections to many other of Chrysologus's sermons, particularly those on the Creed (56–62). See also A. Olivar, "San Pedro Crisólogo autor de la *Expositio Symboli* de Cividale," *Sacris Erudiri* 12 (1961): 294–321. F. Sottocornola, *L'anno liturgico*, 136, concurs with Olivar's findings. The brevity of the sermon Olivar, in *Los sermones*, 383, explains by noting that the original extended introduction of this sermon has not come down to us, and that the commentary on the various tenets of the Creed is itself not much shorter than those in *Sermon* 58. In his *monitum* in CCL 24.353, Olivar goes further and suggests that this *Sermon* 62a could perhaps be a summary of a longer explanation of the Creed that is lost.

2. See *Sermon* 59.5, n. 12.

3. *Commercium.* For other references to this term in Chrysologus's sermons, see R. Benericetti, *Il Cristo*, 101–3. Augustine, *Sermon* 213.3 (FOTC 38.123), also uses this word when preaching on the Creed.

4. Chrysologus uses the same terminology for the Incarnation in *Sermon* 146.3 (FOTC 17.239).

gives birth is something divine and not human. The world does not grasp it, reason does not comprehend it, but faith understands it, and a worldly investigator does not.

5. It is said: *Who was crucified under Pontius Pilate and was buried.* You have heard the name of the judge, so that you would not be ignorant of the date of his persecution. You have heard that he was crucified, so that you would know that life returned through wood. You have heard that he was buried so that you might not suspect that his death was feigned. To have avoided death shows fear, to have conquered it shows power.

6. *On the third day he rose from the dead alive.* That he suffered has to do with only the flesh; that he rose is the glory of the whole Trinity.

7. *He ascended into heaven:* by bringing us, not by bringing himself back, since he was never absent from heaven.[5]

8. *He is seated at the right hand of the Father:* by having everything that belongs to the Father's power and honor.

9. *From there he will come to judge the living and the dead,* either to send them to glory or condemn them to punishment.[6]

10. *I believe in the Holy Spirit.* How will the Holy Spirit be reckoned inferior in divinity? Let us understand that the Father, Son, and Holy Spirit are distinct in names, but undivided in substance; and let us confess that they are perfect in their persons, and not subordinated in a hierarchy.

11. *The Holy Church:* insofar as she herself is the Body of Christ, and her head is Christ.[7] So we profess Christ in the Holy Church.

12. *The forgiveness of sins.* How can one who believes that the kingdom is given him not believe that sins are forgiven him? Heaven receives the innocent, not the guilty. For we believe that all sins must be forgiven us, because unless we are holy we cannot possess what is holy.

---

5. See *Sermon* 58.8 and n. 16.

6. See Niceta of Remesiana, *An Explanation of the Creed* 6 (FOTC 7.47).

7. This notion of the Church, so dear to St. Paul and expanded upon by Augustine, especially in his *Enarrationes in Psalmos* but also in his preaching on the Creed (see *Sermon* 213.7, in FOTC 38.127), is repeated in *Sermon* 57.13 (FOTC 17.109).

13. *The resurrection of the flesh.* Therefore, our flesh will rise so that what shared in our virtue or guilt could also share in either reward or punishment.[8]

14. We believe also *in eternal life:* because the human being only then begins to live when he is unable to die.

---

8. In *Sermon* 83.4 (FOTC 17.136–37) Chrysologus refers to most of the articles of the Creed, without quoting from it directly. In particular, the terminology and explanations found in *Sermon* 62a.12–13 are very similar to parallels in *Sermon* 83.4.

SERMON 63

On the Resurrection of Lazarus[1]

FTER THE READING FROM THE APOSTLE,[2] while we are eager to return to the miracles in the Gospels, the next moment Lazarus comes to meet us upon his return from the underworld, supplying an illustration of how death is to be conquered and providing an example of the resurrection. So if it is acceptable, before embarking upon the waters of the reading, before braving the waves of questions, before penetrating the depths of such a deed, let us consider just the external dimension of this resurrection, because in it we see there the sign of signs, we recognize that it is the miracle of miracles, and we witness the most marvelous of marvels.

The Lord had also raised the daughter of Jairus the synagogue leader, but her corpse was still warm, she was still in the process of dying, her body was still present, she was still a human being lingering among human beings, her spirit was still on its journey, her soul did not yet know the confines of Tartarus,[3] and in short, he restored life to one who was dead such

1. Jn 11.3–27. *Sermons* 63 to 65 consecutively treat the account of the raising of Lazarus in John 11. F. Sottocornola, *L'anno liturgico*, 78–81, considers it possible that these sermons were preached during Lent. The reasons he gives are that Chrysologus preached on John's Gospel only during the seasons of Lent and Easter; John 11 was a text used during Lent in many churches in the West, including Rome, whose liturgical customs Ravenna usually followed; and in the Felician collection of Chrysologus's sermons, these three sermons immediately follow the sermons on the Creed and immediately precede the sermons on the Lord's Prayer, all of which were delivered during Lent.

2. This refers to the reading of and perhaps also the preaching on sections of St. Paul's letters.

3. In *Sermon* 65, the third on the raising of Lazarus, Chrysologus personifies Tartarus; hence the proper name, referring to the infernal abode of all the dead, is retained in this translation.

that the power of the underworld remained intact.[4] He also raised a mother's only son, but such that he stopped the bier, he prevented the burial from taking place, he interrupted the onset of decay, he arrived before the stench set in, such that he restored life to the dead man before he had come fully under the domain of death.[5]

But everything surrounding Lazarus is unique, whose death and whose resurrection have nothing in common with those just mentioned; in his case the complete power of death was operative, and an illustration of the resurrection shines in all its splendor. I dare to say that Lazarus would have usurped the mystery[6] of the Lord's resurrection in its entirety if he had returned after three days from the underworld; but in fact Christ returns on the third day as Lord, and Lazarus is called forth on the fourth day as servant. But to verify what we have said let us now sample a little taste of the reading.

2. *His sisters*, it says, *sent this message to the Lord: "Lord, behold, the one whom you love is ill"* (Jn 11.3). By saying this they appeal to his affection, solicit his love, call upon his charity, and strive to give him a gentle reminder of the duty to assist a friend in need.[7] But Christ, who is more concerned with conquering death than removing suffering, whose idea of love is not to raise someone from a sickbed, but to bring him back from the underworld, was shortly going to provide for the one he loved, not medicine for his suffering, but the glory of resurrection. And so when he heard that Lazarus was ill, as the evangelist says, *He remained in the same place for two days* (v.6).

You see how he allows death to have a foothold, he gives free

---

4. See Mk 5.22–24, 35–43. See also *Sermon* 34.5 on the Matthean version of this account.

5. See Lk 7.11–17. In restoring Jairus's daughter and the widow's son to life Jesus was not performing as momentous a miracle as when he would raise Lazarus, who was already dead for four days. In some rabbinic texts there is the notion of the soul of the deceased hovering around the body for up to three days, but after which any resuscitation would be impossible. See H. L. Strack and P. Billerbeck, *Kommentar zum Neuen Testament aus Talmud und Midrasch* (Munich: Beck, 1924), 2:544–45.

6. *Sacramentum.* See *Sermon* 37.1.

7. A wordplay, *necessitatem necessitudine.*

rein to the grave, he permits corruption to hold sway, he refuses nothing to decay and to stench, and he grants Tartarus the
opportunity to seize, drag, and hold him. He intends for human hope to be completely lost and for the onset of earthly despair in full force, to make the point that what he is going to do
is a divine, not a human, act. But to accomplish this he remains
in the same place to await Lazarus's death, so that he might
both announce that he died, and then declare that he would
go to Lazarus.

For he said: *Lazarus has died, and I rejoice* (vv.14–15). Is this to
have loved him? Christ was rejoicing because the sadness of
death was soon going to be turned into the joy of the resurrection. *And I rejoice for your sake* (v.15). Why *for your sake?* Because
in the death and resurrection of Lazarus a complete prefigur-
ing of the death and resurrection of the Lord was being depicted, and what was going to follow shortly in the Lord was now
happening first in the servant.

He used to say to his disciples, he said to them time and time
again: "Behold, we are now going up to Jerusalem, and the Son
of Man will be handed over to the chief priests and scribes, and
they will condemn him to death, and they will hand him over to
the gentiles to be mocked, beaten, and crucified."[8] And when
he would say these things he saw that they became quite uncertain, sad, and disconsolate, and he knew that they would be so
overwhelmed by the full brunt of his passion that no trace of
life nor of faith would be able to remain in them to enlighten
them, but they would suffer the gloom of an almost completely
dark night of unbelief.

And therefore he prolonged the death of Lazarus until the
fourth day, and he allowed it even to be able to emit a stench,
so that the disciples would have no doubt that the Lord after
three days would be able to rise still unblemished, since they
had seen that the servant after four days rose, already beginning to decay, and so that they would believe that he could easily restore life to himself since he had called another back to
life in so wondrous a fashion. That is why he says: *I rejoice for*

8. Mt 20.18–19.

your sake, so that you may believe (v.15). And so the death of Lazarus was also[9] necessary, so that the faith of the disciples that had been buried together with Lazarus might also rise from the dead.

And I rejoice, so that you may believe since I was not there (v.15). And was there any place where Christ was not? And how was he not at the place from where he was going to announce Lazarus's death to his disciples? Brothers, Christ was there as God,[10] but Christ was not there as man. Christ was there as God when Lazarus died, but Christ was also going to come to the dead man at the time when Christ was going to encounter death as its Lord. And so he was saying that "*I was not there*," that is, in death, in the grave, in the underworld, "where through me and through my death all death's power would be destroyed."

3. *When Martha heard that Jesus had come*, it says, *she went to meet him* and said: "*Lord, if you had been here, my brother would not have died*" (vv.20–21). Woman, do you profess that he is God, yet also say: *If you had been here?* Places or times do not make God absent or present. Lazarus would not be dead, if the Lord had been there, which in fact he was, but only if you, woman, had not been in paradise.[11] Woman, you sought tears, you found groans, you purchased death for the price of your gluttony, and yet you accuse God of being absent, while failing to raise the objection that it was your own presence that was the cause of death.

When you provided an entry for death, then there was reason to weep; but now it has become the occasion for a deed of power, because at one time an occasion for sin was granted re-

9. That is, in addition to being an occasion for Jesus to manifest his love for Lazarus through a sign even greater than a cure of his illness.

10. As in so many of Chrysologus's sermons, here too we find a strong emphasis on Christ's divinity. Without naming the Arians directly, Chrysologus clearly rejects any notion that Christ is anything but fully and completely divine. For the subtle anti-Arian aspects of *Sermons* 63–65, see Bertrand de Margerie, "L'Exégèse de Saint Pierre Chrysologue, théologien biblique," Chap. 3 in *Introduction à l'histoire de l'exégèse: IV. L'Occident latin de Léon le grand à Bernard de Clairvaux* (Paris: Cerf, 1990), 90–96.

11. Chrysologus's harsh words for Martha as a symbol for Eve are somewhat offset in the next sermon (64.2), where he takes her sister Mary of Bethany to represent the Virgin Mary.

sulting in punishment; now there has been permitted an occasion for restoration to life resulting in glory; then Tartarus acquired the human being, now he loses him. But now seek through faith, O woman, what you have lost through being unfaithful. *Lord, if you had been here, my brother would not have died. But even now I know that whatever you ask of God, he will give you* (vv.21–22).

This woman does not believe, but she is trying to believe, while her unbelief is disturbing her belief. *Whatever you ask of God.* God gives of his own accord, he does not ask of himself. Why, woman, do you delay in making your request, when the One to grant it stands before you? Woman, he is the Judge himself whom you desire merely as an advocate. In him there is the power to give, not the need to make any request. *I know*, she says, *that whatever you ask of God, he will give you.* Woman, to believe this means that you don't believe; to know this means that you don't know. The Apostle has indicated this, that the moment when a person thinks that he knows something, he does not know it.[12] But now let us listen to the Lord's response.

4. *Your brother will rise again.* And the woman replies: *I know that he will rise again in the resurrection on the last day* (vv.23–24). Martha, again you know but you do not know. Martha, again do you really know, when you do not know that your brother can rise here and now? Or is it perhaps that God who at that future time is able to raise up all, is now unable to raise up even one from the dead? He is able, yes, God is able to raise up one from the dead as a sign for this time, God who will later raise up all the dead to eternal life. *I know that whatever you ask of God, he will give you*, and *I know that he will rise again in the resurrection on the last day.*

On the last day. Martha, right in front of you is the Resurrection, which you are putting so far into the future. *I am the Resurrection* (v.25), he says. And why does he say: *I am the Resurrection*, and not "I raise him up"? Why is it? It is because he assumed man, and he assumed death,[13] so that he who raises up one per-

12. See 1 Cor 8.2.
13. For other references to Christ's "assuming" or "taking on" humanity,

son by his command would by his own resurrection raise up everyone in himself; so that for those for whom Adam was the pit of death, Christ would be the fountain of life; and so that the following words of the Apostle would be fulfilled: "Just as in Adam all die, so also in Christ all will be brought to life."[14]

I am the Resurrection and the Life, he says. *The one who believes in me, even if he dies, will live; and everyone who lives and believes in me will not die forever.* He asks: *Do you believe this?* And the woman answers: *Certainly Lord, I have believed it,* and I do believe, *that you are the Christ, the Son of the living God, who have come into this world* (vv.25–27). Why does he who had come to Lazarus have such concern for Martha? Why? So that she might rise in faith before he would be raised up in the flesh. Thus does he act who came to help both the living and the dead; he is not afraid of delaying his action, since he always has both the power to act and the means to accomplish it.

5. Brothers, allow me to suspend my remarks for today, if you desire to hear more extensively what follows.

---

death, and other aspects of the human condition, see R. Benericetti, *Il Cristo,* 96–99.

14. 1 Cor 15.22.

SERMON 64

A Second on the Resurrection of Lazarus[1]

 F A BOOK EACH were allotted to each word of Scripture, and not even with that would the mysteries contained therein be entirely clear to those who heard them, what then will an extemporaneous and brief sermon do in providing elucidation? Before it illumines our eyes, it already runs away, and furnishes those who see it not with light but with dread. Pray then, since we dwell in the world's darkness and inasmuch as we are placed in the flesh, the time we spend is night and not day, pray that Christ may enkindle the light of his word for us,[2] and that with it lighting the way we may set out into the darkness of the heavenly mystery, and by walking slowly we may arrive at the clarity of divine knowledge, as far as we can.

May we imitate those magi who took stock of their mind's eyes and did not dare to subject themselves to the sunlight or bright daylight, but at night by depending upon the delicate light of the star with their eyes, more delicate still, they arrived at Christ's crib, most delicate of all.[3] But now, as we promised, let us investigate what remains of the Gospel reading.

2. *When Martha heard that Jesus had come*, it says, *she went to meet him* (Jn 11.20). Was there no servant, neighbor, or friend —certainly there must have been someone there to console her—such that the woman had to go all by herself through the midst of the crowds, through the whole town, outside the city and in the time of mourning, to meet the Savior as he came? Brothers, with regard to these people things do not unfold as one might expect, since mysteries are being signified.

---

1. Jn 11.20–37. For the liturgical season of this sermon, see *Sermon* 63, n. 1.
2. See Ps 118 (119).105.
3. See Mt 2.1–12.

The woman runs on account of a death, she who ran to death; she hastens to receive pardon, she who hastened to her guilt; she reaches her merciful Redeemer, she whom the very wicked seducer overcame; she looks for the resurrection, she who looked for destruction; and the very one who brought death to a man is all out of breath in her quest to restore life to a man.[4] This is why Christ remained in that place, why Christ waited, why he did not enter the crowds, why he did not head for the house, why he did not stop off at the grave, and why he did not hasten to Lazarus, the very reason for his visit. But he takes time with the woman, he lingers with the woman, she is the first one he deals with, since she was the first one the tempter corrupted.

He banishes faithlessness from the woman, he calls her back to faith, so that the very same one who was the accomplice in destroying might assist in saving, and so that, in short, thanks to her faith she might be the mother of the living,[5] who thanks to the devil was for so long the mother of the dead. And because a woman had been the origin of evil, the cause of death, he proceeds to wash away the offense before bestowing his favor; to remove the cause before overturning the sentence; and he takes the precautions necessary for man not to shun as his life-partner the woman through whom he had once been deceived.

And in short, woman would have perished if Christ the Lord had come to the man first. This is why, brothers, Christ is born by means of a woman; this is why the woman always awakens man from the tomb of her womb, so that she may call back with her pains the one whom she drove out with her enticements; so that she might restore through her morning sickness the one whom she ruined by eating.

And so when Martha professed her faith in Christ,[6] and wiped out by her reverent confession whatever blame there was in womanhood, a message is sent to Mary, because without Mary death could not be banished, nor life be restored.[7] Let

4. See Sir 25.23 (24).   5. See Gn 3.20.
6. See Jn 11.27.
7. In *Sermon* 63.3 Chrysologus also interprets the sisters Martha and Mary as symbols of Eve and the Virgin Mary. See as well *Sermon* 74.3 (FOTC 17.124–25)

Mary come, let the one who bears the name of his mother come, so that humanity might see that as Christ dwelt enclosed in the Virgin's womb, so too to that extent the dead will come forth from the underworld, the dead will come forth from the tombs.

3. *When Jesus saw Mary weeping*, it says, *and the Jews who had come with her also weeping, he groaned in spirit, and was deeply agitated, and he said: "Where have you put him?" They answered: "Come and see." And Jesus wept* (vv.33–35). Mary weeps, the Jews weep, and Christ also weeps: do you think with a similar emotion? So be it that Mary the sister wept since she was unable to hold on to her brother, and was unable to prevent his death. Although she was certain about the resurrection, nevertheless, because she was without comfort at the moment, because its delay meant that his absence would be lengthy, and because she was sad about his being separated from God, she could not but weep. At the same time since when death appears it is so grim, so morbid, so very cruel, it could not but unsettle and disturb any mind, no matter how full of faith.

The Jews were in tears. The Jews were in tears, being both mindful of their condition and overcome by despair concerning the future life. Although death is quite bitter to those who are alive, and quite troubling given the fact that someone has passed away, it is even more disturbing by the example it provides. As often as one sees a dead person, that often does he lament that he is destined to die. So a mortal cannot but grieve concerning death.

For which of these reasons was Christ weeping? And if for none of them, then why was he in tears? Certainly he is the same one who had said: *Lazarus is dead, and I rejoice* (vv.14–15). The very one about whose death Jesus rejoices, he laments at the time when he raises him. When he loses him he sheds no tears, but when he lifts him up it is then that he weeps; he pours out mortal tears at the time when he pours back in the

_____

for another example of how, in Chrysologus's view, Christ's interaction with two women serves to reverse and undo the effects of the fall from paradise as recorded in Gn 3.

spirit of life. Brothers, the nature of our human body has this tendency, that the force of joy and the force of sorrow both produce tears. For as often as the inner organs are contracted by too strong a thrust from either happiness or sadness, the very next moment the eyes erupt in tears. This is why Christ wept, not from grief in the face of death, but from calling to mind that happiness when by his own voice, and solely by his voice, he would raise up all the dead to eternal life.

He groaned in spirit (v.33), and he was deeply agitated with his inner organs all in turmoil, because at this point he was going to raise up only Lazarus and not yet all the dead. Who then could think that Christ shed tears on this occasion out of human weakness, when the heavenly Father weeps over the prodigal son, not when he goes away, but at the moment when he welcomes him back?[8] Thus, Christ shed tears over Lazarus because he was welcoming him back, not because he lost him. And, to be sure, it is not when he sees the crowd weeping that Jesus weeps, but when he asks them questions and sees in their responses no trace of faith.[9]

4. He had said: *Where have you placed him?* But they answered: *Come and see* (v.34). They thought that he did not know the place in the ground where he had been placed, he who did know where cruel Tartarus was keeping him. And so by his asking the question he was inquiring into their faith and offering them knowledge, so that those who were standing there might come to know that death, that the tomb, that corruption, that decay, and that the stench did not befall human beings by God's design, but by humanity's sin. For when it is said: *Where have you placed him?* he is reproaching and rebuking women; that is, "Look where you have placed the one whom I placed in paradise, in the realm of the living!"[10]

8. See Lk 15.20.

9. Chrysologus gives three possible reasons for Jesus' tears and groans, none of which has anything to do with his mourning the death of Lazarus, his friend: tears of joy; tears of sorrow that he would now be raising only one person and not all the dead; and tears of agitation at the crowd's lack of faith. See B. de Margerie, *Introduction à l'histoire de l'exégèse: IV*, 94–95. This third reason for Jesus' tears is also noted in Chromatius of Aquileia, *Sermon* 27.2 (CCL 9A.125).

10. The harshness of these words is tempered at least partially by Chryslo-

But the Jews also were responding to the ignorance[11] of the One asking the question: *Come and see.* See what? Him giving a command to death? What? Him giving a command to the underworld? Was this what they supposed when they supposed that he did not see what was right before his eyes, when they were discussing in such a manner the reason for his tears? How could he who was able to open the eyes of the blind man not also prevent this man from dying?[12] He could have, he could have prevented him from dying; but he allowed him to die, since he wanted the dead man to be raised up for his own[13] glory. He allowed him to descend to the underworld, so that he would reveal that he was God when he would bring the man back from the underworld.

But, O Jews, your hearts will be exposed as more impervious than the underworld, your inmost spirit harder than the dead, and your eyes more repulsive than tombs, when his voice, which penetrates Tartarus, does not penetrate your interior life; when his command, which raises the dead man, does not arouse your inmost spirit; when his light, which illumines the tomb, does not illuminate your blindness. But let these remarks suffice, so that we may have more patience to be able to see together with Christ the glory of Lazarus when he rises.

gus's insistence in other sermons that women are the first messengers of the resurrection and the first to see the risen Christ, thereby being the first to be rehabilitated by Christ (e.g., *Sermon* 80.3, in FOTC 17.129), and that the Virgin Mary's role as Mother of Christ indicates woman's significant and necessary contribution to the redemption of humanity accomplished by Christ (*Sermon* 142.9).

11. It is unclear from the Latin who is ignorant: the Jews in not knowing who Jesus really was, or Jesus, who, in their minds, was thought to have asked a question in ignorance.

12. See Jn 11.37.

13. That is, Christ's.

SERMON 65

A Third on the Resurrection of Lazarus[1]

INCE WE HAVE ALREADY touched upon the death of Lazarus, the weeping of Mary, the tears of Martha, and the lamentations of the Jews in two sermons,[2] let us now unburden our spirits, cast aside our cares, and free our understanding, so that with all our minds we may be able both to grasp and drink in[3] the joys of such a resurrection. The evangelist relates that the Savior came to the tomb as follows: *Jesus,* he says, *again groaned in spirit as he came to the tomb. But it was a cave, and a stone had been placed in front of it* (Jn 11.38).

Jesus groaned and came to the tomb. Spirit groans, so that flesh would come back to life; Life groans, so that death would be put to flight; God groans, so that man would rise; Pardon groans, lest the verdict be unfavorable; Christ groans as he subdues death, because one who snatches an unparalleled victory over an enemy cannot but groan. But with regard to the fact that he said that he *groaned again,* he does groan again, in order to provide evidence of a twofold resurrection, since at Christ's voice just as those dead in body are raised to life from their graves, so too those dead in faithlessness rise to a life of faith.

2. *It was a cave,* he says. It would have sufficed for him to have said that he had come to the tomb. Why is it that the evangelist makes special mention of the cave? Certainly it is a cave, where the devil's thievery has lodged human beings; a cave, where a woman's wiles buried the man; a cave, where the greediness of death imprisoned God's handiwork. *And a stone had been placed in front of it.* The door of hard death was bolted

---

1. Jn 11.38–43. On the liturgical season of this sermon see *Sermon* 63, n. 1.

2. Namely, *Sermons* 63 and 64.

3. Reading the textual variant *haurire* for *audire* in Olivar's CCL text.

harder still by a very hard stone. What good does weeping at a grave do since the voice of the one weeping does not penetrate such hard and thick barriers? Christians, let us weep before God for our sins, and let us not weep with the pagans before the dead who do not hear us.[4]

3. *Jesus said: "Remove the stone"* (v.39). With all the divine powers he has Christ needs human help? Isn't the one who is able to put death to flight able to remove the stone? Can't the one who has the power to open the gates of Tartarus unfasten the barriers of the tomb? He had said through the prophet: "I shall remove their heart of stone, and I shall give them a heart of flesh."[5]

He therefore ordered the Jews to remove their heart of stone from themselves, to roll back the rock of faithlessness, to push away the flint of hard unbelief, so that their souls, dead through the absence of faith, might spring forth from the graves of their hearts, and that they might rejoice not so much that Lazarus had risen, as that they had risen with Lazarus. *Remove the stone.* Remove the servitude of wretched humanity so that the works of blessed divinity might now shine forth. *Remove the stone* that you have put in place so that I may now restore the human being whom I have put in place.

4. Martha responded: *Lord, already there is a stench* (v.39). *Already there is a stench.* Woman, and whose fault is it that there is a stench? *Already there is a stench.* Now you are concerned about something that has you at its origin. You would not smell any stench at the grave, if in paradise you had refused to listen to the tempter.[6] *Already there is a stench.* What emits a stench for the wrecker does not do so for the Creator. *Already there is a stench.* What the destroyer of someone else's work finds repulsive does not repel the One who loves his own work.

But by saying this bear witness to death, which you, woman, introduced; broadcast the stench, so that the completeness of his death may become known to the audience, in order that

---

4. See *Sermon* 19.5.
5. Ezek 11.19.
6. See also *Sermon* 63.3 and n. 11, and *Sermon* 64.4 and n. 10.

the raising of Lazarus be attributed to his spirit returning, not to his spirit only lying hidden;[7] that it may be attributed to divine power, not human skill; and so that the Jews may not say— they who say that we cast out demons by the prince of demons[8] —may not say this time that we raise the dead not by God's authority, but by human help.

Now *it is four days* (v.39). She mentions the time so that they may know that he is the Author of time, on whom time imposes no constraint. *Already there is a stench, it is four days.* By saying this she compounds the despair, so that those who are present may see that he is God from the way that he gives life to the dead, salvation to those in despair, and vitality to those who are decaying.

5. *With eyes raised upward* (v.41), it says. He raised his eyes upward in order to show us how to make supplication, not to provide a way for himself to make a petition. For he who is always up with his Father looks up, but the Father is in him, and he is always in the Father. "I am in the Father," he says, "and the Father is in me."[9] *Father*, he says, *I thank you for having heard me* (v.41). Does it say that he gives thanks for what has been granted, and that the Father heard him, yet make no mention of what the Son requested?

Brothers, between the Father and the Son there is a disposition to listen, not any need to make supplication; there is the harmony deriving from charity, and there is never the abrasiveness that comes from giving orders. There all things are accomplished by love, where there is no need to be submissive, as is clear from the following: *Father, I thank you for having heard me; but I knew that you always hear me* (vv.41–42). There is no worry about making a request, when one has sure confidence about being heard. Or what does the effort of making an appeal accomplish there where the means to grant it are held in common? So therefore let no one diminish the Son on the basis of these prayers,[10] nor diminish the role of the Father in human salvation.

7. See *Sermon* 63.1 and n. 5.   8. See Mt 9.34 and 12.24.
9. Jn 14.10.
10. This is another example of the anti-Arian undercurrent in these three

But why the Son speaks in this fashion, he himself reveals when he speaks as follows: *Father, I thank you for having heard me. But I know that you always hear me; but I said it for the sake of the people who are present* (vv.41–42). You see that by speaking in such a way he manifests the affection between him and the Father, he shows gratitude, and he speaks about their unity. He had said: "Everything the Father has is mine."[11] But if everything is his, then how is it that he makes a request? When someone requests what he already has, the request derives not from any need, but from love.

Father, I thank you for having heard me. But I knew that you always hear me: but I said it for the sake of the people who are present, that they may know that you sent me. He said that he was sent, so that the people would know that Christ came from heaven but did not depart from heaven.[12] So then he is sent, so too does he receive what he already has, just as he does not leave from where he came. So then, both the Son receives what he already has, and the Father does not lose what he has given.

Brothers, that he is heard, that he is sent, that he comes, that he receives, that he is born, that he suffers, that he dies, and that he rises, has to do, not with his divinity, but with our infirmity, with our nature; and so, everything that he bore on our behalf in our body, he did not endure for his own sake in his own majesty. But let us return to the subject at hand.

6. What does it mean when he says: *Father, I thank you for having heard me?* What is this? When Christ began to strike the doors of the underworld, to break through the gates of Tartarus, to open the entrance of death, to dissolve the old law of Gehenna, to do away with the age-old right to punish, and to demand the return of Lazarus's soul, the power of Tartarus with all its fury confronted him, brandishing the edict of the Ruler of heaven, bearing the decree of the King Most High, presenting the sentence rendered by the mouth of God and in

---

sermons on Lazarus. See *Sermon* 63.2 and n. 10. See also R. Benericetti, *Il Cristo,* 245–51, for the emphasis that Chrysologus places on Christ's full divinity in the events surrounding the raising of Lazarus.

11. Jn 16.15.

12. See *Sermon* 62.11 and n. 28.

effect for so many years.[13] And upon seeing the Man, he asked
who he was, what were his intentions, what was his purpose,
and why all by himself he was fearlessly challenging and attacking the fearsome entrance to death.

As he asked who he was, the angels serving as ministers of
the Resurrection answered him in the words of the prophet:
"He is the King of glory," he is "the One who is strong and
mighty in battle."[14] But Tartarus responded: "I know that the
King of glory is in charge in heaven of all the celestial powers,
and the whole of creation is unable to bear his will. However,
this one that I see is one of the earthlings, made out of mud,
enclosed in a mortal body, and in his human condition viler
than human beings, and, in short, soon to be handed over to
the grave, and very shortly destined to come under my jurisdiction."

But the angels persisted and kept repeating: "He is 'the Lord
of hosts, he is the King of glory,'[15] he is the Ruler of heaven, the

---

13. The personification of Tartarus, the vivid description of Lazarus's libera-
tion from the underworld, and the dialogue among Tartarus, the angels, God
the Father, and the Son are thought by one scholar to come from a lost apoc-
ryphon (see C. Jenkins, "Aspects of the Theology of St. Peter Chrysologus,"
Church Quarterly Review 103 [1927]: 259). There are, however, some similarities
between Chrysologus's account and one extant apocryphal Gospel in both a
Greek and a Latin version, perhaps as early as the fourth century. This *Gospel of
Nicodemus* 4.20.3–11.27 (NTApo 1.523–26), tells of Christ's own descent into
Hades after his death. The dialogue there between Satan and Hades recalls the
earlier raising of Lazarus, and the fear that once Lazarus has been raised, all the
dead will soon be freed from their imprisonment. Also, there are references
both to a loud voice and to angels, who, like the angels in Chrysologus's ac-
count, shout out verses from Ps 23 (24). In addition, a Greek contemporary of
Chrysologus, Hesychius of Jerusalem, preached two sermons on the raising of
Lazarus, both extant, the second of which contains a personification of Hades,
who laments Lazarus's return to life and wonders who this Jesus is who brought
Lazarus back. See *Homily* 12, in *Les Homélies festales d'Hésychius de Jérusalem*, ed.
and trans. M. Aubineau (Brussels: Société des Bollandistes, 1978), 1:452–55.
See also R. Benericetti, *Il Cristo*, 284–85 and n. 100, and 288–91; and J. Speigl,
"Petrus Chrysologus über die Auferstehung des Toten," *Jahrbuch für Antike und
Christentum* 9 (1982): 140–53, passim. Chrysologus himself in *Sermon* 123.6–7
provides another detailed description of the underworld at Christ's descent
there after his death. Tartarus was described with human characteristics also
among some classical writers. See, e.g., Virgil, *Aeneid* 5.734, 6.543, and 6.577.

14. Ps 23 (24).10 and 8.

15. Ps 23 (24).10.

Creator of the earth, the Savior of the world, the Redeemer of all, he is the One who rendered the death sentence that has you in a fury, he is about to tread on your head,[16] crush your authority, and issue his own judgment of condemnation on you, who, although ordered to seize the guilty, drag away the innocent, abduct the saints, and now threaten the Son of God himself. So give back one before you are forced to release all."

But Tartarus, still not believing the report he received from the customary messengers, and deploring the situation, with a complaint full of envy makes this appeal to heaven: "O Lord, even though I am the lowest of your creatures, even though I am subjected to grim servitude, I am unfailing in keeping your precepts; I am ever vigilant so that no rash innovator alter the age-old authority of your sentence. But a Man has appeared, who is called Christ, bragging that he is your Son, and he reprimands your priests, he rebukes your scribes, he violates your Sabbath, he abolishes your Law, and he compels souls, released from the flesh and assigned now to my custody for punishment, to return to the bodies in which they had lived wickedly.

"And his audacity, which is growing stronger day by day, has reached the point that he has broken the barriers of the underworld and is attempting to rescue Lazarus, already locked in our prison, already bound by our law, and already subject to our authority. Either quickly come to our aid, or, once he opens the doors, you are now going to lose all those whom we have kept in custody for so long a time."

7. To this the Son from the bosom of his Father responds: "Father, it is just that a prison holds, not the innocent, but the guilty; that punishment torments, not the righteous, but the unrighteous. For how long for the offense of one man, on account of Adam's guilt alone, will this executioner continue to drag down to himself with his cruel violence patriarchs, prophets, martyrs, confessors, virgins, widows, those abiding in the chastity of marriage, people of all ages and of both sexes, even little children who do not know good or evil? Father, I shall die, so that all may not die. Father, I shall pay Adam's

16. See Gn 3.15.

debt,[17] so that through me those who die through Adam for the underworld may live for you. Father, on account of your sentence I shall shed my blood; so pressing is it that your creation should return to you. May the price of my blood so dear to you be the redemption of all the dead."

8. To this the whole Trinity agreed[18] and ordered Lazarus to leave, and Tartarus was commanded to obey Christ in giving back all the dead. This is why the Son proclaims: *Father, I thank you for having heard me.* The Apostle bears witness that Christ is our advocate in the presence of the Father.[19] And so, when he is seated he judges together with the Father; when he stands he functions in the capacity of advocate.

9. Then Christ, his appeal as advocate completed, shouts in a *loud voice: "Lazarus, come out!"* (v.43) Then Tartarus with fear and trembling sent Lazarus back up with his hands and feet bound, afraid that while he releases him, while he delays, while he is taking his time in sending one back, he will be forced to give everyone back.[20] Thus he who had become accustomed to being the abductor of the dead became the restorer of the living. For why did Christ, who smashed the chains of the underworld,[21] not untie the bandages of death, unless to manifest to us the underworld's trembling servitude? For if the devil contended with Michael concerning Moses' body,[22] how is Tartarus not going to contend with Christ concerning Lazarus's life and resurrection? Pray, brothers, that we who have taken a sip of the resurrection with Lazarus offering the toast, at Christ's return may merit drinking[23] the whole draft of the universal resurrection.

---

17. *Ego Adae debitum solvam.* The language echoes the *adae debitum solvit* in section 3 of the *Benedictio cerei* or Easter *Exultet* attributed to St. Ambrose, although such attribution is contested by a number of scholars. For the Latin text, see B. Capelle, "L'*Exultet* pascal, oeuvre de saint Ambroise," in *Miscellanea Giovanni Mercati* (Vatican City, 1946) (= *Studi e testi* 121), 1:226.

18. The assent of the whole Trinity to Jesus' own passion and resurrection is noted in *Sermon* 72a.4.

19. The designation "Apostle" refers not to Paul, but uncustomarily to John. See 1 Jn 2.1.

20. This in fact is precisely what happens at Christ's death, as Chrysologus describes it in *Sermon* 72a.1.

21. *Sermon* 81.6 employs this same terminology, but in the context of Christ's own death and descent into hell.

22. See Jude 9.   23. See n. 3, above.

SERMON 66

On Lazarus and Eleazar

ODAY WE HAVE HAD two readings written by two evangelists proclaimed[1] so that your intellect might connect with what we are saying, and that what is hidden might be revealed. Why the occasion of Lazarus's resurrection has compelled us to make mention of the other Eleazar[2] you will hear from what follows. We are attempting presently to bring forth and put before you the astounding reversal of the inhuman rich man[3] and the poor Lazarus, their astonishing outcomes, and their very lamentable conditions.[4] That is, the rich man who had no interest in allowing the poor man in to

1. The two readings were Lk 16.19–31, the focus of this sermon, and either Jn 11.1–45 (the full account of the raising of Lazarus of Bethany) or Jn 12.9–11 (to which he refers in section 9). F. Sottocornola, *L'anno liturgico*, 82–83 and 152–53, n. 54, thinks that the actual reading for the day was Jn 11, while it was Chrysologus himself who introduced Lk 16 fairly spontaneously for emphasis. Thus, Sottocornola considers the liturgical context for this sermon, as for the previous 3, to be Lent. Interestingly enough, Augustine uses the same expression as Chrysologus *(recitari fecimus lectiones)* in a lengthy sermon (362.1, in PL 39.1611), also on the resurrection. In his case the two Biblical texts in question were 1 Cor 15.35–58 and Mt 22.23–33, or one of the parallels in the Synoptics, on Jesus' conflict with the Sadducees on bodily resurrection.

2. The name "Lazarus" is a shortened form of "Eleazar," meaning "God has helped." As such, the two names are interchangeable. See J. Fitzmyer, *The Gospel According to Luke (X–XXIV) (=Anchor Bible* 28A) (Garden City, N. Y.: Doubleday, 1985), 1131, note for verse 20. Here and in section 8 Chrysologus uses "Eleazar" to refer to the beggar of Lk 16, whereas at all other times he uses the more familiar "Lazarus."

3. *Inhumani divitis.* This same expression is found at the beginning of *Sermon* 54.1, in which Chrysologus mentions that the account of Lazarus and the "inhuman rich man" was read "just recently" *(proxime).* This has led A. Olivar (CCL 24A.393) to suggest that *Sermon* 54 was the next one preached after this *Sermon* 66. This was not his opinion, however, in *Los sermones*, 262–63, when he saw this *Sermon* 66 connected with neither *Sermon* 54 nor *Sermons* 63–65. See n. 1 of *Sermon* 54.

4. Chrysologus also preaches on Lk 16.19–31 in *Sermons* 121–24 *(Sermon*

share in his goods in the present was not entitled to have the poor man as a partner in suffering his evils in the future, nor in his scorching thirst did he receive any water to refresh him, since he denied bread to refresh the poor man as he panted with hunger.

2. *When he was in torment,* it says, *he raised his eyes, and saw Abraham far away and Lazarus in his bosom* (Lk 16.23). Now he looks up at Lazarus in vain, he who earlier in his disdain looked down at Lazarus. Concerning those like him the prophet said: "They have cast their eyes down onto the earth."[5] *While he was in torment.* Punishment pierces the one whose conscience was not pricked by penitence,[6] torments plague the one whom the sores of Lazarus did not move, and it is not without purpose that he feels the sting of punishment since he was without gratitude as he wallowed in the lap of luxury.

He saw Abraham far away. Abraham was far away from him who had not considered the poor man his neighbor. He saw Abraham sharing riches and free from inhumanity.[7] And Abraham was rich,[8] but more in humanity than in property; you, O rich man, possessed more inhumanity than you did riches. Abraham, a foreigner in his own right, was a fellow citizen to his guests; you, although you possessed palaces, refused shelter to a poor man. While Abraham welcomed servants, he thus received the Lord, and placing bread before all human beings he welcomed the Lord himself at his table;[9] but you, while you deny crumbs to the poor man,[10] have lost a drop of refreshment.

3. *Raising his eyes while he was in torment he saw Lazarus in the bosom of Abraham, and he cried out* (vv.23–24). Thus was he crying there who had no interest in listening to people crying here; shouting is futile there for a person before whom a cry here

---

122 is translated in FOTC 17.208–13). As might be imagined, Chrysologus repeats some of the same themes in these five sermons.

5. Ps 16 (17).11.

6. I have attempted to capture some of the alliteration and assonance of *pungit poena quem non poenitudo compunxit.*

7. The following praise of Abraham is also a theme of *Sermon* 28.2.

8. See Gn 13.2.   9. See Gn 18.1–8.

10. See Lk 16.21.

goes unheard. Listen to the prophet as he says: "But in the underworld who will acknowledge you?"[11] In the underworld what place is there for mercy? In your torments what hope is there for pardon? And in the hour of judgment who searches for an opportunity to be forgiven? *And he cried out: "Father Abraham, have mercy on me!"* (v.24)

Cruel son, what mercy do you seek since you denied it to yourself in denying mercy to the poor man? *Father Abraham, have mercy on me and send Lazarus* (v.24). Pitiable son, if Lazarus had come to your table, you would not have come to this place. *Father Abraham, have mercy on me, and send Lazarus to dip his fingertip in water and cool my tongue, because I am in agony in this blaze* (v.24). So now the one who shuts his hand to the poor man requests alms from a fingertip, and he who shut off his vat of wine from giving even a drop thirsts for a drop of water.

That he dip his fingertip. The one who amasses his fortune by showing no mercy to the poor man to that extent diminishes mercy for himself. *And cool my tongue.* As though the rest of the body were to be considered free from the fire, but the tongue burns more since it was negligent in bidding mercy to be shown. He feels the fire more strongly on his tongue, which reviled the poor man and refused mercy to the poor man. The tongue is the first in torment, because it blasphemed the Creator of the poor by disparaging the poor. But let us now hear what Abraham responded.

4. *Son*, he says, *you received good things in your life, and Lazarus similarly received evil things* (v.25). Let no one when he hears this think that the rich man received good things in exchange for his good deeds, when for this reason he is more guilty, namely when he received good things from God in exchange for his bad deeds, he did not give any thought to paying God back good for good; for from such great riches neither did he give food to the poor man, nor did he make any sacrifice to God with even the slightest of offerings.

But the poor man, rich in sores, without any property, naked in body, clothed with pains, was offering his life, while it was being consumed solely by its wounds, as a perpetual sacrifice to

11. Ps 6.6 (5).

God.[12] So for this reason he received rest in exchange for his sufferings, glory for disgrace, honor for insults, favor for contempt, immortality for rags, rewards for wounds, a fountain of refreshment for his thirst, the everlasting delights of the heavenly banquet for his hunger, and the one whom the rich man's bastion did not welcome, the bosom of divine consolation envelops.

You, rich man, formerly radiant, radiant in purple, now be covered with smoke, instead of scarlet be adorned with flames, instead of a soft bed endure hard torments, instead of elegant dishes feast on punishments, compensate for your wealth with poverty, let your intoxication quench your thirst, instead of fragrances a dab of decay will suffice, and you who had any pleasure at your beck and call, now be attended there by afflictions, since you brought this kind of reversal on yourself by despising the poor man.

5. But Abraham said in addition: *Besides all this, there is established a great gulf between you and us, so that one who wishes to cross from here to you cannot do so, nor can anyone cross from over there* (v.26). By saying this, he is declaring that there were both unrighteous and righteous in the underworld before the Lord's coming, and he relates that they were kept in distinct places according to their state, but they were not in separate realms.

But after the Lord rose from the dead and rent the underworld, he opened the heavens, he unlocked the bolts of paradise, he granted the saints the privilege of entering the rest of paradise and of attaining to the glory of heaven. The one who trusts that this is so, understands what Christ bestowed upon mortals by his coming. It is foolish then for the rich man to think that places in the underworld can be changed, since by acting well or wickedly here the human being assigns for himself a term there of either punishment or peace.[13]

6. The rich man answered: *Therefore, I beseech you, Father, to*

12. See Rom 12.1.

13. For a more detailed description of what Christ's descent into the underworld accomplished, see *Sermon* 123.6–8. For a brief summary of the lot of the dead before and after Christ's descent, see B. Daley, *The Hope of the Early Church* (Cambridge: Cambridge University Press, 1991), 165–66, and R. Benericetti, *Il Cristo*, 284–87.

send Lazarus to my father's house—for I have five brothers—to bear witness to them, so that they may not come to this place of torment (vv.27–28). The rich man, who was stupid in life, is found to be even more stupid in his punishment, and he who took no heed of when he was prosperous does not recognize either when he is doomed, poor thing! *I beseech you, Father Abraham.* You beseech now? For you now is the time of suffering, not of beseeching.

I beseech you, Father. For what? *That you send Lazarus to my father's house;* in front of that house Lazarus did well to lie down; at that door, on which by his hunger he attached signs of your inhumanity, where he crowned your door posts with his sores, where he painted your crumbs with his blood. So suffer through this reversal of circumstances, and now give up your ploys. Granted that you cannot bear to see Lazarus in this way; it is evident that the happiness of Lazarus inflames you more than the fire of Gehenna.

7. Abraham answered: *They have Moses and the prophets: let them listen to them* (v.29). That is, "If they not only did not listen to Moses who crushed the kingdom of Egypt with the elements fighting on his side, who dried up the sea, hardened the waves,[14] changed stones into water,[15] covered the sun with a cloud, caused a light to shine out of the night,[16] and made the sky rain down flesh and send bread down like dew,[17] but even attempted to kill him,[18] these people will not deem Lazarus worthy of a hearing, who is covered with as many wounds as the virtues with which Moses was girt.[19] Put up with the fact that I experience the consequences of my actions, and put up with the consequences yourself of what you have done."

8. *No Father Abraham* (v.30).[20] Truly he was not his father, because he was not a son of Abraham, but of Gehenna. *No, Father*

14. See Ex 14.21–29.   15. See Ex 17.6.
16. See Ex 13.21–22.   17. See Ex 16.13–15.
18. See Ex 17.4.
19. A similar litany of Moses' mighty deeds is recorded in *Sermon* 43.3 (FOTC 17.91–92).
20. *Non pater Abraham* means more than merely the rich man's plea, "No, Father Abraham!" To Chrysologus it also indicates that Abraham is not the rich man's father *(non pater).*

Abraham, but if someone went to them from the dead, they would believe him (v.30). The rich man says this from the heart of all people, he asks this out of the desires of all people, he speaks these words from the prayers of all the people on earth; for we have all been accustomed to whisper: "Oh, if only someone would have come back from the dead, and relate to us here what goes on there, all would put their trust in him!"

Certainly doubters will say: "Who comes from there? And when no one has come from there, who has ever proven that there is anything after death?" All of us say the words we have just heard, and we know firsthand what these words convey, for the truth that comes from faith we have kept buried and submerged. The reading today that followed [this one], taken from blessed John the evangelist, has shown that this kind of talk, however, is evidence of faithlessness and not ignorance when this is what we believe.[21] For in accord with the rich man's request, God sent Lazarus in place of Eleazar. But why he was sent, why he was desired, and what the benefit was of his rising, listen patiently.

9. "The chief priests intended," it says, "to kill Lazarus, because on account of him many were believing in Jesus."[22] As if it were desired for him to come for this reason, that he endure the perils of death once again. Those who do not want anyone to fail to believe what is heard[23] do not want what is seen to be mentioned. We know, we certainly do, both that life is being provided for the good, and that torments are being prepared for the wicked; but while we are held captive to the vices and do not want the era of the virtues to arrive, we pretend that we do not know what we know, and we want someone to come from the underworld to tell us what happens after death. But all the while, by his coming from heaven and his own return from the underworld, Christ has taught us by his word and confirmed by

21. As mentioned in section 1, two Gospel passages, from Luke 16 and John 11, were read prior to this sermon.
22. Jn 12.10–11.
23. "What is heard" refers to the murmurs of doubt and unbelief recounted in the previous section of this sermon, namely, that no one has ever returned from the dead, and that there is no proof of any existence after this life.

his example[24] both what abides for the good in heaven and what awaits the wicked in hell.

But perhaps the reason that we do not believe these things and do not want Christ to come is that we do not want the world to pass away. It is not that we do not want the world to pass away, but that we grieve that our vices will come to an end. Christ came not to banish life, but death; to banish death, not life; to renew the world, not to do away with it; to destroy the vices, but not to destroy his own creation. But pray, brothers, that when he comes he may find us to be the kind of people he desires and bids to share in his kingdom.

24. That Christ's (and John the Baptist's) pedagogical technique includes both word and example is indicated also in *Sermons* 166.8 (FOTC 17.275) and 167.1.

SERMON 68

A Second on the Lord's Prayer[1]

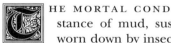HE MORTAL CONDITION, the earthly body, the substance of mud, suspended between life and death, worn down by insecure labor, exhausted by suffering, and destined by its nature to decay and dust, has no capacity to grasp, is inadequate to consider, does not dare to pretend, and is afraid of believing what it is today compelled to profess. Human frailty is powerless to discover how it has ever come to deserve such generous graces from God, such great promises, and such bountiful gifts. I think that Habakkuk the prophet was mentally perceptive enough to recognize this, while after having been struck with such great fear from what he heard he consequently shook and trembled when he said: "Lord, I have heard your reputation[2] and I was afraid; I meditated upon your works, and I trembled."[3]

He feared what he had heard, not because at that time so great a prophet had heard the Lord, but because at that time the servant found out and heard that his Lord had turned into a Father for him; not because he trembled after having considered how harmoniously this world was constructed out of elements so discordant among themselves, but because in meditating at that time upon such great works of kindness towards him, his was the fear and trembling of being awestruck. "I meditated upon your works," he says, "and I trembled." He was as-

---

1. Mt 6.9–13. *Sermons* 67–72 on the Lord's Prayer were preached during Lent, shortly after his sermons on the Creed, to those soon to be baptized at Easter (mentioned in *Sermon* 72.2–3). *Sermons* 67 and 70 are already translated in FOTC 17.115–23. See F. Sottocornola, *L'anno liturgico,* 83.

2. *Auditum tuum,* literally, "what has been heard about you."

3. Hab 3.2. The prophet Habakkuk is mentioned also in *Sermon* 72.1 as a model of holy fear.

tonished that he had been adopted as a son at the time when he had lost confidence in being a mere servant.

2. Therefore, that you may know, by what he then heard from heaven, that the prophet was affected by this prayer, which divinity conveys and imparts to you today, and was in a certain sense undone in his awe at this gift, once again notice what he said: "I kept watch over myself, and my stomach trembled from the cry of supplication on my lips."[4] After he had sensed how great was the generosity of God's gift, he kept watch over himself, so that he would not have to put up with himself once again as an enemy, as a foe, and as a robber as he had in paradise. He becomes a more vigilant and more cautious guard over himself, once he had realized that after having thrown away so great a blessing he had found a heavenly treasure, as Paul says: "We bear this treasure in earthen vessels."[5]

"I kept watch over myself, and my stomach trembled." Here the prophet is calling the depths of his being the stomach of his heart, because the heart just like a stomach with respect to food, is fed and filled by thoughts. "And my stomach trembled from the cry of supplication on my lips."[6] If the thoughts of his heart had imparted the cry into his mouth and had provided the words for his lips, why did his prayers, his longings, and the petition he was about to make cause him to tremble? Because he was speaking not at the suggestion of his heart, but by the inspiration of the Divine Spirit.[7]

Listen to Paul as he says: "God sent the Spirit of his Son into our hearts crying out, 'Abba, Father!'"[8] That is, when he processed what he had heard in the depths of his being, he was amazed that he was considered worthy of such a thing, and the man trembled in the depths of his being. Rightly did he add: "And dread entered my bones,"[9] because the prophet's very inner organs were agitated. "And below me," he says, "my strength was shaken."[10] What does he mean by "below me"? That the very same man, who has now been raised up through

4. Hab 3.16.
6. Hab 3.16.
8. Gal 4.6.
10. Ibid.

5. 2 Cor 4.7.
7. See *Sermon* 72.1.
9. Hab 3.16.

grace, used to lie down below through his old nature, and his earthly strength was unable to sustain the strength from heaven.

Mount Sinai was already smoking when God descended onto the mountain to give the Law;[11] what would flesh do, when God descended into flesh to confer grace on the flesh? He came as Father,[12] because the human being could not endure God, the servant could not endure the Lord; and because he who said: "Open your mouth, and I shall fill it,"[13] is faithful in his words,[14] open now your mouths, so that he himself may fill it with the following prayer and acclamation:

3. *Our Father, who art in heaven* (Mt 6.9). Where are those who distrust God's promise? See how quickly the profession of faith has turned a profit: as soon as you confessed God as Father of his only Son, you yourself were adopted as a son of God, so that you may be an heir of heaven,[15] you who were considered an exile from paradise and earth; and so you now call *Our Father, who art in heaven*, because the one who used to be your father dissolved you into mud, and led you away, dragged you off, and imprisoned you in hell.[16] Let him have no knowledge of earth, let him ignore love of the flesh, let him never seek the father of dust again, let him forbid vice to have any leeway within him, who asks God the Father again for a heavenly nature. And let the one who believes that he is a son of God conform to such a lineage by his actions, by his life, by his morals, by his in-

11. See Ex 19.18.

12. Chrysologus's imprecision here is confusing. After referring to the Incarnation as God's descent into the flesh, he proceeds immediately afterwards to say that "he came as Father." It is unclear whether he is referring to Christ as "Father of Christians" in a functional sense, as in *Sermon* 7.1, for example, or that he means that at Christ's coming in the flesh, the first person of the Trinity is revealed now as Father.

13. Ps 80.11 LXX; Ps 81.10. Chrysologus uses this same verse in one of his sermons on the Creed (58.1 and 2) for a similar purpose: that the candidates be receptive to the Creed and the commentary he is about to present, as here to the Lord's Prayer and his explanation.

14. See Ps 144 (145).13.

15. Being given the privilege of saying "Our Father" means that one receives filial adoption and heirship to heavenly or divine blessings, also emphasized in *Sermons* 69.3 and 71.2, 11.

16. See *Sermon* 65.6.

tegrity, lest by descending once again to earthly things he manage to offend so great a Father.[17]

4. *Hallowed be thy name* (v.9). If the name of Christ gives "sight to the blind,"[18] mobility to the lame, health to those worn down by various illnesses, life to the dead,[19] and sanctifies you yourself, O man, and all creation, how is it that you pray and beseech that his name be hallowed? Because you are called a Christian from "Christ,"[20] and so you beg that the privilege[21] of so great a name may be reinforced in you by your subsequent good deeds.

5. *Thy kingdom come* (v.10). He is demanding devotion, requiring petitions, and seeking prayers, inasmuch as he is in full control when he comes. The faithful soldier is the one who longs for the presence of his king, eagerly awaits the kingdom, and zealously strives for victories. But in this petition you are asking that he come to reign for you and within you, in whom for such a long time the devil succeeded in maintaining a stronghold, death its dominion, and hell its sovereignty. So let us pray, dearly beloved, that Christ may always reign in his soldier, that the soldier may always be victorious in his king.

6. *Thy will be done on earth as it is in heaven* (v.10). Blessed is that day that joins, unites, and makes the wills of earthly creatures equivalent to those of heaven, so that between unequal substances there is one and the same will. This is a secure peace, an unshakable harmony, and a persevering grace, when by the authority of the one Lord among diverse households[22] their nature becomes one in will, and is found to be the same even in their thinking.

7. *Give us this day our daily bread* (v.11).[23] After the heavenly

17. See *Sermons* 70.3 (FOTC 17.120) and 72.3.

18. Lk 4.19.

19. See Mt 11.5.

20. See *Sermon* 69.4.

21. "Privilege" *(praerogativa)* is noted in *Sermon* 72.4 as well.

22. That is, the "household" of human beings and that of angelic beings.

23. On the Eucharistic teaching found in Chrysologus's six sermons on the Lord's Prayer, see B. de Margerie, *Introduction à l'histoire de l'exégèse: IV*, 97–106, and A. Olivar and A. Argemi, "La Eucaristía en la predicación de San Pedro Crisólogo," *La Ciencia Tomista* 86 (1959): 612–19.

kingdom who would ask for temporal bread?[24] But every day he wants us also to ask for the daily[25] provision[26] of bread in the sacrament of his Body,[27] whereby from this we may arrive at the eternal day[28] and the very table of Christ,[29] so that from having consumed a foretaste here, we may later receive there the full portion in all its abundance.

8. *And forgive us our debts as we also forgive our debtors* (v.12). The one who makes such a petition and does not forgive debts accuses himself even in the very prayer he utters. The one who asks that as much be given and forgiven him as he himself forgives, also gives howsoever the Lord decides and in this way invites God into the arrangement. As much as each one grants another, that much does he demand to be likewise granted to him.[30] But debts must be forgiven, brothers, not only of money,[31] but also of all lawsuits, offenses, and charges. Whatever debt, O man, you may incur, in these matters forgive another when he incurs such a debt to you. The one who is willing to forgive a sinner confidently asks pardon for his own sin.

9. *And lead us not into temptation* (v.13). It is necessary that many make this petition in many ways, brothers, so that frailty that is more bold and recklessly presumptuous about itself, and fails to consider the limit of its own strength, may not succumb in the conflict by being poorly prepared. Then God, having been offended, would abandon them and deliver them over to their temptations.[32]

24. Similar rhetorical questions are asked in *Sermons* 70.7 (FOTC 17.121–22) and 71.7.

25. "Daily" *(cotidie)* does not necessarily imply a celebration of the Eucharist every day in Ravenna: see *Sermons* 33.5, n. 13, and 34.3, n. 7.

26. *Viaticum* is also employed to describe the Eucharist in *Sermon* 95.2 (FOTC 17.158).

27. Chrysologus refers to the Eucharist with these same words *(sacramentum sui corporis)* in *Sermon* 95.4 (FOTC 17.150).

28. This eschatological orientation of Eucharistic participation is noted also in *Sermons* 71.7 and 72.7.

29. The altar is called *mensa Christi* in *Sermon* 30.4 as well.

30. This *quid pro quo* arrangement is also noted in *Sermons* 67.8 (FOTC 17.118), 70.8 (FOTC 17.122), and 72.8.

31. That a monetary debt is only one of a variety of debts implied by this petition, see also Augustine, *Commentary on the Lord's Sermon on the Mount* 2.8.28 (FOTC 11.135–37).

32. See *Sermons* 67.9 (FOTC 17.118), 70.9 (FOTC 17.122), and 71.9.

10. *But deliver us from evil* (v.13). The one who implores that
he be delivered from evil by the action of God is appropriately
humble in his own regard and does not presume to be saved by
his own resources.

11. Make the sign of the cross![33] Understand, little children,
how very glorious, how truly mighty are the perfected and the
strong, when such great power is revealed merely at conception, and when such great majesty is revealed at birth. The one
who is not yet born calls upon his Father, asks for holiness,
seeks the kingdom, gives laws to the earth, puts earthly wills on
a par with heavenly ones, and from the moment he is consecrated he requests rations so that his labors will be profitable.
Give us this day, he says, *our daily bread* (v.11).

Blessed are you who have begun to conquer even before the
battle, to be victorious even before living,[34] to reach the lap and
storerooms of your Father even before reaching the lap of your
mother; to enter the pasture of the flock before taking a whole
drink of milk; to shout with the cry of victory before responding with a wail from the cradle. Truly, as the Apostle has said,
"God's weakness is stronger than human beings."[35] Or who will
be able to tell of the mystery of so great a conception, where
the virgin mother gives birth on a daily cycle?[36] She does not
abandon her posterity to distress, but she sends her offspring
ahead to eternal glory.

33. See *Sermon* 56.5, n. 15.
34. Chrysologus mentions others who have achieved greatness "before living": John the Baptist, who while in his mother's womb recognized his Creator
(Lk 1.41: *Sermons* 69.6, 70.3 [FOTC 17.120], 72.3, 88.4 [FOTC 17.141], and
91.7); Jacob, who struggled with his twin Esau in their mother's womb (Gn
25.22–26: *Sermons* 69.6, 70.3, 72.3, and 154.2 [FOTC 17.260]); Tamar's twins,
who competed to be the first one born (Gn 38.27–30: *Sermon* 72.3); and the
Holy Innocents, who were soldiers of Christ even while still infants (Mt 2.16–18:
Sermon 153.2).
35. 1 Cor 1.25.
36. Or, alternatively, "in the world every day" *(orbe cotidie)*. F. Sottocornola,
L'anno liturgico, 144, even suggests that *cotidie* cannot mean literally "every day,"
but rather "frequently" or "always." It could be rendered "on a regular basis."
See also above, n. 25.

SERMON 69

A Third on the Lord's Prayer[1]

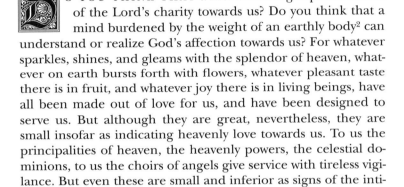O YOU THINK THAT a mortal heart grasps the extent of the Lord's charity towards us? Do you think that a mind burdened by the weight of an earthly body[2] can understand or realize God's affection towards us? For whatever sparkles, shines, and gleams with the splendor of heaven, whatever on earth bursts forth with flowers, whatever pleasant taste there is in fruit, and whatever joy there is in living beings, have all been made out of love for us, and have been designed to serve us. But although they are great, nevertheless, they are small insofar as indicating heavenly love towards us. To us the principalities of heaven, the heavenly powers, the celestial dominions, to us the choirs of angels give service with tireless vigilance. But even these are small and inferior as signs of the intimate bond God has with us, and as paltry in value as the creature is inferior to his Creator.

2. God, whose face cannot be seen, who is imperceptible to our sight, who cannot be grasped by our senses, who is inaccessible to our mind,[3] and not even completely known when his voice is heard, how often, in how many ways, with how many varieties, and with what diversity has he adapted himself to hu-

---

1. Mt 6.9–10. In his *monitum* to this sermon in CCL 24A.412, A. Olivar notes that unlike the other five sermons on the Lord's Prayer, this one comments only through the verse "Thy kingdom come." Either Chrysologus himself finished his remarks at that point on account of this sermon's lengthy preamble, or the complete text did not come down to us. F. Sottocornola, *L'anno liturgico*, 83, mentions another possibility, that Chrysologus only intended to preach on the first several verses of the Lord's Prayer at a time of the year other than Lent. But the explicit reference to those preparing for baptism—*nondum natus* ("not yet born") in section 6—makes this unlikely, as Sottocornola himself admits.

2. See Wis 9.15.

3. See 1 Tm 6.16.

man vision! How he has offered and submitted himself to communion and familiarity with human beings, when he made Noah a partner in his design! He forewarned him that very shortly the world was to be purified by a flood, and he carried out his plan for the whole world under his supervision over the little seed-vessel that was the ark.[4]

When he came as a guest to Abraham, he very graciously accepted the invitation, he did not refuse what was offered, he ate what was served like one who was hungry and weary, and in this divine exchange he received and accepted human kindness like one who was in need.[5] Shortly thereafter the dead members of the old man revive, the sterile womb of the childless old woman is now awakened, and the nature that had been buried in a living corpse rises to life to reveal its Author, and although her time had already passed, she who had believed the one Creator produces very many descendants.[6]

To Moses he comes as a ball of fire in the bush, then he discusses with his servant what must be done, he is busy in Egypt with various acts of power, and he is revealed at the will of his servant. He imposes scourges or he removes them, and in the sea the avenging waves show by their obedience how great he is and how much he has given to the human being, when with its swell all dried up the wave yields to the holy ones, and it provides a wall out of water that solidified, it offers a defense for those to be freed, and with all its might it crashed down in triumph over the fiercest of enemies.[7]

In his wondrously intimate bond with the Israelites God keeps company with them in their camp; at one moment he strikes a number of pagans with a thunderbolt, at another he pours down hail, at yet another he levels them with the noisy din of trumpets, so that without a battle and without a wound, God goes ahead of the battle lines and leads them to victory.[8] He was present to their needs, he granted individuals their prayers, he responded quickly to what was asked, he revealed

4. See Gn 6–9.
5. See Gn 18.1–15.
6. See Gn 21.1–8; 22.17.
7. See Ex 3–14.
8. See Jos 10.11 and 6.1–24.

what was hidden, he foretold the future, he brought to light what was sought, he conferred the kingdom, he bestowed wealth, he provided rain in due season, he supplied fertile lands, and with prosperity and honor he endowed his children who kept holy the bond of marriage.

But he considered this to be still too little, if he were to show his affection towards us by bestowing blessings on us, but not also by enduring adversities. After all this he entered his own world in poverty, he lay in a cradle: thus as a human being by his crying he implores, he seeks, he pleads for the loving kindness that he himself has shown to you. The Parent of all[9] has made use of you as a parent, and the One who is higher than every height lived under your authority;[10] the One whom terrifying things fear was frightened, the Refuge of all fled, the Ruler of the heavens is a guest in the homes of sinners, the Judge of the guilty is fed on their bread.

And why should I say more? The Ruler of all ages[11] is seized, the Founder of the earth is arrested, the Bestower of pardon to humanity is judged, the Examiner of hearts is struck, the Giver and Restorer of life is punished, the Resurrection of all is buried, so that the slow mind of human beings and their very dull intellect would learn of God's fondness towards them by his death at least. For that intellect had not perceived or recognized God's charity towards humanity from his prophecies and innumerable gifts. God, therefore, who made us exist, who granted us life, also taught us how to pray, because he wanted to furnish everything, since he willed that he be invoked by means of his own prayer.[12]

3. *Our Father who art in heaven* (Mt 6.9). Notice, O man, how with your own voice Christ today adopts you as a son of God the Father, in order to make you a coheir with him,[13] while he says:

---

9. See *Sermon* 33.2 and n. 4 on the expression *parens omnium.*

10. See *Sermon* 140a.5 for similar antitheses.

11. A Grecism, *Pantocraton.*

12. The idea that God alone could teach humanity the proper way to pray is found in Tertullian, *Prayer* 9.3 (FOTC 40.167).

13. See Rom 8.15 and 17. See also Augustine, *Commentary on the Lord's Sermon on the Mount* 2.4.16 (FOTC 11.123), on linking calling God "Father," be-

Our Father. What belongs to his dignity he has willed to be in your power, according to the words of the prophet:[14] "To all who believed in him he gave the power to be called sons of God."[15] And nevertheless, he commands us to say these words, to indicate that it depends on the One who gives and not on one who is rash and presumptuous.

Who art in heaven. It is not that he is not on earth, but you, who now invoke him in heaven, he wants to strain towards and seek once again the heavenly nature, so that your life may correspond to so great a lineage, and so that your conduct on earth may not defile what the heavenly nature has now bestowed and conferred.

4. *Hallowed be thy name* (v.9). It is not that his name is to be made holy by your prayer, but that his name makes you holy. But since one is called a Christian from the name Christ, you must ask that this name be kept holy by your actions and honored in you; because just as a good reputation arising from virtue brings so much glory to one's name, so too the infamy of one who lives wickedly heaps insult on the very same name, as the Apostle says: "Because of you God's name is blasphemed among the gentiles."[16] And truly, children, a pagan does dishonor the name Christian whenever he sees a Christian living differently from what he professes and what he is called.[17]

5. *Thy kingdom come* (v.10). We do not pray that the kingdom may come to God, who always has it, but you ask that it may come to you who do not have it,[18] and that you may receive what the Lord promises in his fondness for you, when he says: "Come, blessed of my Father, receive the kingdom that has been prepared for you from the foundation of the world."[19]

---

coming coheirs with Christ, and receiving filial adoption. See also Chrysologus, *Sermons* 67.2 (FOTC 17.115–16), 68.3, and 71.2 and 11.

14. Not his customary designation for the Evangelist of the Fourth Gospel.

15. Jn 1.12. For the use of this same verse in elucidating the first words of the Lord's Prayer, see also Chromatius of Aquileia, *Sermon* 40.2 (CCL 9A.172), and idem, *Tractatus in Mathaeum* 28.1.3 (CCL 9A.329).

16. Rom 2.24.

17. See *Sermon* 67.4 (FOTC 17.116).

18. See Augustine, *Letter* 130.11.21 (FOTC 18.392).

19. Mt 25.34. Chrysologus makes use of this verse again to interpret "Thy

"Come, blessed": he did not say, "Let us come"; "Receive": he did not say, "Let us receive."

6. Let no one wonder that one who has not yet been born[20] invokes his Father, for John leaps,[21] and Jacob wrestles in the womb.[22] Let the prudent person consider what the divine nature can do, if a human being conceived through God's intervention can do so much.

---

kingdom come" in *Sermon* 70.5 (FOTC 17.121). So too did Cyprian, *The Lord's Prayer* 13 (FOTC 36.137); and Augustine, *Sermon* 56.6 (FOTC 11.243); *Sermon* 57.5, in P. Verbraken, "Le *Sermon* 57 de saint Augustin pour la tradition de l'Oraison dominicale," in *Homo Spiritalis: Festgabe für Luc Verheijen OSA*, ed. C. Mayer and K. H. Chelius (Würzburg: Augustinus-Verlag, 1987), 416; and 58.3, in P. Verbraken, "Le sermon LVIII de saint Augustin pour la tradition du 'Pater,'" *Ecclesia Orans* 1 (1984): 120.

20. This refers to those still preparing for baptism and hence "not yet born." See also *Sermons* 67.11 (FOTC 17.118), 68.11, and 71.2.

21. See Lk 1.41.

22. See Gn 25.22 and *Sermon* 68.11, n. 34.

SERMON 71

A Fifth on the Lord's Prayer[1]

ROTHERS, HE WHO HAS BESTOWED upon you the gift of faith has also taught you how to pray,[2] and he has fitted the whole formula[3] of supplication into a few words, because when asking something of his father, a son does not have the arduous task of making a lengthy petition. For just as need forces a child to make a request, so too charity compels a father to give. Therefore, the Father, who gives willingly, shows us not so much that he should be asked as what should be asked for, in order that the son should please him by asking for what is right, since he can displease him by making a request for what is foolish. Listen to the Father, and believe that you are already his children, so that you may obtain without delay what you are asking for.

2. Today it is made clear to you what faith can accomplish, what belief can do, and how great it is to profess it. Notice that the threefold profession of faith in the Trinity[4] has raised you up from earthly servitude to the status of an offspring of heaven. Notice that the faith that has spoken of God as Father has today for your benefit acquired God as your Father. Notice that the voice that has professed faith in the Son of God has made you adopted sons of God.[5] Notice that the belief that has proclaimed God the Spirit has transformed you out of the mortal

1. Mt 6.9–13. See *Sermon* 68, n. 1.

2. See *Sermon* 69.2 and n. 12.

3. *Forma.* See *Sermon* 67.1 (FOTC 17.115), Cyprian, *The Lord's Prayer* 2 (FOTC 36.127–28), and Chromatius of Aquileia, *Sermon* 40 (CCL 9A.172).

4. The explicit Trinitarian references in this section point to the profession of faith in the Trinity and to the Trinitarian formula of the baptismal ceremony.

5. Filial adoption is likewise indicated also in section 11 of this sermon, as well as in *Sermons* 68.3 and 69.3.

substance of flesh into the living substance of spirit. Who is found worthy to declare such bountiful kindness?

God the Father deems human beings worthy of being heirs, God the Son does not disdain having his mere servants as co-heirs,[6] God the Spirit welcomes flesh to partake of divinity;[7] heaven is made the possession of earthlings, and those who had been consigned to the underworld administer justice in the celestial realm, as the Apostle attests when he says: "Or do you not know that we shall judge angels?"[8]

So call God your Father, and even now believe that although you are not yet born,[9] you are, nevertheless, already designated as his children, and see to it that you possess a life reflective of heaven, that your behavior be divine, and that God's pattern be revealed in its entirety in your pattern of life, because the heavenly Father enriches with divine gifts those children that correspond to their lineage, but backsliders he reduces once again to penal servitude.

3. *Our Father who art in heaven* (Mt 6.9). We would be overwhelmed in our awareness of being slaves, we would disintegrate in our earthly condition, if the authority of the Father himself and the Spirit of his Son were not rousing us to make this acclamation. "God sent," it says, "the Spirit of his Son into our hearts crying out, 'Abba, Father!'"[10] Our mind grows faint, our flesh falters at divine matters, if God who gives the command were not to carry out himself what he commands to be done. When have mortals dared to call God their Father, except now, when the deepest recesses of the human being are enlivened by power from heaven?

Our Father who art in heaven. O man, what do you have in common with earth, you who profess that your lineage comes from heaven?[11] Therefore, manifest a heavenly manner of life

6. See *Sermon* 69.3 and n. 13.

7. In *Sermon* 60.14 Chrysologus holds that it is through membership in the Church that one partakes of divinity. See also *Sermons* 57.13 and 67.2 (FOTC 17.109, 115).

8. 1 Cor 6.3.

9. *Nondum natos.* See *Sermon* 69.6 and n. 20.

10. Gal 4.6.

11. This notion of having a heavenly lineage is also mentioned in *Sermon*

while dwelling on earth, because if earthly considerations have any hold on you, you have brought a blemish upon heaven, and an injury upon your heavenly lineage.

4. *Hallowed be thy name* (v.9). We ask that God sanctify his name, that name which by virtue of its own holiness saves and sanctifies all creation. Brothers, this is the name at which the celestial powers tremble, to which they submit with dread and homage; this is the name that puts demons to flight, this alone is what frees souls held captive by the devil's savagery; this is the name that gives salvation to a world that was lost. But we ask that God's name may be made holy in us by our actions.[12] Indeed God's name is blessed when we behave well, but it is blasphemed when we behave wickedly. Listen to the Apostle as he says: "God's name is blasphemed among the gentiles because of you."[13] And so we ask, we ask that as holy as God's name is, we may be counted worthy of that much holiness in our conduct.

5. *Thy kingdom come* (v.10). As though it has not always been and continues to be, we pray in this fashion that Christ's kingdom may come now. And what about this passage: "The kingdom of God is within you"?[14] It is within us by faith, but we ask that it come in reality. Brothers, as long as the devil by various kinds of wickedness and by manifold methods of deception disturbs the face of the universe, throws into confusion the minds

---

67.3 (FOTC 17.116) and 70.3 (FOTC 17.120). That having such a heavenly pedigree demands equally lofty conduct was something indicated by Cyprian, *The Lord's Prayer* 11 (FOTC 36.136).

12. This sentence encapsulates how Chrysologus and most Latin-speaking early Christian preachers interpreted this verse. See Chrysologus's *Sermons* 67.4 (FOTC 17.116), 69.4, 70.4 (FOTC 17.121), and 72.4. See also Tertullian, *Prayer* 3.4 (FOTC 40.161); Cyprian, *The Lord's Prayer* 12 (FOTC 36.136); Ambrose, *The Sacraments* 5.4.21 (FOTC 44.316); Chromatius of Aquileia, *Sermon* 40.2 (CCL 9A.172) and *Tractatus in Mathaeum* 28.2.2 (CCL 9A.330); and Augustine, *Sermons* 57.4 (*Homo Spiritalis*, 415), 58.3 (*Ecclesia Orans* 1 [1984]: 120), and 59.3 (SC 116.188–89).

13. Rom 2.24: this Pauline verse is used to explicate "Hallowed be thy name" in all the references in the previous note to Chrysologus's sermons except *Sermon* 72.

14. Lk 17.21. Chrysologus refers to this verse in expounding on "Thy kingdom come" in *Sermon* 70.5 (FOTC 17.121), as did Ambrose in *The Sacraments* 5.4.22 (FOTC 44.316).

and morals of humanity, rages with idols, drives people insane with sacrilege, deceives them with omens, tells lies with soothsaying, tricks with signs, deludes with stars, captivates them with the shows, besets them with the vices, wounds them with sins, injures them with offenses, and overwhelms them with despair, he keeps Christ's kingdom at a distance and far away from us. And so we ask that the time may come when the author of such evil will perish and the whole world and all of creation will reign and be victorious when the fullness of glory will belong to Christ alone, and that the following occur:

6. That there be only the Lord's will *on earth as it is in heaven* (v.10). Then heaven will be our earth, God our life, eternity our time, rest our homeland, innocence our wealth, immortality our reward, chastity our peace, and God our all. He added:

7. *Give us this day our daily bread* (v.11). After the Fatherhood of God, the holiness of the Lord's name, and the kingdom of heaven, are we commanded to ask for daily bread?[15] Christ is not subject to forgetfulness, nor does he demand something contrary to his commands. He it is who said: "Do not worry about what you are to eat, or what you are to drink."[16] But since he himself "is the Bread that came down from heaven,"[17] which has been ground into flour by the millstone of the Law and grace, molded in the passion on the cross, and leavened through the great and sacred mystery of his compassion,[18] which has raised up from the tomb dough that is risen, which, in order to be cooked by the heat of his divinity, has melted down the furnace of the underworld, which is offered daily[19] as heavenly food at the Church's table,[20] broken for the forgive-

15. See *Sermon* 68.7 and n. 25.

16. Mt 6.31. See also *Sermons* 67.7 (FOTC 17.117) and 70.7 (FOTC 17.121–22). Augustine also employs Mt 6.31 in interpreting this verse of the Lord's Prayer in *Commentary on the Lord's Sermon on the Mount* 2.7.25 (FOTC 11.132–33).

17. Jn 6.58.

18. See 1 Tm 3.16; the "great and sacred mystery" in question is the Paschal Mystery.

19. See *Sermon* 33.5, n. 13.

20. See *Sermon* 95.3 (FOTC 17.149) on the continuing presence of Christ at the Church's table.

ness of sins, and which feeds and nourishes those who eat it for everlasting life,[21] this is the Bread we ask to be given to us each day, until we enjoy it fully in the everlasting day.[22]

8. *And forgive us our debts, as we also forgive our debtors* (v.12). O man, you have the power to pardon, you have the authority to show indulgence, and you have been appointed as the author of your own forgiveness. In vain do you ask for pardon if you refuse to be indulgent to another.[23] O man, you yourself have become the measure of mercy for yourself; show as much mercy as you seek.[24]

9. *And lead us not into temptation* (v.13). Temptation, brothers, is the deceptive appearance that hides prosperity in adversity and adversity in prosperity, and through trickery misleads human beings in their ignorance into falling. And so we ask that we do not stumble into the pitfalls of temptations, to which sins entice us. But God is said to *lead* when he abandons those who rush into offenses.[25]

10. *But deliver us from evil* (v.13). Here he is indicating the evil author of evil, that is, the devil.[26] And so we ask that by means of this one favor we may be free from all evils together with the author of evil.

11. *Our Father who art in heaven* (v.9). Let no one be amazed, when he calls himself a son, that he remains in the condition of a servant; you have been designated today as a divine offspring, but not promoted; you should realize that you have acquired the hope, not the reality. Listen to the Apostle: "By hope you

21. For finding in the details of the manufacturing, baking, and consuming of bread an analogy for aspects of the Paschal Mystery of Christ sacramentally present in the Eucharist, see *Sermons* 67.7 (FOTC 17.117) and 172.6. See also Quodvultdeus of Carthage, *Liber Promissionum et Praedictorum Dei* 1.39.56 (CCL 60.64–65). Augustine employs the same analogy of bread but applies it to the process of a catechumen becoming fully initiated: see, e.g., *Sermons* 227 and 229 (FOTC 38.196–97, 201–2), *Sermon Guelferbytanus* 7.2 (=227A) (*Miscellanea Agostiniana*, 1:463), and *Sermon* 272 (PL 38.1247–48).

22. See also *Sermon* 68.7 and n. 28 on the eschatological dimension of the Eucharist.

23. Literally, "if you refuse to be indulgent to yourself in another."

24. See *Sermon* 68.8 and n. 30.

25. See *Sermon* 68.9 and n. 32.

26. See *Sermons* 67.10 and 70.10 (FOTC 17.118 and 122–23).

have been saved. But a hope that is seen is not hope. For why does one hope for what he sees? But if we hope for what we do not see, we await it with patience."[27] Today is the day of adoption, today is the time of promise.

Hear, trust, await: trust your Creditor, who has trusted you; wait a little while for him to come, who has been so long suffering in your regard waiting for you to come. Give him more time to fulfill his promise, since he has already forgiven you whatever debt you owed. Or why are you made weary by your hope in God, when the whole human race exists by hope and lives by faith?

The farmer would not exert himself so strenuously in sowing seeds, if he did not have hope concerning the eventual fruit of his labor. A traveler would not undergo the trouble of a long journey, unless he believed that he would reach his destination. A sailor would not incur the risks of traversing the sea, if he did not have hope that he would compensate for his perils with subsequent profits. A soldier would not spend the whole period of his youth confronting dangers, if he did not hope for the most abundant honors in his old age. A son would not endure the period of submitting to his father's authority, if he did not have hope that he would inherit his father's property.[28]

And you, if you believe that you are already a son of God, in the prophet's words: "Wait, be strong, and let your heart take courage";[29] so wait, so that you may acquire the inheritance of God from your faith in what you await and from the strength[30] of your patience. Listen to the Apostle:[31] "We are God's sons, but it is not yet evident what we are; when he appears, we shall be like him."[32] And again:[33] "Your life is hidden with Christ;

27. Rom 8.24–25.
28. Some of these same examples are also mentioned by Zeno of Verona, *Tractatus* 1.36.1.3 (CCL 22.92). Zeno refers to a student, a sailor, a soldier, a farmer, and a Christian.
29. Ps 26 (27).14.
30. Or, alternatively, from the "virtue" of patience.
31. Here the reference is to John, rather than Paul, who is more usually designated as "the Apostle."
32. 1 Jn 3.2.
33. Here, a Pauline text.

when Christ your Life appears, then you also will appear in glory."[34] Brothers, blessed are the sons of God, because they will possess the inheritance of all the universe, and they will face no period of grief over the death of their Father.

34. Col 3.3–4.

SERMON 72

A Sixth on the Lord's Prayer[1]

HAT I AM NOW about to say with great trembling, what you are now about to hear fearfully, or rather what you are about to invoke fearfully, causes the angels to be astounded and the celestial powers to tremble. It is something that the sky does not grasp, the sun does not see, the earth does not endure, and all of creation does not comprehend. In the face of these things what is the mortal heart, what is limited human intelligence, what is the breath of a human voice, and in the face of this what is the human tongue that will soon be silent? When Paul had seen this without physically seeing it, he revealed it by not revealing it when he said: "Eye has not seen, ear has not heard, nor has there come into the heart of the human being what God has prepared for those who love him."[2]

Since Isaiah had had difficulty grasping this with his own ears, he still had doubts about being able to penetrate the ears of other human beings when he said: Lord, "who has believed what we have heard?"[3] When Jeremiah had conceived this by listening to God, he endured the birth pangs attending heavenly understanding, as he cried out: "I ache in my stomach, and the understanding of my heart has been going into convulsions."[4] Habakkuk spoke of this through the inspiration of the Divine Spirit,[5] when he said: "I kept guard over myself, and my stomach trembled at the sound of the supplication on my lips, dread has entered my bones, and my strength has quivered beneath me."[6] Having been raised up by the strength of God, he felt his own strength sink below him.

---

1. Mt 6.9–13. See *Sermon* 68, n. 1.   2. 1 Cor 2.9.
3. Is 53.1.   4. Jer 4.19.
5. See *Sermon* 68.1–2.   6. Hab 3.16.

2. It would take too long to elaborate upon and enumerate how the saints trembled before this mystery; time does not allow me to linger for long on this fear; the heavenly birthing process cannot slow down the forceful arrival of those being born. And so I say, and I urge you with a voice that penetrates all the way into the womb, and I exhort you with a word to the wise, that before you see your Mother, you invoke her Father; that you be intent on hastening to the Father's kingdom before your Mother's caresses; that you reach the Father's bread, before you hang onto your Mother's breasts; and that neither your need for your Mother nor your time of life may make any claim on you, but that everything in you may respond to and be directed toward the divine Father, the heavenly creator.

3. *Our Father who art in heaven* (Mt 6.9). This is what I was afraid to say, this is what I trembled at professing, this is what the condition of their own servitude prevented any heavenly or terrestrial creature from even imagining: that so great an interchange[7] between heaven and earth, between flesh and God would suddenly be able to occur, that God would be turned into man, that man would be turned into God, that the Lord would be turned into a servant, that the servant would be turned into a son,[8] and that in an ineffable fashion divinity and humanity would become relatives once and for all.

God's gracious favor toward us was so great that it is impossible for a creature to decide which deserves the most amazement: that God has lowered himself to our level of servitude, or that God has carried us off to the dignity of his divinity. This is why, O man, divinity comes into contact with you, why it is aflame now with such great love for you, why through the words you speak God adopts you as a son while you are still in

7. *Commercium.* For the ways Chrysologus uses this term, see R. Benericetti, *Il Cristo,* 101–3, who claims that the antitheses Chrysologus presents should not be understood as monophysitism, whereby Christ's human nature is absorbed by his divinity, but as mutual interpenetration between Christ's divinity and humanity ("la mutua compenetrazione tra divinità e umanità in Cristo," 103).

8. In one of his Christmas sermons (*Sermon* 371.1, in PL 39.1659), Augustine uses language very similar to Chrysologus's. Augustine says, "God became man, so that man might become God; and so that the servant might be turned into a lord, the Lord took the form of a servant."

the womb,[9] why he wills, not that you become free, but that you be born free, and why for your sake he liberates that very nature, so that birth in ancient servitude may not inflict upon you any birthmark or blemish. O how blessed are you to have been permitted to exercise dominion before being born, to rule before living, to attain to the glory of God the Father before recognizing your own inferior stock!

The Church is a happy mother who has such regard for you,[10] and who, while remaining ever a virgin, marvels that she has given birth to such as you and in such a fashion! In former times this birth was prefigured by earlier examples. So it is that Jacob engages in conflict in the womb, and makes off with the spoils.[11] So it is that in Tamar's womb twins battle to win first place, slow the birth process, and do not want to see the light of day before gaining victory.[12] So it is that John leaps for joy and meets his Creator before coming forth from his mother's womb;[13] and so human offspring fight in God's service before being born to their parents and before living in the world.[14] What is so wondrous if the divine offspring of the Church, if God's own children, while still in the womb acknowledge before him that they are of heavenly stock?

Our Father who art in heaven. The wonder increases: Christ from the breast of God the Father invokes and acknowledges his mother on earth, and the human being from the womb of his mother invokes and addresses his Father in heaven. *Our Father who art in heaven.* See where grace has brought you all of a sudden, O man, where the heavenly nature has carried you off, such that while you are still placed within flesh and on the earth you do not now know the flesh and the earth when you say: *Our Father who art in heaven.* So let the one who professes and believes that he is a son of so great a Father have his life

---

9. This of course refers to those who will soon receive the new birth of baptism at Easter.

10. Olivar's CCL text erroneously has *nos* instead of *vos,* the correct reading. See PL 52.405.

11. See Gn 25.22.   12. See Gn 38.27–30.

13. See Lk 1.41.

14. See *Sermon* 68.11, n. 34, on these and other pre-natal accomplishments, as recorded in Scripture.

correspond to his lineage, his behavior to his Father, and his mind and his actions confirm what he has obtained by means of the heavenly nature.[15]

4. *Hallowed be thy name* (v.9). We are certainly called by the name of him whose stock we have begun to be, and so we ask that the sanctity of his name may abide permanently in us; that the privilege[16] of his name may bring honor to those whom so sublime a Father has raised so high.[17]

5. *Thy kingdom come* (v.10). We do not ask on his behalf who never is or was without the kingdom, but who is himself the kingdom unto himself and holds all the power of the kingdom within himself.[18] But he who wants us to reach the glory of his kingdom as he has promised, advises us to seek this with all our prayers, and wants us to long for this with all our mind. For as rash as one is who debates about the stock, so is one ignorant who is not bold, eager, or desirous in aiming and pressing on for the promised kingdom.

6. *Thy will be done on earth as it is in heaven* (v.10). *On earth as it is in heaven:* then everything is already heaven, then the one mind of God directs all,[19] then all are in Christ "and Christ in all,"[20] when all know and do only God's will; then "all are one,"[21] rather all are of One, when the one Spirit of God lives in all.

7. *Give us this day our daily bread* (v.11). Just as we read in the Psalm: "Blessed be the Lord from day to day,"[22] so also here:

15. See *Sermon* 68.3 and n. 17.

16. *Praerogativa:* see also *Sermons* 68.4 and 70.4 (FOTC 17.120–21).

17. See *Sermon* 71.4 and n. 12.

18. That God always reigns in his kingdom is a point made also in *Sermon* 67.5 (FOTC 17.116). Likewise, see Tertullian, *Prayer* 5.1 (FOTC 40.163); Cyprian, *The Lord's Prayer* 13 (FOTC 36.137); Chromatius of Aquileia, *Sermon* 40.2 (CCL 9A.172); and Augustine, *Sermon* 56.6 (FOTC 11.243), *Sermon* 57.5 (*Homo Spiritalis*, 415–16), and *Commentary on the Lord's Sermon on the Mount* 2.6.20 (FOTC 11.128).

19. This same notion about God being the directing mind is found in *Sermon* 67.6 (FOTC 17.117); Augustine too emphasizes the mind *(mens),* but in his case it is the human mind, which has heaven as its focus, and is in fact identified with heaven: see *Sermon* 56.8 (FOTC 11.245) and *Sermon* 57.6 (*Homo Spiritalis* 417).

20. Col 3.11.   21. Jn 17.21.

22. Ps 67.20 LXX; Ps 68.19.

Give us this day our daily bread. By *daily* we mean "perpetually"; that perpetual bread is he who "came down from heaven." "I am the Bread that came down from heaven."[23] So it is characteristic of perfect beatitude to live already on the food of that bread "today," that is, in the present, from the perpetual, that is, *daily*,[24] supply of which we shall be fed in the future.

8. *And forgive us our debts as we also forgive our debtors* (v.12). The fountain of pardon wells up out of the heart of the suppliant, and whatever kindness abounds and flows forth for another will flow back for pardon, since a person gives himself as much indulgence as the forgiveness he has shown to another.[25] *Forgive us our debts as we also forgive our debtors.* A human being can be satisfied with the degree of his mercy if he rivals God in showing kindness, since as much is given to him as he has given; he desires to have as much bestowed on him as he has bestowed. O man, let pardon be always in your heart, if you do not want to worry about your sins.

9. *And lead us not into temptation* (v.13). This needs no interpretation, because temptation is the devil's forerunner and is a bitter attendant. But as long as we are confined to this frail body, it is necessary for us to pray that there may be in us no access to temptation, and the devil may find no way to enter.

10. *But deliver us from evil* (v.13). But may our Lord God himself deliver us from evil, and lead us to every good.

23. Jn 6.58, 51. In *Sermons* 67.7 (FOTC 17.117), 70.7 (FOTC 17.122), and 71.7, Chrysologus uses a verse from Jn 6 to elucidate what the "bread" of this petition in the Lord's Prayer is, and he concludes that it is the Bread of Life in its specifically Eucharistic connotation.
24. See *Sermon* 33.5, n. 13.
25. See *Sermon* 68.8 and n. 30.

INDICES

GENERAL INDEX

Aaron, 111, 187
Abel, 68, 186–87
Abihu, 111
Abraham, 54, 55, 63, 68, 116–17,
    172, 211–12, 214, 268–72, 281;
    bosom of, 44, 116, 268, 270
Adam, 59, 84, 188, 207–8, 254,
    265–66
Adelphius, 9
adversus Iudaeos tradition, 16
Africa, 13–14, 64
Agnellus, author of *Liber Pontificalis*,
    1, 2, 3n, 4, 5, 6n, 7, 11, 12
Agricola, 3n
Ahab, 59
Alaric, 5
allegorical exegesis, 22–25, 27, 84–
    85, 151, 194; *see also* typology
Ambrose of Milan, 3n, 6n, 9, 22,
    35n, 69n, 79n, 122n, 134n, 185n,
    186n, 193n, 197n, 219–220n,
    266n, 287n
Andrew, apostle, 115
angel, angels, 17–18, 61, 68, 88,
    111, 186, 202n, 264–65, 277n,
    280
Antioch, 2, 9
Apollinaris, name, 24n, 28n
Apollinaris, saint, 2, 3, 4
Aquileia, 9, 10, 17
Argemi, A., 142n, 146n, 216n,
    277n
Arianism, 19, 93n, 98n, 99n, 101n,
    104n, 233n, 244n, 252n, 262n
Arius, 19
Arles, 10
astrology, 16

Athaulf, 5
Aubineau, M., 135n, 264n
augury, 16, 86
Augustine of Hippo, 5, 19n, 64n,
    79n, 92n, 102n, 148n, 174n,
    176n, 178n, 193n, 202n, 216n,
    219n, 219–20n, 222n, 226n,
    229n, 233n, 236n, 243n, 246n,
    247n, 267n, 278n, 282n,
    283–84n, 287n, 288n, 289n,
    293n, 295n
autocephaly, 1n
avarice, 38–39, 44, 51, 58, 61, 65,
    76, 103, 108, 117–19, 120–22,
    125–26, 136, 168, 207

Balaam, 190
Baldisseri, D., 28n, 30n
Banterle, G., 131n, 186n
Baptism, 52n, 54–55, 81n, 205n,
    218n, 231n, 239n, 274n,
    294n
Baxter, J., 29n, 130n
Bede, 92n
Benericetti, R., 6n, 68n, 72n, 81n,
    99n, 124n, 131n, 132n, 175n,
    186n, 189n, 192n, 194n, 195n,
    197n, 227n, 233–34n, 246n,
    253–54n, 262–63n, 270n, 293n
Bertrand, G.-M., 191–192n
Billerbeck, P., 250n
Böhmer, G., 17n
Bologna, 3n
bread as image of Christ, 63, 128,
    215, 288, 289, 296
Bussi, E., 211n

299

INDEX OF HOLY SCRIPTURE

Old Testament